The
Loft
Conversion
Manual

LABC

Local Authority Building Control
www.labc.uk.com

Published in May 2008

British Library Cataloguing in Publication Data:
A catalogue record for this book is available from the British Library

ISBN 978 1 84425 446 0

Published by Haynes Publishing,
Sparkford, Yeovil, Somerset BA22 7JJ, UK
Tel: 01963 442030 Fax: 01963 440001
Int. tel: +44 1963 442030 Int. fax: +44 1963 440001
E-mail: sales@haynes.co.uk
Website: www.haynes.co.uk

Haynes North America Inc.
861 Lawrence Drive, Newbury Park, California 91320, USA

Printed and bound in Great Britain
by J. H. Haynes & Co. Ltd, Sparkford

While every effort is taken to ensure the accuracy of the information given in this book, no liability can be accepted by the author or publishers for any loss, damage or injury caused by errors in, or omissions from, the information given.

Acknowledgements

SPECIAL THANKS TO
Basil Parylo, The Rooflight Company, Paul Bagley @ PBdrylining.co.uk, Godfrey Rawlings Building Contractors, Kingspan Insulation, Gillam Wood Architectural Design, Paddick Engineering, CharlesGrosvenor.co.uk, South London Lofts.

PHOTOGRAPHY
Basil Parylo, Dave Davies, Helen @ The Rooflight Company, Peter Morgan @ Kingspan Insulation, and the Author

Thanks also to
Ian Douglas / Aylesbury Vale District Council
BSW Timber
Celotex Insulation
DCLG
Ed Smith
Robin Clevett
EGLO Lighting
Environmental Seals Ltd
Nigel Griffiths
Juice Property.co.uk
Loft shop
LondonandKent.co.uk
Specialist Roofing Contractor A.J. Green
Stewart Saunders and Gregor Developments Edinburgh
The Velux Company
The Wooden Hill Company

The
Loft
Conversion
Manual

Ian Alistair Rock MRICS

Technical Editor – **Basil Parylo** MBEng

CONTENTS

Loft Conversion Manual

INTRODUCTION

Photo: Juice Property

Loft conversions are consistently voted the nation's Number One home improvement project. Creating a new room in the roof is reckoned by experts to be about the best way to conjure up extra living space seemingly out of nowhere, whilst at the same time boosting the value of your property.

Easier than building an extension and cheaper than digging out a basement, it's no wonder that houses with large empty lofts ripe for conversion often sell at a premium. The real puzzle is why so many homes were built with such huge amounts of wasted space in the first place. In a typical two-storey house, the volume of the roof space is equivalent to about a third of the combined two storeys below, and in bungalows it can comprise as much as 75 per cent of the existing living space. So it makes sense to use it.

A brief history of attics

The concept of 'loft living' has a cool, modern image – something that Victorian servants shivering in cramped attic rooms certainly wouldn't recognise. But there's nothing new under the sun – in 19th-century Paris lofts gained creative credibility when fashionable artists of the day moved their studios into 'garrets' high up in the rafters. In Britain, however, lofts have traditionally been regarded as something of a waste of space, some builders even neglecting to fit access hatches. These cold, sometimes damp spaces needed ventilating blasts of cold air running through them to deter rot and beetle attack to the timbers, thereby limiting their appeal as a cosy living space. Often lacking party walls from one end of a terrace to another, they instead provided a useful dumping ground for water tanks and assorted junk. The final death knell to loft-living ambitions arrived with the advent of manufactured trussed rafters in the mid-1960s, with their typically shallow concrete-tiled roofs and intricate webbing of timber components.

But in recent years, as property prices have soared, we have rediscovered the potential of under-used spaces in our homes, and it has now become economically viable as well as technically possible to convert most lofts. That, however, does not mean it's a simple job.

Popular lofts

Loft conversions have never been more popular. The vast majority involve adding an extra floor to an existing two-storey house or enlarging a bungalow; consequently much of the following guidance relates to projects of this type. Although larger conversions are discussed, on the whole we assume that no more than two habitable loft rooms will be required (a bedroom with an en suite counting as one habitable room) and that you won't need to raise the height of the roof above the present ridge line.

Before we go any further, it might be worth taking a moment to ponder whether a roof space should be called a *loft* or an *attic*? Surely the term 'attic' is just a posh word that someone like Stephen Fry might use to describe a loft?

Strictly speaking, a loft is defined as 'a roof space used for storage', whereas an attic is 'a roof space used for living'. So the term 'loft living' is actually a bit of a misnomer, conjuring up images of a sad existence amongst old packing cases and dusty Christmas decorations. But the advent in the 1990s of stylish 'Manhattan loft apartments' changed all that. So 'loft rooms' can now be considered as habitable space in a *converted* roof, while attics can be defined as *purpose-built* living space.

Be prepared

A recent full-page magazine advertisement from a spray-foam contractor makes the following claim: '*With a roof window installed and some flooring laid, your cold damp loft is transformed into a clean, dry, warm, useable*

Photo: Loft shop

room.' Unfortunately, this isn't an entirely honest description of what's needed, as this manual will show, and the Advertising Standards Authority have since ordered the firm in question to withdraw it. The truth is, converting a loft is a major structural alteration, so it's essential that the works are done correctly. Also, not every loft can be successfully transformed into a fabulous living space. So before planning a whole extra storey of accommodation for your home, you first need to be sure that your loft is suitable for conversion.

WEBSITE

For further technical information, plus sample plans and details of specialist firms, visit our website at **www.loft-rooms.com**

Photo: Velux

1 BEFORE YOU START

Photo: Velux

There is one essential measurement that must be checked before your conversion to loft living can begin, and that's the height of your loft. If you find yourself stooping, caveman-like, inside the roof space then there's a good chance that the overall building height will need to be raised – more of which later. In the meantime there are a

number of searching questions that need to be asked before you can be certain that all the expense and time, and the general hassle involved will really be worth it.

Is it practical?

Loft conversions typically fall into two categories. Either a property is crying out to be converted, and it will be quite easy to do; or it's the job from hell, with awkward floor and stair layouts and minimal headroom.

By the time you've installed a bed in a small loft room, you might find there's nowhere left to stand up because the pitch of the roof is so low. Also, homes with open-plan layouts downstairs can be expensive to convert, because complying with fire regulations is more troublesome. So in some cases you have to question whether the job's actually worth attempting. On the bright side, however, most technical problems can be overcome, as we shall see.

It's obviously important at the planning stage to consider what you want to use the extra space for. The majority of converted lofts are used as bedrooms, very often with a new en suite shower room and WC. But loft rooms can provide 'flexible accommodation' – anything from small offices that allow you to work in peace, to games rooms or home cinemas. However, rooms at the top of the house may not be suitable for young children with a natural curiosity about roof windows, or for oldies to whom steep stairs could be a challenge. Home gyms and music rooms are also a better suited to ground floor extensions and garage conversions, where noisy activities, heavy loads and grand pianos can all be better accommodated.

Photo: Velux

Photo: Loft shop

Photo: Charles Grosvenor

Will you get your money back?

Loft conversions are regularly cited by leading mortgage lenders as the best way to increase a property's value – as long as they're done properly and don't uglify the architecture. Estate agents routinely define residential property in terms of the numbers of bedrooms, so when it comes to adding value an extra bedroom is always a welcome addition. Even if you're hell-bent on building a loft room devoted exclusively to train sets, when the time comes to sell buyers will very likely perceive it as a valuable additional bedroom.

Is it neighbourly?

At this stage, it pays to consider what effect your proposed building work is likely to have on your neighbours. Even if the loft conversion itself is not a problem for them, the inevitable noise, mess and deliveries of building materials at all hours of the day surely will be. Builders have an endearing tendency to commence work on site at the crack of dawn accompanied by much whistling, singing, swearing, thudding and crashing, the precise mix depending on how the job is going. This can strain even the best relationships. Involving the neighbours in your plans at this early stage not only helps prepare them for

Photo: Velux

Photo: Velux

Photo: Velux

Of course, it's only too easy to underestimate the amount of work involved and to bite off more than you can chew. So unless you really know what you're doing, and have good experience, especially at carpentry, you might want to make it easy on yourself and get the professionals in. If you're not used to doing heavy building work it's probably better to pay someone else to lug all those heavy beams and giant sheets of insulated plasterboard around.

If you're keen to tackle some of the work, one golden rule is to never put yourself under pressure to rush a job. It's best to only select jobs that aren't too time-critical. Also bear in mind that the different trades will need space to work without tripping over you. To save money, it may be easier to have a bash at doing some of the decoration and finishing jobs at the end of the project, once the contractors have completed the main structural works.

With a bit of luck your project should be able to sidestep the planning process, as many loft jobs are currently permitted without the need for a formal application (see Chapter 4). This will considerably speed things up by cutting out a huge amount of hassle. However, you'll still need to provide detailed drawings for Building Control. These drawings will require professional input, as there is less scope for drawing your own plans here than for relatively simple planning applications. However, it's still a good idea to sketch out what you want

inconveniences to come, but may also help sweeten things a little for any co-operation that may be needed with future planning applications or party wall issues.

How much should you do yourself?

Lofts are a fairly specialised area. Major structural alterations will need to be carried out to your roof and significant changes made elsewhere in the house. But that doesn't mean you can't make a major contribution personally. Even if you don't do any of the structural work, there are plenty of tasks suitable for those with general building skills or an aptitude for DIY. If you employ contractors, it's essential they're experienced at precisely this kind of work – you don't want some clown with zero qualifications and knowledge learning on the job.

There are several alternatives when it comes to selecting the best way to have the works carried out, depending on how much work you can personally contribute, and the amount of money you're willing to spend. Options range from employing a specialist loft firm to do the full monty – a design-and-build 'package deal' (normally the most expensive choice) – through to employing individual trades direct and doing much of the work yourself. The various alternatives are discussed in Chapter 5.

to achieve at an early stage so that this can form the basis of discussions with professional designers, who should also be able to give you a fair idea of what the build is likely to cost.

Project management

Achieving a successful outcome is largely about planning ahead and applying a little common sense to problems as they arise – which isn't always as easy as it sounds.

Any decent firm of contractors will be aiming to achieve a successful completion within the agreed timescale, with or without someone standing over them. This is the way most package-deal specialist loft firms operate, and in many cases this works perfectly well. The problem is, you're effectively handing over control to the contractors, and the job will get done the way they think is best. So if you want something more than an 'off-the-peg' loft conversion, it's often better to play a more active role (see Chapter 5).

Getting builders in is inevitably going to be a bit of a pain. No matter how angelic they are, the works will clearly involve a lot of bashing, noise, vibration and dust. Trying to lull the baby to sleep or study for those crucial exams is more of a challenge when there are angle grinders screeching and hammers thudding in the background. But careful programming of the works can significantly minimise disturbance. A good contractor will suggest working mainly from the outside and leaving the 'breaking through' from the loft into the house below as late as possible. This is where a considerate package-deal firm can be worth the extra expense.

Will it blend in?

Happily, in many cases the size and style of loft you want to build will fall within the 'permitted development' rules, so you may not need to worry about getting planning consent. Nonetheless, it's worth taking a squint at what other people in the neighbourhood have been allowed to build. Pay special attention to the rear elevations, since this is where the more dramatic alterations can normally be seen. But a word of warning: in the course of this research, you may encounter some truly monstrous old dormers sprouting from roofs facing the street that would not be allowed today.

Unless you plan to totally rebuild the roof in order to make it taller (which would definitely require planning consent) the range of possibilities externally is actually fairly limited. Basically, the available options are either to fit skylight roof windows that are flush with the roof slopes, or to build projecting dormers of varying sizes and styles. The simplest and cheapest conversions may only need a

couple of small roof windows to be installed, just the job for larger lofts with sufficient internal space. However most will require a large dormer to the rear plus skylights or small dormers to the front. Having decided which combination works best for you, the next step is to develop the design details that will bring it all to life.

Can you afford it?

The total cost of getting your loft converted should be fairly predictable. If you want to get a rough idea of the likely costs now, run your plans past a friendly local architect or surveyor, or if you call a specialist loft firm they may be willing to give you a ball-park figure. But builders' prices sometimes bear little relationship to the actual cost of materials and labour. Like other businesses they ride the waves of supply and demand, perhaps with a bit added for 'what your postcode area will take'. Fees for a designer (not including project management) can add another 5 to 10 per cent, and Local Authority charges for planning and building regulations can add upwards of £1,000.

That just leaves the small matter of coming up with the ready cash. It's essential to arrange funding early on, as nothing sours relationships with builders more than delayed payment.

A few money matters worth pondering at this stage are:

■ Don't finance building work on your credit card – the interest rates can be ruinous. Mortgage funding is normally the cheapest option, and because banks know that a loft conversion will significantly enhance the value of your property this should be fairly straightforward. Personal loans are dearer, but are still better than credit cards.

■ Keep a contingency sum of around 10 per cent in reserve, as there will inevitably be some unforeseen extra expense.

Photo: Ian MacMillan

Photo: South London Lofts

VAT

One of the great iniquities of life in this country is the way VAT is charged on building works. Essential maintenance, improvements, conversions and extensions are all charged at the full rate, whilst property developers building new houses get away with paying nothing. The cost of paying VAT to the government will add a significant amount to the price of your new loft room. Builders' quotes are often rather vague on this subject, so make sure it is clarified early on. There are, however, some possible small consolations. Your contractor may agree to you deferring payment of VAT to him until completion, and if you're VAT-registered you might even be able to claim some of the tax back.

VAT on Listed Buildings is reduced to 0 per cent for 'approved material alterations' when undertaken by a VAT-registered contractor. Work to houses left empty for ten years or more should also be free of VAT, and those left empty for three years or more may be chargeable at only 5 per cent, the same reduced rate as for flat conversions. One of the attractions of directly employing individual trades is that it's often possible to quite legitimately avoid paying VAT because 'subcontractors' whose annual earnings are below the legal threshold may not need to register for VAT. Main contractors, on the other hand, will have a higher turnover and won't fall into this category.

Is it legal?

It's always a good thing to keep one step ahead of the lawyers, by spotting any legal nasties before they jump out and bite you. For example:

Photo: Velux

- If your house is a terrace or semi, the party walls will be jointly owned with the neighbours. It's very common for loft conversions to require new structural beams to be inserted into party walls. So before letting rip with the sledgehammer, it's essential to follow the rules set out in the Party Wall Act (see Chapter 4).
- Altering your home may be legally prohibited by a 'restrictive covenant'. These are conditions sometimes written into the deeds of the property by the original developer at the time of construction. Their intention is to prevent residents 'lowering the tone of the area' by activities such as parking kebab vans in driveways, running brothels or erecting enormously ugly dormers on their roofs. So even if you have planning permission to build, in theory the developer's

permission may be required before converting. In reality such restrictive covenants are often unenforceable, or the original developers have disappeared without trace. Fortunately it's usually not too difficult for solicitors to overturn them and at worst you can always insure against any risk of enforcement.

■ Ex-Local Authority properties may have a sting in the tail. Local Authorities tend to apply restrictive covenants to Council houses sold under Right To Buy rules, and these commonly require you to obtain approval from the Council's Housing Department before extending or converting. However, judging by the large number of ex-Local Authority properties that have been successfully extended this is unlikely to prove too draconian a restriction.

■ Houses and bungalows are almost always Freehold, but if your property is Leasehold (normally flats and maisonettes) you won't usually be permitted to make structural alterations without the prior written consent of the Freeholder.

■ Mortgage lenders like to know in advance of any significant alterations that are proposed to their security (*ie* your home).

■ Check that your buildings insurance cover remains fully valid during the works. If not, will the builder's insurance cover the cost of any damage? You'll also need to take out special insurance for the works (see Chapter 5).

■ Got bats in your belfry? These are tricky little devils to shift, indeed it's an offence to remove or disturb them without first notifying the relevant Nature Conservation body.

Personal safety

You could be forgiven for assuming that some builders actually welcome a spot of self-harming. Everyone knows that building sites are dangerous places, but the reality is that health and safety is routinely ignored on small sites. Make no mistake, it's essential to protect yourself. There's no point building the most spectacular new loft accommodation but having to be winched up on a stair-lift to appreciate it.

A brief guide to body-care on building sites would have to include:

Brain: A 'Bob the Builder' safety helmet is essential anywhere you might cut your head open (or where stuff could drop on you from a great height).
Hands: Gloves must be worn when shifting materials around – especially bricks, blocks and steels.
Arms: Not half as much fun as it sounds, 'hand-arm vibration' is a safety concern resulting from the repeated use of nail guns to 'shot-fire' bolts through steel beams. Limit the extent of such work.

Toes and feet: Dropping an RSJ on your tootsies won't do a lot for your goal-scoring prowess, so protect them with steel-capped footwear.
Eyes: Wear eye protectors, especially when operating power tools. It just takes one tiny shard to fly into your face to blind you for life.
Ears: Operating noisy machinery in a confined space means risking partial deafness in later life – like some sad old heavy metal guitarist, but without the fun. Wear ear protectors.
Lungs: A dust mask is a cheap and easy way to stop you wheezing and coughing like a 20-a-day man.
Back: Back injuries are surprisingly common – from trying to lift too much or in the wrong way, or from falls. Take special care with steel beams. Keeping the site tidy will help avoid tripping up.

2 THE SURVEY

Photo: Jonathan Rock

The good news is that most lofts can be successfully converted or extended. Unfortunately however, there are some that can't. The critical factor, quite simply, is that of headroom.

If you own a house with a very shallow roof (common in 1960s and 1970s properties) you may have no option but to physically raise the existing roof in order to create sufficient height inside. The problem here is that planning permission is required, and this could be refused. Even if your loft already has sufficient headroom, you need to consider how much space will be consumed by installing a new flight of stairs to the floor below, since sacrificing valuable living space for stairs could effectively mean losing one room in order to gain another, making the whole exercise a bit pointless.

So the first step is to carry out a survey. This is essential to help figure out how best to design your new loft room so that it's structurally compatible with your existing property. If you live in a recently constructed house you may be able to cheat and save on drawings, since the plans may still be available, either from Building Control or the original developers.

The survey will first need to identify which type of roof you have and how easily it will lend itself to conversion. As a matter of fact, it's not just the roof that we're interested in. Parts of the house quite remote from the roof can affect the project's feasibility. For example, if you have an open-

plan layout downstairs it will make complying with the fire escape rules harder, and you may end up needing to build partition walls to create a separate hallway to the front door (See Chapter 4). While we've got our surveyor's hat on, it's also important to check the condition of the roof and walls. If any repair work is needed, then having the scaffolding in place for your conversion will provide an excellent opportunity to retile an old roof, replace leaking flashings, or re-point the walls.

But the main objective at this stage is to work out how the property stands up, by identifying its 'skeleton' support structure. Converting your loft will make a big difference down below, with substantial extra loadings needing to be transferred down to the foundations, via the walls, so their condition needs to be checked.

Photo: Velux

The survey will not only reveal how the house is put together, but it will also form the basis of your drawings. Before detailed plans can be produced, accurate measurements will be needed, and the obvious place to start is up in the loft. Sticking a foot through the ceiling wouldn't be a great start, so unless the joists are already boarded over, access can be made safer by laying some planks across them. If there's a lot of dust and fibre flying around it's best to don a facemask.

Six key loft questions

- Is there enough headroom?
- What type of roof is it?
- Are the internal walls taking any loading?
- Where will the new stairs go?
- Is there an entrance hall?
- Are there tanks and pipes that need to be relocated?

Max headroom

This is the acid test. It's obviously pretty fundamental that you should be able to walk around your new accommodation proud and erect, so it's a good start if you can stand in the centre of your loft without having to crouch. It's even better if you can raise your hand straight up above your head without hitting anything. If you can perform both these tasks, there's every chance that the conversion will be feasible.

The most common complaint about new loft rooms is that the ceiling heights are lower than expected. This may not be such an issue if you live in a quaint thatched cottage with protruding ceiling beams, where the need to stoop has become second nature, but for most of us height matters. So it's a little surprising that the Building Regulations don't actually stipulate a minimum ceiling height for rooms. The general view is that 2.3m is a desirable distance between the finished floor surface and the ceiling, although a minimum of 2.2m should be adequate. If the ceiling height is much less than this, any exposed beams will be a head-banging hazard.

By raising an arm, a person of average male height (officially 1.77m) can normally reach about 2.2m with fingers extended. However, the area with generous headroom in your loft may be restricted to only the narrow 'centre aisle' directly under the ridge. This needn't necessarily be a problem because adding a large box dormer to your roof can massively extend this

high ceiling area, transforming the amount of useable living space. But if you're planning to simply add some roof windows to the roof slopes, or perhaps some small traditional dormers, the existing

headroom at the apex will need to be more plentiful – at least 2.8m.

When calculating the final floor-to-ceiling height, remember that once the new floor joists and floorboards are installed they'll probably be around 175mm above the old ceiling joists on which you're currently standing.

If headroom is limited, and you don't think the planners will be too keen on the idea of raising the height of the roof, there is an alternative. Lowering the ceilings in the rooms below may be a practical solution if the existing ceiling heights are reasonably generous, although this would add significantly to the cost.

What type of roof is it?

Before putting on your surveyor's hat you need to know what sort of roof you've got, since some property types are naturally more welcoming to conversion than others. It's obviously a good start if your home has a cavernous loft just begging to be occupied. The age of the property will have a big influence on how the new loft accommodation will need to be designed. Fortunately the majority of houses from the later Victorian period right through to the early 1960s have good-sized lofts. Properties dating from

the 1960s and 1970s are probably the most challenging, thanks to the fashion at the time of ultra-shallow roofs. If there's an ideal property type for conversion it would probably be 1930s to 1950s bungalows, with their giant roof voids large enough to accommodate a Grand Prix.

Before venturing any further, let's recap on some basics. As everyone knows, the structure of a pitched roof takes the form of a simple triangle with the slopes constructed from timber rafters. At their feet the rafters are fixed to timber wall plates – the strips of timber that run along the

tops of the walls. To stop the rafters pushing the walls outwards the ceiling joists tie them together. As we shall see, this arrangement becomes a little more complex in modern houses (post 1960s) with roofs constructed from factory-manufactured timber trusses.

Since the 1950s it's been common for roofs to have a layer of underfelt beneath the tiles, providing a secondary line of defence against wind driven rain getting under the roof coverings. But don't be alarmed if you find yourself staring directly at the naked underside of your tiles or slates. If your roof is pre-war or older it was probably built without any underlay, although some better-quality properties of the period employed timber 'sarking boards' under the tiles. But in most lofts what you see is a layer of black, bitumen-soaked, hessian underlay drooping ponderously between the rafters. In newbuild construction this type of traditional underfelt has now been superseded by modern high-performance lightweight polyester

Impregnated paper underlay circa 1950s

roofing material. Rather like high-tech mountaineering clothing, these cleverly prevent rainwater from getting in, yet allow water vapour to escape outwards from the loft. They are thinner yet tougher than the old felt, which was always prone to being ripped and torn on installation.

ROOF TYPES
There are 3 basic roof types:

The traditional cut timber roof

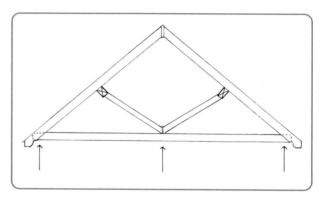

Most houses built before about 1950 have traditional timber roofs known as 'cut roofs', *ie* roofs made from pieces of cut timber. These are the easiest type to convert, as the loft space is relatively unobstructed. With the exception of thatched cottages and some Georgian and early Victorian properties with very shallow-pitched slate roofs, most traditional roofs offer fairly generous headroom.

Cut roofs are usually supported from below via internal 'spine walls', typically the ones separating the main

bedrooms upstairs and the front and rear reception rooms on the ground floor.

Most cut roofs are technically known as 'close coupled', which simply means they comprise a pair of lean-to roofs propped up one against the other. The rafters are typically made from 100 x 50mm ('four by two') timbers, spaced very approximately at 400mm or 600mm centres. At the top they're nailed to the ridge board, and at the base they're skew-nailed (nailed at an angle) to the wall plate and secured with a birdsmouth joint (a small V-shaped cut

made in the rafters). Most require additional support in the form of a large horizontal timber purlin running across the underside of the rafters, anywhere between a third and two-thirds of the way up the rafters.

Purlins aren't meant to be built perfectly at right angles to the underside of the rafters – they should be in an upright position, which gives better support. In larger roofs with rafters spanning more than about 5m an additional purlin is often needed a little higher up. Purlins are often supported with timber struts. These transfer the roof loadings down to internal load-bearing bedroom walls.

Finally, traditional roofs are sometimes strengthened with additional timbers known as hangers and collars. Hangers are central vertical beams (traditionally called 'kingposts') that hang down from the apex, helping to hold up the ceiling joists below. Collars are horizontal beams that join the two main roof slopes sometimes provided to help prevent the roof 'spreading'. They are more structurally effective at lower levels – hence the importance of ceiling joists which act as collars, tying the roof together.

'Butterfly roofs' are a special type of cut timber roof, commonly found on Georgian and early Victorian townhouses. These are a unique and somewhat peculiar design. Imagine looking at the front of a Georgian terrace from the street: the butterfly roof is M-shaped, with the highest points on each side above the party walls. From street level, however, the roof may appear flat, being hidden behind the front parapet wall. Butterfly roofs actually comprise two small separate lean-to roofs, each propped up against the party walls either side, from where the rafters slope downwards, meeting at a central valley at the low point in the middle of the 'M'. Rainwater runs into

the hidden central valley gutter and is then fed out to a downpipe at the back of the house. The valley is supported from below by an internal spine wall. Butterfly roofs are normally built to a very shallow angle – often less than 20° – which means their lofts are too small to convert. The solution is drastic, involving the construction of a new roof by infilling across the valley, building up the walls to the front, rear and sides and then topping it off with a new flat roof structure. This will all be very much subject to getting planning consent. (See Chapter 8.)

The TDA truss roof

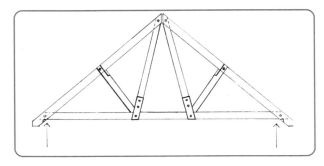

The trussed rafter roof

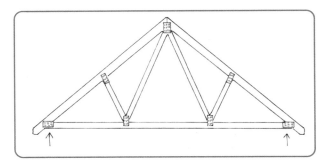

Between the late 1940s and late 1960s, although traditional timber roofs were still being constructed, a large number of properties came to be built with a new kind of roof construction – the TDA roof truss. At the end of World War Two building materials were in short supply, timber being especially scarce, so the boffins at the Timber Development Association (TDA) came up with an ingenious new roof truss design – a distant cousin of the massive structures used in wartime aircraft hangars. Despite using substantially less timber this was extremely strong, allowing larger spans without support from internal walls below. TDA trusses comprise A-shaped hangers coming down from the ridge, forming a 'W' when combined with struts to the purlins. Some versions feature a central vertical timber hanger. A distinguishing feature is that the trusses are bolted together and are spaced quite widely apart (about every 1.8m), so there may only be about three sets of trusses in a typical loft. The rafters and ceiling joists are typically spaced approximately every 450mm.

From a conversion point of view, TDA roofs are considered more difficult to convert than traditional roofs, but not as awkward as the trussed rafter roofs that replaced them.

Most houses built since the late 1960s have roofs constructed from prefabricated trussed rafters, which use about 30 per cent less timber than traditional roof structures. Trussed rafters are factory-manufactured and delivered to the site on the back of a lorry, being quick and easy to install. Their greatest advantage is that they can normally span well over 6m without needing any support from internal walls, with consequent savings on construction elsewhere in the house.

Unfortunately, the arrival of trussed rafters on the scene some 40 years ago also coincided with the fashion for extremely shallow 'Californian-style' roofs (along with 'avocado' and 'dark chocolate' coloured bathroom suites, but that's another story).

The trusses themselves are rather weedy-looking things, held together with primitive metal 'nail plates' (punched

metal plates), or sometimes plywood gussets nailed in place. However, when combined together they form a strong yet lightweight load-bearing frame. As a result such roofs cannot easily be modified, since cutting bits off here and there will drastically weaken the overall structure.

The trusses are manufactured from surprisingly thin strips of timber, perhaps only 72 x 35mm (or 72 x 47mm), and it is this slimness, together with the rectangular metal nail plates, that makes them so distinctive. Another distinguishing feature of a typical prefabricated roof truss is its W-shaped webbing, which blocks you from easily walking through the loft. The trusses are spaced fairly close together, typically at 600mm centres. The exact design will depend on the age of your house, as shapes and construction techniques have evolved over time.

A potentially very serious problem arose with some early roof structures of this type. It was discovered that in storm conditions some roofs collapsed quite spectacularly, like the proverbial deck of cards. Consequently the regulations were swiftly changed requiring roofs of this type to be strengthened with extra timber bracing strips, improving sideways rigidity. This 'lateral bracing' takes the form of long 100 x 25mm planks nailed horizontally and diagonally across the trusses, together with timber binders across the top of the ceiling joists. The net result is that the loft space cannot easily be used for living accommodation due to the intricate network of struts and bracing timbers. For this reason, many firms refused to tackle such loft conversions until a few years ago. Today, however, it's accepted that conversion is entirely feasible, provided, as always, that there's adequate headroom.

If your house is of fairly modern construction with the ceilings sloping around the edges of the bedrooms, it's likely that the trussed rafters in your loft are strengthened with large steel purlin beams near ceiling level. This allows for a currently popular traditional-looking design featuring small dormer 'cottage' windows.

The manufacturers of trussed rafters must have taken note of all the moaning and groaning from struggling loft converters, because in the 1990s they launched a new version known as the 'room-in-roof' or RIR truss. These now comprise over 30 per cent of all new roofs, and are a dream for anyone contemplating a

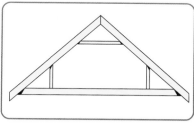

conversion since they're specifically designed in the form of a ready-made shell for a loft room. RIR trusses are ideal for replacing and rebuilding old shallow roofs should the planners agree to you raising the height of your existing roof to create a new loft room.

Hipped or gabled

Whichever type of roof structure your property was built with, when it comes to the side of the roof, there are

basically only two designs: gabled or hipped (unless, of course, it's a mid-terrace property). This matters a great deal when you're planning to convert the loft, for the reasons explained below.

The majority of houses have their side walls built up in the form of trangular gables. Hipped roofs, on the other hand, have a roof slope instead; these classic pyramid-shaped roofs were all the rage in the 1930s.

When you're contemplating a loft conversion, gabled roofs are normally preferable because they offer the greatest space inside the loft. The problem with hipped roofs is that their 'streamlined' design effectively cuts the amount of headroom and shrinks the useable floor area. Unfortunately, the position of the hipped roof slope may coincide with the preferred location of your new loft stairs. As a result, shallow hips often need to be converted to gables, or else have large side dormer windows installed on them, both of which will be subject to getting planning permission. But hipped roofs aren't always bad news. Many 1930s lofts are so cavernous that you can afford to sacrifice some space and thereby avoid the need for major surgery.

Are the internal walls taking any loading?

As noted earlier, adding new loft accommodation to your home is likely to increase the loadings on the existing structure by at least 10 per cent, so it's essential at the design stage to calculate how it's all going to be supported. If your house has a traditional timber roof, then there's a high probability that an internal wall is taking some of the load from the roof and floors. In modern houses with trussed rafter roofs, on the other hand, the internal walls are not normally 'structural'.

Most loft conversions are designed so the new loadings don't need support from internal walls. However, in some cases, utilising existing 'spine walls' makes sense, and can save money by allowing the design to be kept as simple as possible. So the first task is to establish which internal walls are load-bearing with foundations below them. Walls built of solid brick or blockwork are most likely to be load-bearing structural walls. Timber stud walls, which sound hollow when you tap them, are often just partitions, which will be useless for providing support to the new loft floor. But there are exceptions to this rule, especially in Victorian and older houses where timber frame walls are sometimes structural. Conversely you may discover slim 50mm internal blockwork walls (or thin 'brick-on-edge' walls) whose role in life is simply to separate upstairs rooms, without supporting any loadings. Because these are commonly just built off floorboards, adding extra loadings could have disastrous consequences.

To be certain, you need to check which way the floor and ceiling joists run. In the loft, inspect the ceiling joists, noting how far apart they're spaced, and whether they overlap above a supporting wall. Floor joists normally run

in the opposite direction to the floorboards, as can be seen from the lines of nails on the surface. In order to check where the joists end, and what they're resting on, some floorboards will need to be lifted. It's also worth checking that upstairs solid walls are actually built directly above the downstairs ones, and not offset to either side – ie check that there's vertical continuity between the walls on different floors.

Some years ago, knocking through the front and rear reception rooms to make one large open-plan room was a popular home improvement. But if these structurally important spine walls have been removed how do you know whether adequate structural support was provided to the remaining bedroom wall and floors above, such as a suitable steel beam? Structural alterations should always be carried out with Building Regulations consent. So if no completion certificate was issued for the work, it's fair to assume that the job may have been botched, and a structural engineer will now need to inspect it. Alternatively, it will probably be simpler to design the new attic floor construction so that it simply spans right across from new beams in the loft, and doesn't require any support from internal walls. (See Chapter 7.)

Where will the new stairs go?

One of the first things to consider at the design stage (Chapter 3) is the location of the loft stairs. In many traditional houses, such as typical Victorian terraces, the new stairs can normally be run directly above the existing ones, providing a very neat solution. In most semi-detached houses the main flight of stairs runs next to the side wall, and this arrangement will also often allow the loft staircase to be positioned directly above. But there's just one potential snag with this idea. If the roof is hipped (as many semis are), the resulting lack of headroom may necessitate building a large side dormer window, or else converting the hip to a gable.

Normally the simplest solution is to run the new stairs parallel with the ceiling joists, which usually run front to rear. Alternatively, the new stairs could enter the loft room sideways. One popular design is to run the loft stairs across the house, parallel to the internal wall that divides the front and rear main bedrooms. Here the loft stairs are approached from the upstairs landing, perhaps via a redundant airing cupboard. (See Chapters 3 and 10.)

If it turns out that there just isn't the space to accommodate a new flight of conventional stairs, you may

be allowed to fit a compact 'alternating tread' staircase (except that Building Control are generally not keen on them, so they may only be accepted as a last resort).

The most important measurement to note at this stage is from the surface of the floor below up to the proposed new loft floor surface. This will determine the precise dimensions of the new loft staircase. To be absolutely accurate and avoid red faces at the end of the project, take this measurement twice!

Is there an entrance hall?

The layout of your ground floor rooms and the position of the main entrance doors will have a major impact on the cost of getting your new design to comply with the fire regulations. As we shall see, the ideal existing ground floor layout is the traditional one, comprising an entrance hall or lobby leading in from the front door to the main stairs. Other layouts will need to be modified to meet the regulations. Make a note of the construction of the internal walls to the hall and upstairs landing. Once you add an extra floor of living space to your home, these walls will form your main defence against fire as part of a 'protected escape route' through the building. Fortunately, the existing walls – be they masonry or timber stud partition walls with skimmed plasterboard or lath and plaster to either side – should provide adequate fire resistance. (See Chapter 4.)

Are there tanks and pipes that need to be relocated?

Many lofts have a large cold-water tank sitting smack in the middle, just where you want to build your new room. But water tanks aren't the only offenders. Assorted suitcases and ancient TV aerials, along with tonnes of hoarded

clutter and sentimental junk, will all need to find a new home. But at this stage the main consideration is to identify any tanks and pipework that the services in your house depend on to operate effectively. These will later need to be moved with the minimum of disruption. The purpose of the cold-water tank is to feed stored water to baths, basins and WCs (kitchen sinks are normally fed direct from the mains). There will also normally be a 'feed and expansion' tank or header tank serving the vented hot water cylinder. Plus it's not unknown for boilers and hot water cylinders to also be found residing in lofts.

Tanks and pipework can often be successfully relocated to new eaves cupboards created at the edges of the new loft room. If the system is getting on a bit it may be due for renewal anyway. An increasingly popular option is to eliminate the need for tanks altogether by installing an unvented hot-water system such as a combination boiler or a Megaflo pressurised system. (See Chapter 12.)

Survey checklist

In addition to the six key points above, there are a number of other important areas that must be checked. Taking accurate measurements, particularly within the loft itself, and converting these into draft scale drawings should save some money. Working from this information together with photos, it's often possible for structural engineers to carry out the necessary calculations without needing to charge you for a site visit.

Roof loadings

Whilst you're up in the loft, it's essential to note the size of the rafters and how far apart they're spaced. Also record the sizes and positions of purlins and any collars. Note especially how the loads are taken, such as via struts to the purlins, and whether they rest on internal walls below. Consider whether any roof timbers are likely to obstruct your new stair access or will interfere with the location of the new roof windows.

Roof condition

You don't want your expensive new loft room to be ruined by water leaking through the roof. So this is a good time to assess whether the roof will need to be overhauled prior to the conversion works. It's obviously sensible to repair any defects now rather than having to cough up for expensive damage once the room is occupied. On many conversions it's the front roof slopes that are the most important area to check. The front coverings generally remain largely unaffected whereas the rear slopes are commonly modified with the construction of large dormer windows. If you do need to replace any tiles, it may be possible to recycle some of the discarded ones due to be stripped from the rear to make the opening for the new dormer. Externally, keep an eye open for any slipped or missing slates or tiles, and check condition of common weak points such as valleys and flashings.

Above: Slate roofs painted with sealant won't last long

Right: Beware wasps' nests

Inside the loft, check for signs of rainwater leaks, especially around flashings to chimney stacks. If there's no underlay, are any large areas of daylight visible, especially at joints to party walls and stacks, where rain could penetrate?

Chimneys

It's sod's law that you'll find there's a large chimney stack obliterating the view just where you want to put a new roof window. So the design may need to be revised to

accommodate such obstacles.

Take a look in the bedrooms and note whether any chimney breasts have been removed, then go up a level and check inside the loft that the remaining brickwork above them has been properly supported. Such structural works require Building Regulations consent, and you would hope to see some beefy metal 'gallows brackets' or a steel beam supporting the old chimney breast in the loft.

Adding a large new dormer can potentially interfere with airflow to shorter stacks, such as those found on some rear additions. Stacks need to rise at least 900mm above ridge height, so in some cases it may become necessary to increase their height or fit a suitable cowl to prevent downdraughts pushing smoke back down the flue. Note also any significant leaning, or outstanding maintenance works. It's very common for mortar joints to need re-pointing. If your roof is hipped with a chimney

rising up a main wall, and you're planning to convert the hip to a gable, it should be possible to incorporate this stack within the new structure. Large dormers can sometimes be designed to neatly embrace a 'rogue' stack.

Party walls

At the heart of many loft conversions are some hefty new steel beams bedded into the old party walls, thereby substantially increasing the loadings. So for semis or

Party wall in loft omitted by Victorian builders

terraced houses it's obviously important to check their condition first. Party walls are normally the length of one brick thick, *ie* approximately 225–230mm, but on some older properties the builders saved money by laying all the bricks lengthways to form a narrow single leaf of only half this thickness. An easy way to check this is by ensuring that there are plenty of 'headers' (the ends of bricks) visible, which should confirm that the wall is a full brick-length thick.

But this is by no means the worst thing you could discover. It was not unusual for loft walls in rows of Victorian terraces to be omitted altogether, so if your 'firebreak' party walls are missing or undersized they will need to be rebuilt. In some more modern properties the party walls are often built from concrete blockwork, which in some cases may only be 115mm thick, and will need upgrading. Where party walls are only of 100mm single-

Left: Leakage to stack 'back gutter' will rot timber

Right: New blockwork firebreak party wall – but only 115mm thick

Many loft conversions include a new en suite shower/bathroom and WC. This needs to be located as near as possible to your existing bathroom. The key thing here is to make a note of the position of your existing soil and vent pipe (SVP). In pre-war properties these wide-bore vertical pipes are normally run on the outside, up a side or rear main wall near the bathroom, but in more modern houses are usually run internally and boxed in. (See Chapter 11.)

Main walls

skin thickness, beams or joists should not rest in them. Instead, a design solution needs to be found that avoids penetration of the wall. (See Chapter 6.)

A further obstacle to your plans may occur in the form of chimney breasts, which commonly follow the party wall on their way up through the roof. The problem here is that it's not permissible to fit structural beams or joists directly into a chimney breast. Make a note of their dimensions so accurate plans can be drawn.

As part of the survey, it's important to note whether next-door have already converted their loft. If they have, there's a high probability that steel beams have already been inserted into the party wall from the other side. Even in normal thickness walls there's potential for 'beam to beam conflict', because beams normally need at least 100mm end-bearing support. Try to identify the position of any neighbouring steelwork by checking for any disturbed brickwork just above ceiling joist level.

Rooms

You'll shortly need to produce drawings, not just of the proposed loft room but of all the rooms in the house, so now is a good time to measure the dimensions of each room. Note also the ceiling heights of the bedrooms in case you need to 'borrow' some space at a later stage as a means of increasing the available headroom in the loft.

What type of main wall construction does your house have? Cavity walls are found in most homes built since the 1930s and are normally about 260–300mm thick. Older properties often have solid brick walls about 230mm thick or traditional solid stonework that is considerably thicker,

Timber frame construction visible from loft

perhaps 400mm or more. Then there's modern cavity wall construction incorporating a timber frame inner leaf. This is only a generalisation, so if you plan to add serious loadings to your walls it's clearly important to carefully check their type and condition first.

Loft conversions often take their support from new beams embedded in party walls. One reason for this is that all the window and door openings in the main walls means they are already weakened and may not be able to cope with much extra loading. If it is intended to rest new beams in the main front, rear or side walls, the lintels over doors and windows must be checked, especially where they span wider openings such as to bays. In many houses the lintels weren't designed to cope with loadings from an extra floor above, and in some cases they were omitted altogether, especially to upper storeys with only a few courses of brickwork over them.

Any cracks or bowing to the walls may need further investigation before additional loads can be applied. Check the condition of mortar joints, and where necessary carry out localised re-pointing. Lime mortar was generally used until the 1930s, and on period properties the bricks and the mortar will not be as strong as on modern buildings.

As a general rule, older buildings are more prone to defects, making them potentially riskier to convert. Some cheaper Victorian terraces which might appear to have good solid 9-inch thick brick walls actually comprise two perilously thin separate leafs which aren't tied together. Adding extra loadings here could have disastrous consequences. Bay windows in period properties are also unlikely to be much use when it comes to taking extra loads, since many have shallow foundations and thin brickwork that can be prone to bowing and movement.

However, living in a modern house doesn't mean you can carry on regardless. Some inner leafs of lightweight

concrete blocks will have limited load-bearing potential, although engineers can normally factor this into their calculations. In modern timber-frame houses the loadings are primarily taken by the timber framework inner leaf, and the outer walls of brick, stone or rendered blockwork aren't intended to support significant structural loads.

Foundations

It's very unlikely that you'll need to carry out any foundation work in order to provide adequate support for your loft room. Although the loadings on foundations are often increased by around 10 per cent (and sometimes as much as 30 per cent), routine conversions rarely affect foundation stability. Only in extreme cases, where the old foundations are very shallow, or the ground is very prone to subsidence, would Building Control insist that underpinning is required.

The last resort

If you return downhearted from the survey, don't despair. In some cases you're actually better off rebuilding the roof from scratch. If it's simply too shallow to provide decent headroom this may be the only option. The only real obstacle here is the need for planning permission. Or it may be that your roof is on its last legs and you would have had to replace it anyway, in which case this is a good opportunity to rebuild it, perhaps using 'room-in-roof' trussed rafters that incorporate the ready-made shell of a loft room. Complete roof replacement is not as dramatic or excessively expensive as is sometimes thought, and is should be no dearer than building an equivalent-sized home extension. (See Chapter 8.)

Photo: Charles Grosvenor

You are about to transform the appearance of your home forever. Getting it right means reaping huge benefits, improving your property's 'kerb appeal' and significantly adding to its value. But there is one major catch that faces all aspiring loft-converters. To get the maximum space inside the new loft room, a large box dormer window normally needs to be built into the roof; yet to create a pleasing design that looks attractive externally, small 'cottage style' dormers and skylights are usually preferable. In other words, the designer will need to carefully balance the demand for room space inside with the desire for maintaining or enhancing the property's external appearance.

You don't have to look far to find examples of stupendously ugly loft conversions around town. Prior to 1988 the planning rules allowed free rein to lovers of the grotesque, and as a direct result a plethora of clumsy, clodhopping front dormers now blight our townscapes. Sticking a giant box dormer with off-the-shelf UPVC windows onto the roof of an elegant Georgian or Victorian period property can, at a stroke, trash its character and reduce its value. The trick is to minimise the visual impact of a loft conversion by building in sympathy with the surroundings. If that's not possible, all the big stuff should be tucked away from view. This is why the planners will normally restrict the location of big dormers to the rear, to minimise any significant visual change to the main façade as seen from the street.

Photo: Charles Grosvenor

Photo: Velux

Conversion options

Other than totally rebuilding your roof, there are basically two design options:

Roof-space only conversions

This is the easiest and cheapest option for lofts that are already reasonably roomy. In some cases the only necessary new window could simply be built into an existing gable wall. But roof-space only conversions normally require the installation of roof windows, flush with the roof slope, into new openings cut between the rafters. This should be a fairly straightforward job (see step-by-step project Chapter 9).

All habitable rooms need opening windows for light and ventilation, and rooflights can happily fulfil this

Hipped roofs needn't be hard to convert

Dormer conversions

Dormer conversions are the most popular type of loft conversion because, in many cases, the existing loft is of insufficient size to accommodate the proposed new rooms and stairs. So a strategically placed large dormer is often the key to achieving the required additional space and can also solve the problem of how to get the new stairs into the loft without banging your head.

A dormer is defined as 'a window that projects from a sloping roof'. There's a clue in the name as to which rooms are most likely to feature dormer windows, being derived from the French *dormir*, meaning 'to sleep'. Because they're built vertically and stick out, they also have another distinguishing feature – they have their own roofs.

For shallow-pitched roofs (*ie* less than about 30°) the most effective way of providing light and headroom is normally with a big rear box dormer. But building dormers onto shallow-pitched roofs means the side 'cheeks' are consequently long and thin, stretching further back and thereby creating a tunnel effect inside the rooms. This also reduces the amount of daylight, unless, of course, you choose to glaze the sides.

requirement at about a third of the cost of an equivalent dormer window. Apart from not having to perform the major surgery on your roof that would be needed to install large dormers, this method should also free you from possible planning problems, since you're not making any alterations to the external shape of the roof. But you do need a decent-sized loft to start with. With this method in properties with traditional cut timber roofs, once the floor structure has been beefed up and the stairs fitted, much of the main structural work is done.

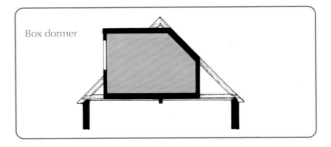

Box dormer

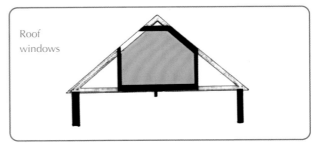

Roof windows

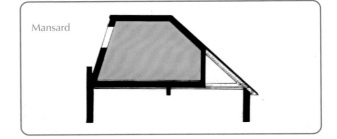

Mansard

Photo: South London Lofts

Full width dormer

Dormers

There are many styles of dormer, from bulky flat-roofed boxes that double the size of your loft, to a wide variety of small 'cottage' windows that can transform the tired front elevation of a downright boring-looking house into a vision of architectural splendour.

Box dormers

Large flat-roofed 'boxes' are popular because they dramatically boost the amount of useable room space, are fairly quick to install, and are reasonably cheap to build.

Unfortunately they're also the clumsiest-looking design, and are therefore usually restricted to the rear of the property.

Boxes can either be built straight up from the main wall or, more commonly, set back up the roof a little. They're normally constructed from timber framework and usually clad with tiles, timber boarding, render or sheet metal. Large flat dormer roofs typically join the existing main roof just below its ridge, and slope down slightly to the front.

Construction involves first removing a section of the existing roof tiles, battens and underfelt, and then constructing the timber stud framework for the side walls. Next a flat or pitched roof is built. The window frame can then be inserted and the stud framework covered with plywood and a suitable external cladding. Unlike flush rooflight windows, dormers impose significant new loadings to rafters and floor joists, which need to be calculated in advance.

Full-width dormers

These are similar to box dormers but, as the name suggests, they extend across the full width of the roof slope. Here the existing party walls or side gable walls of

the house are usually built up in matching brick or rendered blockwork to form the new sides that will enclose the dormer. The front faces are normally constructed of timber studwork and clad in tile, timber boarding or UPVC.

Like box dormers, the full-width variety have the advantage of maximising room space, but can look overbearing externally. They're best suited to terraced houses, especially those originally built with parapet party walls projecting above the roofline (a Victorian by-law requirement in London designed to show at a glance that the builders hadn't omitted the firebreak party walls in the loft).

Mansards

Crazy name, crazy roof, attributed to the 17th-century French architect François Mansart. The term describes a roof with a combination of a very steep lower slope and a very shallow or flat upper part. Mansards are essentially mega-dormers, the main difference being the front wall, which leans back at an angle becoming in effect a very steep front roof slope. They're a good way of visually reducing the bulk and ugliness of big dormers whilst maximising room space inside, thereby achieving the best of both worlds. Set within the large front face of mansards you often find two or three neatly recessed windows.

In some historic inner-urban areas the planners may consider the addition of a large mansard to be the most architecturally appropriate style of loft extension to a period house. Such conversions are regarded as 'roof extensions' rather than pure conversions, necessitating the complete rebuilding of at least one roof slope.

Mansards can provide struggling loft designers with a secret weapon to get round strict planning rules. Whereas big box dormers are usually not appropriate for front elevations, mansards may be acceptable, especially on historic Georgian and Victorian butterfly-roofed 'townhouses'. Their limitation, however, is that they only really suit buildings of three or more storeys, as they tend to make smaller properties look bizarrely top-heavy.

Mansards are usually built full-width. The sides are built up in brick from the existing party walls or end gable walls in a similar fashion to full-width dormers, except that here the walls have to be constructed to a slope that matches the steep pitch of the front roof slope. Where neighbouring roofs have already been extended in a terrace it makes sense to match the existing pattern. The planners may in any case want to specify the required front roof pitch, typically sloped at a very steep 60° to 70° angle.

The front is normally clad to match the original roof, often in slate, and the shallow or flat upper roof may be clad with lead or even copper. Because flat roofs actually slope slightly towards the front, the detailing at the junction with the steep front face needs to be super-watertight and usually comprises a lead flashing fixed beneath the upper roof and dressed over the lower front face. It's best to avoid cheap felt coverings due to their short lifespan.

Traditional small dormers

Before the days of giant box dormers, massive mansards and mega full-width loft extensions, the humble dormer was a charming, well mannered architectural nicety. Today, quaint 'cottage dormers' are still very popular, and are an excellent way of giving otherwise bland, charmless buildings a character-makeover. But their good looks come at a price. In contrast to clunking great modern box dormers, they add relatively little space and headroom

Dormer styles

Gabled

The majority of 'cottage-style' pitched roof dormers are built to the classic gabled Λ shape, a.k.a. 'pitched' or 'bonnet' dormers. Their small size means ceiling joists can sometimes be omitted within the dormer itself, with ceilings formed by plasterboarding the underside of the insulated rafters, creating a pleasing open ceiling up to the apex.

Hipped

Similar to the gabled version but with a laid-back hipped front roof slope – usually appropriate when matching a hipped main roof.

Flat

Flat roofs are the easiest type to construct because they don't need a lot of tricky valley detailing where they join the main roof. Traditionally they're clad in lead or zinc, or more rarely in copper (the most expensive option). Modern roofing felt not only looks cheap, it also has a short lifespan and is best avoided. Most flat roof dormers actually slope forwards, but occasionally they're designed to fall gently back towards the main roof to discreetly disperse rainwater.

Recessed

Strictly speaking these aren't dormers at all, because they're set back into the roof rather than projecting outwards. Being inset they need a small flat roof laid out in front, which means you lose more space inside the room than you would with a roof window, which would also be a lot cheaper. So why bother? Well, they're a traditional design in some localities, and may be visually appropriate with their

pleasant 'balcony' detailing, so planners may favour designs that include them. Recessed roof windows look best on steeply pitched roofs, especially mansards.

Eyebrow

Eerily peering out of the roof, curved eyebrow dormers are a traditional design found on many thatched cottages. Of

course, thatch lends itself to bends rather better than rigid tiles, which is why a certain amount of head-scratching may occur on the part of the roofers when they first see the drawings. Probably the most complex of all dormer types, both in terms of the timber frame structure and the laying of tiles over the curve.

Cat slide

What do you call a sweeping 'flat' roof built at a steep angle? A distinctive feature of these small dormer roofs is their incredibly long, thin triangular cheeks. More accurately known as 'swept' or 'wedged' roofs. These only work if the main roof is steeply pitched.

Hybrids

Occasionally you come across some intriguing hybrid styles…

indoors yet are expensive to build, plus they're only really suited to houses with roofs steeper than 40°.

The front of your house is always going to be highly sensitive from a planning perspective, so large front dormers are normally a no-no. Which means you are left with two basic window options: rooflights or small dormers.

The relatively light weight of small dormers means that traditionally they only required support from the adjoining roof rafters (trimmed around the opening). Modern versions, however, are heavier, with their thick insulation boarding and double glazing, so additional support from the floor structure is sometimes required. If you're lucky,

you may be able to construct a small dormer without having to move any purlins, especially on large roofs with two purlins per slope and plenty of clear space between them.

Most traditional dormers have little pitched roofs, and to look right these normally match the angle of the main roof. Guttering is often dispensed with since it tends to look rather awkward.

Half-dormers
Whereas 'real' dormers are set back up the roof a little, traditional 'half-dormers' have their fronts built directly up from the main wall in matching masonry. Here, the windows will often slot straight down into the top of the wall. Common on Victorian houses, half-dormers are making something of a comeback today on new 'cottage style'

houses where the bedrooms extend into the lower part of the loft, and the ceilings slope around the edges of the rooms.

Window styles
Just when you thought the choice of dormers couldn't get any more diverse, you can further customise your design by picking from a variety of styles for the windows set within them.

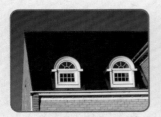

Pediment, bow or arched roof dormers
These classically inspired window designs are found on mansards and steep roofs.

Canted bay dormers
A bay window on your roof – how very Scottish. Victorian 'roof bays' with gabled, hipped or flat roofs are a widespread period feature north of the border.

Photo: Stewart Saunders / Gregor Developments

Design considerations

Hip to gable conversions
If your roof was originally built with a hipped roof slope to the side, the chances are that the available headroom will be restricted just where you need it most – over the new loft stairs. If you're lucky, the main part of your loft will be so spacious that you won't need to worry about sacrificing

some space around the sides, especially if you can design the stairs to surface centrally into the loft room.

Conventional gabled roofs are generally easier to convert than hipped roofs. This is not just on account of their more generous headroom, but also because gable end walls are useful for supporting new structural floor beams. So if your hipped roof turns out to be a major obstacle, the obvious answer is to convert it to a gabled roof. This is done by building the existing side wall straight up, to form a new triangular gable end. The space between the new gable wall and the existing roof can then be filled in with a timber rafters, increasing the amount of useable loft space. New gable end walls are commonly constructed of masonry, such as brick or rendered thermalite blockwork, to match the existing walls. But a popular alternative is to build them in lightweight timber studwork, especially where they're to be clad with tiles, slates, or rendered metal lathing. Timber frame walls can be designed to support new floor and roof beams if required for the main loft conversion works.

So what's the downside of a hip conversion? Hipped roofs were especially popular from the 1930s and to the 1950s, and are famously found on many semis of the period. The thing is, if you convert the hipped roof of your semi to a gable it can arguably make the pair of semis look rather imbalanced, even hunchbacked. It's also a relatively expensive option. A good compromise might be a more subtle-looking 'half-hip'. This is a traditional barn-style treatment in which the side gable wall is only partially built up, finishing with a small hipped roof at the top. This way you should get sufficient headroom without the awkward-looking shape. Or you could be even more adventurous and do completely the opposite. A hipped roof slope can be designed with a 'gablet' or 'baby gable' wall poking out about halfway up.

Side dormer conversions

If the prospect of converting your hipped roof to a new gable all seems a bit drastic, it might be simpler to opt instead to build a side dormer. The beauty of this

solution is that the dormer needn't be too overpowering in order to simply create enough internal headroom above the new loft stairs, and it means you don't need to completely sacrifice your property's original character. A sympathetic architect should be able to design one that blends in pleasingly, perhaps incorporating its own tastefully hipped mini roof echoing the original style of the house.

Lean-to conversions

This has to be the easiest loft conversion of them all. If your main house has a secondary roof leaning against it,

Hip and gable styles

Right: Gable
Below: Half-gabled (or half and a bit!)
Below right: Lean-to

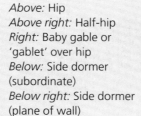

Above: Hip
Above right: Half-hip
Right: Baby gable or 'gablet' over hip
Below: Side dormer (subordinate)
Below right: Side dormer (plane of wall)

perhaps from an adjoining garage or single-storey extension to the side or rear, this may offer great potential. Such lean-to roofs can provide very useful loft space without the need to fit new stairs. Simply knock through a new door opening and you have the makings of a great new room. (See Chapter 7).

Existing attic rooms

Many grand (and some not so grand) Victorian houses were originally built with small attic rooms, used as nurseries or occupied by maids. Although these obviously won't comply with modern Building Regulations and there's no obligation to upgrade them, any new work that you carry out – such as adding an en suite bathroom to an existing attic room – will need to comply. However, just because Victorian servants were expected to put up with cold draughty rooms without complaint doesn't mean you have to, so it's well worth upgrading the insulation and improving fire protection at the very least.

Galleries

Galleries are the oldest form of habitable loft, found in some barn conversions and older period houses. They're defined as 'a raised area or platform around the sides or at the back of a room which provides extra space'. Sometimes an adjoining loft can be accessed via a door high up in an internal wall. Installing a fixed ladder with handrails can make this into a potentially handy hidey-hole for teenagers, or priests on the run. Such quirky design features are sometimes also found in more expensive new 'designer' loft apartments.

However, larger galleries can prove rather taxing from a Building Control perspective, as they don't fit neatly within the standard criteria, especially where they contain an 'inner room' potentially making access rules tricky to resolve. Normally, where such a feature is included in your design, it should be no more than 4.5m above ground level

and have guard rails fitted along the gallery edges. Also, any cooking facilities in a gallery must be enclosed within a fire-resisting construction, or alternatively be positioned well away from the stairs so that they don't hinder escape.

External design

The real challenge is to design your new loft accommodation so that it's as spacious as possible on the inside without making your home look top-heavy and stodgy when viewed from the street. This normally means

picking the appropriate type of dormer that best suits the existing architecture. For example, large flat roof dormers can look peculiar on steeply-pitched roofs, and conversely small cottage dormers would look a bit odd on 1970s-style shallow-pitched roofs. It generally pays to respect the property's original architecture, especially when converting pre-war or older houses. To successfully blend the new with the old, there are three key design points to consider: the dormer cladding style; the windows; and the roof detailing.

Dormer cladding

Adding dormer windows to your roof will obviously have a major impact on the way your home looks. The bigger they are, the more important it is to get them looking right. Your choice of materials for the external finish will have a dramatic effect, either enhancing your property's natural charm and character or blighting the

practicalities to consider, such as access for cleaning, increased heat loss, and possible concerns from the planners about 'overlooking'. UPVC cladding is a popular choice on some large dormers, but because plastic and timber are combustible their use is restricted within 1m of the boundary to restrict the potential spread of fire between buildings.

Less popular coverings include copper, which develops a pleasing green patina over time but is expensive, and cheaper GRP fibreglass and zinc materials with relatively short lifespans.

Many modern houses have pitched roofs clad with large concrete interlocking tiles, and some older properties have traditional pantiles of a similarly large size. Trying to match these with vertical tiling on dormers tends to look clumsy, since the detailing is often poor, and you may find that a contrasting material works best, such as smaller 265 x 165mm plain tiles that are widely available and can look very neat.

Windows

neighbourhood. Popular choices include cladding with plain tiles or slates that match the roof, or lead sheeting, a traditional finish that seems to blend well with roof coverings of all types. Alternatively, the triangular dormer cheeks may look good finished with barn-style timber cladding or rendered over metal lathing applied to the studwork frame. It's even possible to glaze dormer cheeks, boosting the amount of daylight in an otherwise dark room, but there are

When designing your dormers you may need to work backwards. First consider what type of window would best fit the 'face' of the house, and then how it can be incorporated into the dormer structure. To look right, the new windows should respect the basic proportions of the existing ones in the rest of the elevation. Accurate detailing is especially important in period houses. Rebating the windows within their openings to match those elsewhere in the property should not only improve their appearance but can also provide enhanced protection from the elements.

You don't want a house that looks boss-eyed and wonky, so where possible it's always best to align the new windows vertically with those below – it just looks better that way! At the very least windows should be spaced evenly, which isn't always as easy to achieve as it sounds when you have to consider the position of internal dividing walls and light requirements in different rooms.

Roof detailing

Experienced designers know the tricks of the trade that make buildings look good. Some might say they've learned from their mistakes, judging by the number of architectural eyesores that grace our streets. But in order to look good there are some golden rules to bear in mind at the design stage. Getting your detailing right is the hallmark of a quality job.

- All the slopes of a pitched roof should be built to the same angle, so if possible new dormer roofs should match the main roof.

- Avoid building big box dormers and mansards on short, dumpy buildings; it makes them look top-heavy.
- New fascias should be of a similar style to the existing ones – but remember that white ones tend to draw attention to the guttering.
- Ugly waste pipes can spoil an otherwise great design, so it's important to plan their routes at an early stage, minimising the number of changes of direction and joints, which tend to look conspicuous at higher levels.
- Chimneys can pose design problems, but a stack that runs straight through the centre of your loft may not actually be as big an intrusion as you might think. Once plastered and painted to match the decor, it's surprising how unobtrusive they can be. Disused flues however are often best removed.

Chimney breast through loft room

Internal design

Stairs

Floor area is a precious commodity when designing loft rooms, so it's a little disappointing to realise that your new staircase and landing may eat up an unexpectedly large chunk of this space.

Selecting the best position for the stairs has traditionally been a potential headache for loft-converters. You don't want to sacrifice any more valuable floor space than is really essential, but there are strict fire regulations to consider, as well as the question of where to join the new staircase to the floor below so that it fits with the existing room layout. In most conversions, the new loft stairs can rise up from the landing. But where there are space restrictions they may

Chimney View

Photo: Solalighting.co.uk

They have a mirror-like reflective lining and work via a prism and reflector arrangement to direct daylight into dark areas where it would otherwise be difficult to admit natural light. The lens at the top of the tube at roof level doesn't have to be directly over the area to be illuminated, and can therefore be located to blend in discreetly on the roof. Light tubes are completely sealed so as not to need cleaning. They're available from 230mm up to a super-sized 2m diameter. It's claimed that a 300mm tube can light up a $10m^2$ room to normal daylight level. Best of all, they still work on cloudy days and have no maintenance requirements.

Fitting is fairly simple, as even a 350mm size can fit happily between closely spaced rafters found on older buildings. A larger 550mm light tube should be fine for most modern trussed rafter roofs spaced at 600mm centres.

The latest models incorporate ventilation, as they have a double tube that allows light to pass down the centre, whilst air can pass through the space between the walls of the two tubes. This makes them useful for high-humidity rooms such as bathrooms, WCs and kitchens. Some even incorporate discreet electric night lighting.

Light tubes

Sometimes adding a new window or skylight in the roof is not practical. One solution may be to fit a discreet 'light tube'. As the name suggests, these are metal tubes through which daylight is channelled. For loft conversions, they can be run through eaves cupboards or new mini-lofts, and connected to the ceiling or wall of the room below. They're especially useful for brightening bathrooms and stair landings.

Photo: Charles Grosvenor

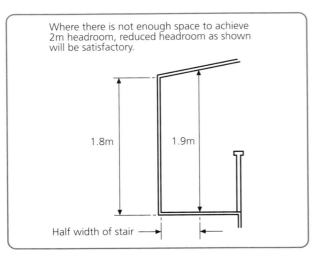

Where there is not enough space to achieve 2m headroom, reduced headroom as shown will be satisfactory.

1.8m   1.9m

Half width of stair

Main stairs (left) with loft stairs above

Photo: Charles Grosvenor

need to steal some of the space from an existing bedroom, in which case a lobby will need to be created with (fire-resistant) partition walls so that you don't have to go trooping through someone's private room to get to the attic.

The killer question with stairs is how to achieve sufficient headroom. Normally a clear space of 2m is required, but recent changes to the Building Regulations have introduced some welcome flexibility. For example, you often find there's a sloping ceiling just where the new stairs enter the loft. But as long as you can achieve 1.9m headroom above the centre line you only need a minimum of 1.8m height at the lowest edge of the stair. This concession can make all the difference, allowing shallower lofts to become habitable rooms. If you're still stumped with your stair design, there are other possible alternatives, such as compact stairs and spirals. (See Chapter 10.) To designers, spiral stairs are liberating and sexy. However, they generally take up more space than is popularly imagined, and using them routinely day in, day out, can become a tad tedious, especially as they sometimes develop a mildly alarming tendency to vibrate (and the initial love affair can start to wear a bit thin once furniture has to be carted up and down them).

Bathrooms

If you plan to use your loft accommodation as a bedroom,

it makes sense to also include a new en suite bathroom and WC. But this means doing some extra careful planning at the design stage. As noted earlier, there's the practical issue of how to connect your new waste pipes to the existing system. Then there's the architectural challenge of how to disguise bulky new soil and vent pipes (SVPs) if they're run externally, so that they don't protrude very obviously in all the wrong places. In modern houses they're usually run on the inside, which should make matters easier.

But if you need to connect to an external soil pipe, it will be less conspicuous where dormers have their front faces built straight up from the main wall rather than being set back up the roof. Inside, it's best to keep new waste pipes above floor level, to minimise cutting through the structure. Locating the new bathroom as near as possible to the existing SVP waste stack will help limit the amount of branch pipework. A restricting factor with bathroom fittings is the permitted length that you can run new waste pipes from sanitary fittings to the SVP stack, so it's important to plan the position of sanitary fittings early in design process. (See Chapter 11.)

Fireproof design

It's perfectly possible to go through life blissfully unaware of the hazards posed by fire. But as soon as you decide to

add an extra floor of habitable space to your house there will suddenly be a lot to discover in a short time. The fire regulations (Part B of the Building Regulations) are a major factor to consider when designing your new loft room. They not only apply to the loft itself, but can significantly affect the interior of your home all the way down from the roof to the main entrance doors. If you live in a period property or Listed Building the desire to preserve old features may conflict with regulations designed to resist fire. For example, the requirement to replace existing internal doors with new fire doors may be unacceptable in some properties, so

a suitable compromise will need to be agreed.

Apart from fireproofing the new loft room as a self-contained 'compartment', the key area where the Part B regulations are going to influence your design tends to centre around the need to provide a fire-resistant escape corridor through the house, which in some houses could mean having to enclose the staircase – all of which is discussed in Chapters 4 and 11.

Valleys

Many roofs have valley gutters running along the 'V' junctions between adjoining roof slopes. The problem is that within lofts, the undersides of valleys take the form of sharp corners that jut out inconveniently – which is why you need to duck every now and again in some badly planned loft conversions. So the layout of your new loft accommodation needs to make the best of such obstacles, which are not always obvious when looking at plan drawings. The least intrusive place to accommodate projecting valleys is probably the landing area, as they're best kept away from entrances to rooms and any other areas where good headroom is essential.

Escape windows

Until April 2007, emergency exit windows (a.k.a. 'egress windows') were an important component in most loft conversions. Essentially the idea was to create a fire-resistant box around the new loft room with an escape route provided either internally down through the

Photo: Charles Grosvenor

A load of party walls

Before going any further, there's one thing that needs to be thrashed out as early as possible.

Anyone contemplating a loft conversion in a semi-detached or terraced house is obliged under the terms of The Party Wall Act 1996 to first notify their adjoining neighbours. Like a particularly embarrassing illness, this is a subject that everyone seems to pretend doesn't exist, and would rather not get involved with. But it is the law, and you are legally required to carry it out.

The Party Wall Act may sound like a lot of unnecessary hassle, but its objective is to prevent serious disputes arising between neighbours. The Act has nothing to do with Planning or Building Regulations but is a totally separate piece of legislation, which applies to any work to an existing shared wall. The official boundary line between terraced and semi-detached properties runs through the middle of the party wall. Strange as it may sound, both owners legally have rights to the whole wall. This is because both buildings rely on the same wall for structural support, as well as for protection from fire and noise intrusion. So each side needs to know in advance if the other is planning to muck about with it.

Most loft conversions involve building new structural beams into shared party walls and you can understand neighbours not being entirely overjoyed at the prospect of having massive steel joists suddenly thrust through their walls. Not unreasonably they may want some reassurance that the structural work won't damage their property. Right now you probably want to crack on with the job without undue hindrance, but even if your new beams need less than half the width of the wall for support – say 100mm in a 229mm wall – you are still legally obliged to notify the adjoining owners.

For loft conversions, relevant party wall works would typically comprise:

- Cutting into a party wall to insert and support a new beam.
- Building new firebreak party walls in the loft if there are none.
- Building up the existing party walls above roof level to form new sides to a full-width dormer. (Note that half of any new party wall will actually be in next door's territory.)

What needs to be done?

You need to serve a formal 'party structure notice' on the owner of the adjoining property at least two months before doing any work to an existing party wall. To get full co-operation, the best approach is always to discuss your plans with the neighbours on friendly terms *before* the formal notice is served.

Surprisingly there's no official form for the notice itself and you'll need to draw up your own document. This must state your name and address (as the building's owner), confirm the date when you plan to start, and include details and drawings of the proposed work. The notice is only valid for a year. See the website for sample forms.

Even where the adjoining owner's written agreement is forthcoming, you still have a legal obligation to avoid all unnecessary inconvenience to them whilst the work is carried out.

But what if your neighbours have already got a massive dormer extension on their roof that comes right up to your boundary? In such cases, if you want a new full-width dormer you'll probably need to build right up to theirs, so that it effectively becomes your new party wall. Again, you must give them notice and hope they agree.

The catch with the Party Wall Act is that unless the adjoining owner writes back within 14 days the law assumes that they do *not* give their consent, and that a dispute has arisen.

Disputes

If your neighbour doesn't respond or don't agree, you can either:

- Jointly with your neighbour appoint a single surveyor acting for you both, who will draw up a legal agreement detailing your proposed works. This is known as an 'award'. The agreement will confirm that you'll pay for any damage caused by your building activities.
- Alternatively, each side can appoint their own surveyor to produce an award. If any differences arise between the two that can't be settled, a third surveyor may need to be appointed to mediate.

Option one is clearly the better and cheaper route. Note that surveyors are duty-bound to act impartially and fairly regardless of their client. Unlike lawyers, they don't bat for just one side, but must consider the interests of both the building owner and the neighbour. Incidentally, the fees for all the surveyors are down to you!

Photo: Velux

building, or else externally via an escape window in the roof. Most converters chose the latter option because it was often easier and cheaper. However, the rules have now changed. Today, unless you're converting a bungalow, you can no longer rely on windows from loft rooms to provide an alternative means of escape. (See Chapter 4.)

Drawing it

If you decided against employing an expensive package-deal loft firm to design and build your attic rooms, you may want to employ your own architect or draughtsman to prepare the plans instead. But there's still a fair bit you can do yourself to start the ball rolling. It's certainly possible for you to draw the preliminary outline plans, and a good place to start is by drawing a scale plan of your existing top floor, and then superimposing the proposed loft rooms over it on tracing paper. This shows what's not

Photo: David Davies

practical for such things as the position of new stairs and bathrooms.

But because drawings for Building Control require a lot of structural detail, a professional designer will need to be involved. For conversions to Listed Buildings it's particularly important to employ someone who has good experience with and empathy for period properties.

Package deals

The most popular approach to loft conversions is the package deal where a specialist firm does it all. Or at least, they claim to do it all. Often things like the Party Wall Act (see opposite) are left solely up to the client, and it's not unknown for dodgy firms to 'forget' to notify Building Control.

Loft specialists normally prepare the necessary drawings in-house and obtain all required Local Authority consents together with the necessary completion certificate at the end of the job.

It's important to be sure that your contractors have appropriate experience converting lofts, and are not just being over-confident. Builders sometimes regard the deskbound 'white collar' part of the job as a bit of a

What to look for in a set of drawings

- The right scale. Scale drawings don't use perspective like a sketch, so in more controversial cases, such as raising roof heights, it's worth submitting a good sketch or photo mock-up of the finished building to help demonstrate how attractive the design will look. (See 'Submitting a planning application' in the next chapter.)
- The accompanying text and notes should be easy to read, so avoid the use of fancy handwriting or bizarre fonts. The design details should be clear.
- Drawings are needed for each of the required elevations, floor plans, cross-sections etc, as described in the next chapter.
- Show plenty of measurements, usually in millimetres, marking the dimensions of any new walls and dormers and the positions of window openings.
- The drawings for Building Control need a considerable amount of text explaining how the design will comply with the regulations in key areas. This may be explained in detail on the drawings, perhaps in addition to a separate 'specification' document. If you just write something lazy like 'work to comply with Building Regulations approved documents' it may well get sent back for clarification.

doddle, perhaps not fully appreciating the sometimes confusing array of forms, procedures and rigorous Local Authority requirements you need to satisfy before getting anywhere near starting on site. With a package deal you'll also need to trust the firm implicitly, since the designer won't be 'on your side' if things go wrong. In such cases good communication, explaining exactly what you want, is paramount from the outset. The risk with package-deal firms is that they may simply provide a thinly disguised duplicate of the last 200 jobs they've done, regardless of any special requirements you have. Also, the legal contract they ask you to sign will be skewed very much in their favour. On the other hand, if you're a busy person it's sometimes convenient to let someone else take the strain of running the entire project.

If you do decide to use a specialist loft firm, many of the following points still apply – especially checking what the price includes (see Chapter 5).

Finding a designer

By getting your loft rooms designed independently you should be able to achieve maximum personal input in the design. But that doesn't necessarily mean having to appoint an architect. Converting lofts can be a technically challenging task, especially with older buildings. So what matters most is finding someone with specialist knowledge and experience. A warmly recommended local draughtsman or structural engineer with a good reputation from similar projects could be a better choice than an eminent firm of architects renowned for their landmark luxury hotels.

It always helps if your designer is already familiar with

Photo: Wooden Hill

the Council's planning policies and how to overcome technical queries with the Building Regulations. A 'free consultation' visit should normally be offered to discuss your ideas.

Note that designers have a legal responsibility for their designs to minimise on-site safety risks associated with building work. Some may also be able to fulfil the Project Manager role, if required. Although local recommendations are a good start, you'll also want to see examples of previous work, both drawings and completed buildings. A list of local architects and designers may be available from the Council, but they're not allowed to make recommendations.

The style of drawings varies to a surprising extent between different designers, so compare several before confirming the appointment. A badly drawn set of plans will be confusing for everyone including the builders on site.

What does the price include?

It's important to be sure exactly what you're getting for your money. Agree a fixed fee with your designer only once the following points have been clarified:

Are all necessary drawings included?

Does the price include all the drawings needed to get planning permission and building regulations consent?

Photo: David Davies

Are all fees included?

Legally it's the homeowner who's responsible for paying the fees for the Planning and Building Regulations applications, so the cost of these may not be included in the price. The designer should be able to confirm how much the fees will be, or you can check on your local Council website. It's normally a good idea to give the designer cheques for these fees made payable to the Council.

Are minor amendments included?

The price should always include the need for any small revisions to the plans required by the Council. If amendments are due to the designer omitting information on their original drawings, the cost of revisions shouldn't be down to you. Small amendments shouldn't be too difficult, particularly if plans are drawn on a computer. Always be sure to get fresh copies of any amended plans. To avoid later confusion, the first drawings are usually numbered version 'A' and subsequent revised versions are numbered 'B', then 'C' etc. To be on the safe side it's best to mark all old plans very clearly as 'superseded'.

Are structural engineers' calculations included?

All loft conversions involve making structural alterations, sometimes of a complex nature. Building Control applications will therefore require accompanying structural calculations. These fees may not be included in the price, but the designer should at least be able to provide a rough idea of the cost. It is with the structural engineer that the buck finally stops, since everyone else is relying on their calculations to prove that the finished loft extension won't come tumbling down in the first gust of wind.

It may help at the design stage to bear in mind some structural facts of life. The walls and foundations of your house need to support not only substantial extra loadings from the new loft accommodation (dormers, floors and stairs etc) but also from the occupants and furniture. Plus the structure has to be strong enough to withstand forces unleashed by extreme storms or freak blasts of wind, or from heavy layers of snow. The designer has therefore to assume the worst possible combination of circumstances – perhaps a sumo-wrestling loft-rave whilst a storm-force blizzard rages outside.

Is project management included?

Do you want your designer to play an additional role, overseeing the project on site through to completion? Project management is a major task involving frequent site visits, approving stage payments, and ultimately signing the job off, for which professional indemnity insurance is required. This tends to limit the role to architects (ARIBA qualified) or suitably qualified chartered surveyors (MRICS or FRICS). But how much will this cost and what exactly will it include?

Photo: David Davies

Builders' drawings

For the more complex parts of the work (such as joints between beams, major structural alterations and the position of new stairs) the builders should ideally be provided with additional large-scale drawings that clearly explain the precise details. This will help ensure it all gets built right first time. If you don't, the builders will always 'know better' and will do it their way – which may be fine with an experienced contractor, but could be a disaster if they're unaware of some important element at a later stage that depends on getting this part exactly right. Without guidance, they may get hacked off and be tempted to do the job badly.

At the early stages, contractors don't need to know the precise location of every single switch, power point and radiator, but don't neglect this information for too long. Soon after works start on site you'll need to provide modified drawings showing exactly where the various pipes are to be run and sockets placed. Otherwise things will inevitably get positioned in the wrong place (and there may then be a charge for the trouble of repositioning them). Finally, because drawings tend to get rather mashed up on site it's worth laminating a couple of copies of the approved plans in an effort to make them builder-proof.

Loft Conversion Manual

4 PLANNING AND BUILDING REGULATIONS

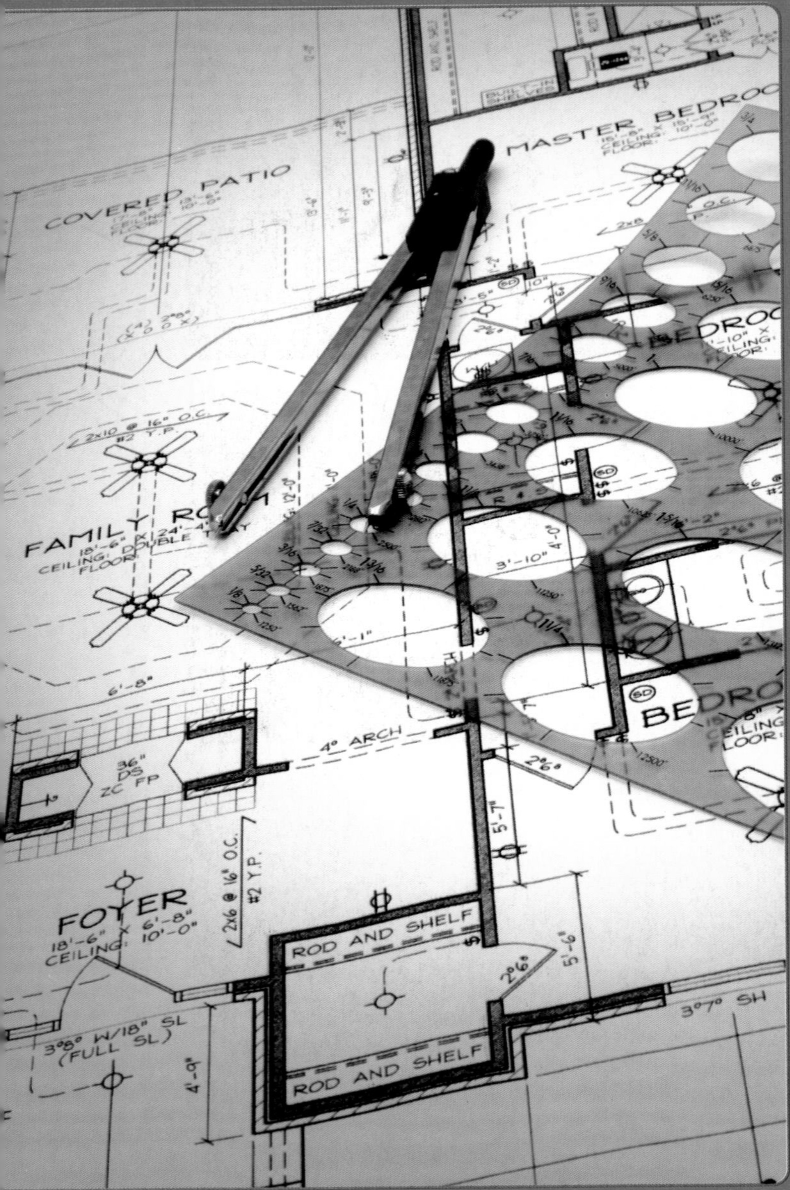

Photo: South London Lofts

One of the great joys of converting lofts is that the job can often be done without the need for a formal planning application. Even if consent is required, in most cases it's pretty clear in advance what's likely to be acceptable and what isn't. Things are only likely to get tricky if you need to raise the height of the roofline.

It's important to note that Planning and Building Regulations are two totally separate things. However, both departments are normally run by the local Council. The chief concern of the planning department is essentially to balance one person's right to build with the rights of other interested parties, such as the neighbours. They will also aim to protect the character of an area from being blighted by hideous, overbearing new mega-structures or from potentially disturbing changes of use. Basically, the planners will want you to achieve a decent-looking, unobtrusive loft extension that doesn't detract from other local residents' enjoyment of their homes.

Converting your loft will almost inevitably involve making major structural alterations to the property, so regardless of the planning situation you'll need to satisfy the folk at Building Control. Without their approval you would find it virtually impossible to sell your house since prospective buyers and mortgage lenders could assume it was structurally unsafe. The objective of Building Control is to ensure compliance with basic safety standards. The kind

of stuff that will interest them for a typical loft project would include protection from fire and how you could escape in an emergency, structural alterations (such as those to party walls, floors and roofs), the quality of thermal insulation and whether there is safe stair access to the new loft rooms. This is pretty much the bare minimum, as we shall see later in this chapter.

If your loft happens to be one of the lucky majority that can effectively bypass the planning system under the current 'permitted development' rules, you may want to skip this stage and move straight to the section on Building Control. But don't be too hasty. Rather cunningly, local Councils can choose to remove permitted development rights where they feel the character of an area is particularly vulnerable, by slapping on an 'Article 4 Direction'. Also, loft conversions to flats and maisonettes as well as those to Listed Buildings are excluded from permitted development. So it's always worth checking with the planners first.

Planning

New planning rules

The Government is currently proposing to simplify the planning system – which cynics claim will inevitably result in more red tape and confusion. Essentially the idea of the mooted new 'Unified Consent Regime' is for proposed building works to be assessed by the Planners in terms of their impact on the local area. Any that are deemed 'low impact' or 'no impact' will be automatically permitted. Sounds good, until you consider that in high-density urban Britain there's a good chance that most works would still be deemed to have a significant impact, and therefore could require a planning application. The proposals seem to be aimed at broadening the permitted development rules so that relatively minor projects such as conservatories, small extensions and installing solar roof panels will not require planning permission where they clearly have little impact on the street scene and on neighbouring properties. The general view is that whilst

this could make getting permission easier for some home extensions, because the existing rules for lofts are already fairly relaxed there's a risk that it could actually make it harder to get consent. See website for updates.

Will my loft conversion need planning permission?

Most loft conversions are carried out as 'permitted development'. This means that you don't need planning consent, subject to meeting some basic rules on maximum size and height. In terms of size, the 'free allowance' is very generous. New loft rooms should be exempt from planning where they enlarge the volume of the existing house by less than 50m³ (40m³ for terraced properties). This should be more than ample, because your original loft space is already included within the volume of the existing house. Therefore only additional projections from the original roof count as enlargements. In other words, if you create a new room in your loft without adding any new dormers there will be no enlargement at all. Incidentally, the volume of your property is measured externally, including the main walls and your half of any party wall.

However, regardless of volume there's another basic rule. You cannot alter the shape of the building without consent. An exception to this is often where dormer roof

Photo: Velux

Grey areas and definitions

Just in case this all seems too easy, some aspects of loft conversions are grey areas, where local interpretations may vary depending on the Planning Authority. Some common works that can prove controversial include:

- Building up an existing party wall above roof level to form the new side walls of a full-width dormer. Because half the party wall is officially in next door's territory, planners may regard this as disqualifying such works from 'permitted development'.

- Large dormers built on side hipped roof slopes. Although they may not face a highway as such, their sides are still visible from the front.

- Fitting a skylight window to a roof slope facing a highway in a Conservation Area.

- Converting hips to gables can sometimes prove controversial depending on their visual impact and the local planning authority's general feeling about such roof extensions.

In some cases, the sequence of making planning applications can affect the outcome. Suppose your existing house has a hipped roof, and you want to build a full-height side extension with a gabled roof. For such an application, the planners may very well insist that the new extension roof is

extensions don't face a highway and don't raise the overall height of the roof. Roof slopes facing highways, usually to the front of the house, are always a sensitive area. As a result, large dormers on the front are unlikely to be approved. The definition of a highway includes footpaths and bridleways, so loft conversions in properties on corner plots or where there's a road or footpath to the back or side of the house, may be more controversial.

Because roof windows or skylights are visually flush with roof slopes they are normally acceptable on the front, although the planners may prefer them fairly small and positioned away from more visible areas. Small, traditional 'cottage dormers' may also be acceptable to the front, but will normally require a planning application.

Before spending money producing detailed drawings, it's always a good idea to have a friendly chat with the planners. Some Councils produce guidance leaflets and design guides specially for loft conversions to show what can and can't be done.

Big front-facing dormers - unlikely to be permitted today

Not much of a view. Box dormer permitted without windows to improve internal headroom

hipped, so it matches the roof on the main house. But suppose the original hipped roof had already been converted to a gable, some time ago; you may find that a subsequent application for the new extension with a gabled roof would be viewed more favourably – as it now matches the existing roof.

The decision to grant or refuse consent can sometimes depend on the definition of a single word. For example, you're not usually allowed to build any higher than the highest part of your existing roof. But where exactly is the highest part? What if you live in a Victorian house topped with elaborate crested ridge tiles that project about 150mm above the apex? Similarly, some terraced houses have their party walls extended about 400mm above roof level in the form of small parapet walls. Or houses with butterfly roofs, which may have the main front wall higher than the roof behind it?

Small dormers that respect the character of the house are often acceptable

Illustration: Aylesbury Vale District Council / Ian Douglas

Box-like roof extensions impoverish the street scene ✗

Illustration: AVDC / Ian Douglas

As a rule, it's safer not to assume that such features will buy you any extra loft height. The planners may very well consider that the roof ridge itself represents the high point, excluding any fancy crestings and finials, thereby limiting the height to which you can build. And you can't count chimneys either!

One major planning consideration that your design must take into account is 'overlooking'. In some cases otherwise acceptable roof windows may run into planning problems where they glare down onto the neighbours, so consent may still be required. One solution is to design loft rooms with skylight windows high up, so they gaze harmlessly out into space. Or you may be able to compromise by fitting obscured glass that lets light in, but restricts occupants from easily seeing out.

In terms of design, planners tend to prefer new dormer roof extensions to complement the existing building rather than totally dominate it. You're more likely to win approval if its shape is traditional and blends in with the surroundings.

Listed Buildings and Conservation Areas

Special rules apply for Listed Buildings and for properties in Conservation Areas. Here your freedom to build without consent is far more tightly controlled. If your property is listed in any form (Grade I, II, or II star) it means that it's

been deemed to be of 'special architectural or historic interest', and particular importance will be placed on retaining its character, identity and appearance.

So in addition to submitting a normal planning application, you'll also need to apply separately for special Listed Building Consent, which will be required for any alterations, including internal changes that normally wouldn't interest the planners. The new unified consent regime should hopefully streamline this process. On the plus side, qualifying building work on Listed Buildings should be zero rated for VAT purposes, so you should be able to claim back VAT paid on materials. In fact the

contractors shouldn't charge VAT at all on their labour, but you do need to first notify them in writing that it's a Listed Building.

Conservation areas are defined as 'areas of special architectural or historic interest', and there are currently over 9,000 of them in the UK. It's crucial to check whether you're located in one, since the permitted development allowances (which includes extensions) are restricted in Conservation Areas to a 50m³ maximum (the same limits apply in Areas of Outstanding Natural Beauty, Areas of Special Control, National Parks and in the Norfolk and Suffolk Broads).

Here the planners have a duty to ensure that any external alterations 'preserve or enhance' the character and appearance of the area. Essentially this is intended to prevent incompetent DIYers from blighting a neighbourhood with a plague of artificial stone cladding and clumsy plastic porches. In effect, this gives the planners carte blanche to get closely involved (or interfere, depending on how you look at it) with the style of your design, even down to your precise choice of materials. They may, for example, stipulate that your dormer windows are built to a traditional design using expensive clay tiles or natural slate for the roof. In other words, having to pay for any fancy historic detailing that they deem necessary may cost you more, but at the same time may well enhance the 'kerb appeal' and value of your property.

Bulky dormers can be unsympathetic to the original architecture

Illustration: AVDC / Ian Douglas

Summary: lofts and planning

In summary, your loft conversion should be OK without planning unless:

- ■ You raise the height of the main roof, or build a new dormer higher than the ridge of the existing roof.
- ■ You construct a new dormer window on a roof facing a highway (normally the front).
- ■ You increase the volume of the original house by more than 50m³ (40m³ for terraces). Note that if you're extending other parts of the house as well as the roof, then the overall increase must be no more than 70m³ or 15 per cent of the property's volume (50m³ or 10 per cent for terraces), whichever is the larger, subject to a maximum limit of 115m³.
- ■ Your building is Listed or in a Conservation Area, or where permitted rights have been removed by an Article 4 direction or planning conditions.

Submitting a planning application

Right now, you'd probably like to crack on and get the building work started. But the planners have extreme enforcement powers, and can force you to demolish and remove any unauthorised building work at your own expense. Alternatively, they may arrange for the demolition to be done on your behalf and send you the bill. As a last resort they can even impose a jail term.

So your best bet at this stage is to ensure that any necessary planning application is organised well enough to sail swiftly through the system. There is, however, one possible shortcut you could take. Because planning applications normally have a timeframe of eight weeks, and a 'full plans' application for Building Regulations can take five weeks, it can save time if you apply for both simultaneously rather than wait until planning is granted. The downside is that if you steam ahead on both fronts and then things go pear-shaped with the planners, you're looking at additional expense and delay getting revised Building Regulations drawings submitted.

Detailed or outline?

There are two types of planning application – detailed and outline. Outline is only for large, complex, controversial developments where the general principle needs to be agreed first, and design details such as choice of materials can be left for a later application. For loft conversions and home extensions it should all be done in one go with a full application. Having discussed your initial ideas with the Council planners, assuming they're generally happy and don't foresee any major difficulties you should now be in a position to submit the required drawings.

What drawings to submit

You need to submit a full set of scale drawings clearly showing the work you propose to carry out, drawn in metric measurements. Some Councils prefer smaller A3-size drawings rather than the traditional monster A1-size plans that flap about on windy days on site. Drawings must clearly show all openings such as windows and doors. Elevation plans should show architectural details such as timber cladding. Each drawing needs to be clearly labelled with its title (eg 'Existing Front Elevation'), along with its number ('001 A' etc), the scale, and the address of the property, not forgetting to include your name and phone number. You'll need to run off at least six sets of drawings to distribute, plus a few more to keep for yourself.

Existing elevations 1:50 or 1:100 scale
– showing the relevant front, side and rear elevations from the outside *before* any work is carried out.

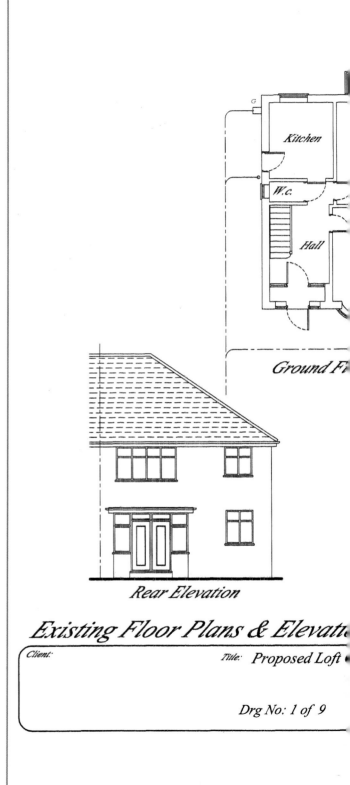

Kitchen

W.c.

Hall

Ground Fl

Rear Elevation

Existing Floor Plans & Elevati

Client:

Title: Proposed Loft

Drg No: 1 of 9

EXISTING DRAINAGE

*THE DRAINAGE SHOWN IS INDICATIVE ONLY AND THE
CONTRACTOR CARRYING OUT THESE WORKS MUST
CARRY OUT EXPLORATORY EXCAVATIONS TO DETERMINE
THE EXACT LOCATION OF ALL UNDERGROUND SERVICES
BEFORE WORK STARTS ON SITE AND ALL NEW CONNECTIONS
INTO THE EXISTING DRAINAGE SYSTEM MUST BE INSPECTED
AND APPROVED BY THE LOCAL AUTHORITY BUILDING CONTROL
OFFICER BEFORE THE EXCAVATIONS ARE BACK FILLED
ON COMPLETION THE EXCAVATED AREA MUST BE RETURNED
TO ITS ORIGINAL CONDITION UNLESS AGREED OTHERWISE
WITH THE CLIENT ENGINEER*

EXISTING FOUNDATIONS

*THE EXISTING FOUNDATIONS ARE TO BE EXPOSED BY
THE CONTRACTOR BEFORE WORK STARTS ON SITE FOR INSPECTION
BY THE LOCAL AUTHORITY BUILDING CONTROL OFFICER AND
REINFORCED BY THE CONTRACTOR IF REQUIRED
BY THE LOCAL AUTHORITY BUILDING CONTROL OFFICER*

EXISTING WALLS

*THE EXISTING WALLS ARE TO BE EXPOSED BY
THE CONTRACTOR BEFORE WORK STARTS ON SITE FOR INSPECTION
BY THE LOCAL AUTHORITY BUILDING CONTROL OFFICER AND
REBUILT BY THE CONTRACTOR IF REQUIRED
BY THE LOCAL AUTHORITY BUILDING CONTROL OFFICER*

EXISTING LINTELS

*THE EXISTING LINTELS ARE TO BE EXPOSED BY
THE CONTRACTOR BEFORE WORK STARTS ON SITE FOR INSPECTION
BY THE LOCAL AUTHORITY BUILDING CONTROL OFFICER AND
REINFORCED OR REPLACED BY THE CONTRACTOR IF REQUIRED
BY THE LOCAL AUTHORITY BUILDING CONTROL OFFICER*

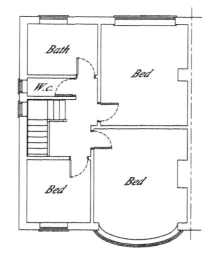

First Floor Plan

Side Elevation

Front Elevation

Scale :- 1-100

Paddick
Engineering
Limited

3 Falkland Mount,
Leeds,
LS17 6JG.

*This drawing is the sole property of
Paddick Engineering Ltd
and must not be reproduced or
copied without the written permission
of Charles Tidmarsh.*

LL ACT
TH THE PARTY WALL ACT THE OWNER OF THE ADJOINING
T BE INFORMED OF THIS PROJECT AND HIS PERMISSION
RITING BEFORE ANY WORK IS DONE ON OR NEAR THE
DIVIDING WALL BETWEEN THE TWO PROPERTIES

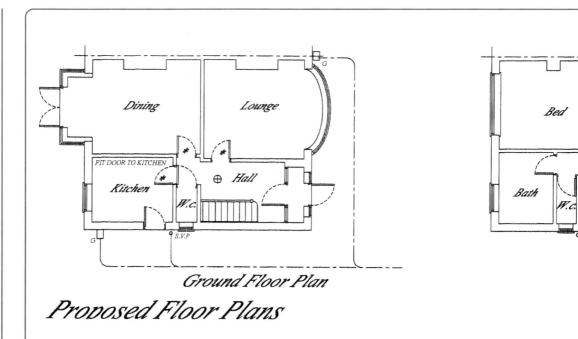

Dining

Lounge

FIT DOOR TO KITCHEN

Kitchen

Hall

W.c.

G

S.V.P

Ground Floor Plan

Proposed Floor Plans

Bed

Bed

Bath

Down

Up

W.c.

Bed

S.V.P

First Floor P

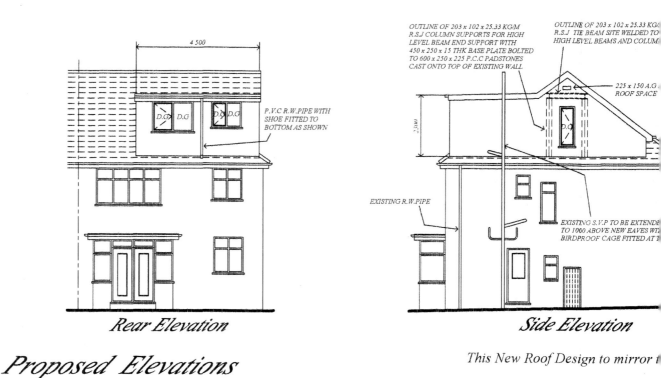

4 500

D.G D.G   D.G D.G

P.V.C R.W.PIPE WITH
SHOE FITTED TO
BOTTOM AS SHOWN

Rear Elevation

Proposed Elevations

OUTLINE OF 203 x 102 x 25.33 KG/M
R.S.J COLUMN SUPPORTS FOR HIGH
LEVEL BEAM END SUPPORT WITH
450 x 250 x 15 THK BASE PLATE BOLTED
TO 600 x 250 x 225 P.C.C PADSTONES
CAST ONTO TOP OF EXISTING WALL

OUTLINE OF 203 x 102 x 25.33 KG/
R.S.J TIE BEAM SITE WELDED TO
HIGH LEVEL BEAMS AND COLUM

225 x 150 A.G
ROOF SPACE

D.G

EXISTING R.W.PIPE

EXISTING S.V.P TO BE EXTENDE
TO 1000 ABOVE NEW EAVES WITI
BIRDPROOF CAGE FITTED AT T

Side Elevation

This New Roof Design to mirror t

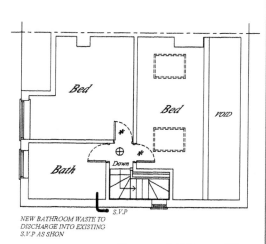

Second Floor Plan

NEW BATHROOM WASTE TO
DISCHARGE INTO EXISTING
S.V.P AS SHON

Front Elevation

g roof on adjacent house

Proposed elevations 1:50 or 1:100 scale
– the front, side and rear elevations showing what the outside of the property will look like *after* the work is completed.

Existing Layout plan 1:50 scale
– showing the existing floor layout of each level (*ie* ground floor and first floor, shown from above), with the name of each room clearly marked.

Proposed Layout plan 1:50 scale
– showing the proposed floor layout of each level including the completed new loft or roof extension, with the name of each room clearly marked.

Area or Location plan 1:1250 scale (not less than)
– a large-scale copy of the Ordnance Survey plan of your street, available from the Council for a smallish fee. Your house and garden must be outlined in red.

Site or 'Block' plan 1:500 scale or larger, commonly 1:200
– a close-up plan of your plot showing the position of site boundaries, roads, drains, trees and other buildings. This shows how the proposed works will relate to your immediate neighbours and the boundaries. Mark the orientation compass points. It may be acceptable to combine this with the Location plan.

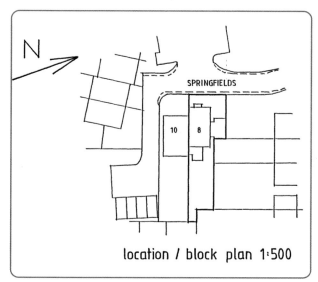

location / block plan 1:500

A 'Section' plan – showing a cross-section through the building – is not always necessary for planning but will definitely be needed for your Building Regulations application, and is normally the most technically detailed of all the plans. (See the section on 'Submitting your Building Regulations application' on page 71.) However, this could be required for planning applications for mid-terrace houses, because their sides aren't visible.

Registering new applications

With the drawings now prepared, you should be in a position to formally apply for planning permission. The only remaining task is to complete the Council application form, which can be done on paper or online at www.planningportal.gov.uk. The form asks for confirmation of ownership of the property or land being developed. Not a hard question to answer normally, but if the works happen to include building up a party wall above roof level to construct a new full-width dormer, then strictly speaking it will include a piece of party wall belonging to next door. But in nine out of ten cases the property will be entirely owned by the applicant.

If some of the questions seem a bit tricky, it's always best to phone the Council planners for assistance rather than guess, otherwise it will only get sent back and hold things up. You can then submit your completed application form to the planning department, together with the various sets of drawings and site plans, not forgetting to include the appropriate fee.

Within a few days, the Council should acknowledge receipt of your application by writing to you confirming the name of the case officer who will be dealing with it. Having checked that all the right documents are enclosed your application will then be placed on the 'planning register', which means that anyone can wander into their offices and take a look. Small laminated notices (often coloured yellow) may be physically posted on or near your site, and the application may be advertised in the local press and listed on the Council website. The Council may also write to your neighbours, alerting them to your intentions by giving them a couple of weeks to lodge any objections (should they feel strongly enough). It's always advisable to consult neighbours personally at an early stage, in order to quell any worries and hopefully deter them from objecting.

The case officer will normally visit the site within two weeks of the registration and the Council will aim to decide your application within a period of eight weeks. They can't reject a proposal simply because a lot of people oppose it; there must be good planning reasons for refusing permission. So they'll consider whether your proposals are consistent with the development plan for the area, and will assess its impact on the surrounding locality including any associated loss of amenity or possible traffic problems. If minor changes are needed to resolve a problem, they'll ask you to amend the design and resubmit it so that a decision can still be made within eight weeks.

Eventually, having completed the site visit, and after considering all the various consultations together with any objections, the case officer will prepare a report with a recommendation either for approval or refusal. This will then be submitted to the planning committee (made up of elected councillors). However, most loft applications are fairly straightforward cases where the decision can be made by senior planning officers under delegated authority, without the need to go to committee.

Planning conditions

When you finally receive the formal planning permission document that will hopefully approve your plans, there will normally be a number of conditions attached. Read these carefully, because legally the approval is conditional upon them being actioned. Some conditions can significantly affect the final appearance and cost of the building work. Others may relate to only very minor details. The most common stipulation is that work must be started on site within three years of the date of the consent.

Planning conditions are legally referred to as 'charges' and are recorded in the Local Authority land charges register. Such conditions are being increasingly applied to new housing in order to restrict otherwise permissible future development, such as loft and garage conversions. This is because much modern housing is built to high densities with limited parking. There's a potential trap here. Owners may not be aware that their rights have been removed and could embark on an otherwise acceptable conversion without permission – thereby unwittingly performing an illegal act in a loft!

For more sensitive developments, such as those in Conservation Areas, approval is sometimes subject to more onerous restrictions, such as the requirement for samples of your choice of materials (typically bricks and roof tiles) to be submitted for the planners to have a good look at and hopefully approve, prior to commencement of any building work.

Refusals and appeals

A refusal will be accompanied by specific reasons for the decision. Frustrating though refusal is, this may actually leave the door open to resubmitting modified plans that the planners are prepared to accept. The reasons tend to be expressed in planning jargon with references to policy numbers, so it's best to have a chat with the case officer to understand in plain English how you can best revise your design to get it approved next time. You're normally allowed to submit another application free of charge within 12

months of a refusal and are entitled to see background papers – such as comments from highways, objectors and supporters – that may have influenced the final decision.

If you feel the reasons for refusal aren't valid, you can appeal to the planning inspectorate within six months of the decision. This is an independent body, but your chances of success are fairly slim, since only around a third of appeals are successful. Although there's no great expense in submitting a written appeal if you put it together yourself, it normally takes four or five months before the planning inspector visits the site, and then another couple of months for a decision. Employing a planning consultant to process your appeal means having to pay fees, but it could be money well spent if they know the ropes. Appeals can also be made against individual planning conditions if they're unreasonable.

The basic procedure is to submit evidence that proves the Council's refusal was inconsistent with its relevant policies and with Government planning guidance. What can help clinch a result is being able to demonstrate that similar local developments have recently been permitted. Above all, it's essential to stick to the facts and avoid emotional arguments. The inspector's visit takes place after both sides have made their written submissions. The decision is final unless you want to take it all the way to the High Court. At the time of writing, the government is proposing to change the appeals procedure for applications decided under 'delegated authority' – ie for simpler cases that didn't need to go to committee. The intention is for appeals to be considered by the Council – the same organisation that refused your application.

One reason for thinking very hard before appealing is that it can actually make matters worse. For example, a design that would have been acceptable if the windows were modified so as not to overlook the neighbours could now be totally rejected as unacceptable by the inspector.

Building Regulations

Regardless of the planning situation, Building Regulations consent will normally be required for loft conversions. Of course over the years, various ingenious bluffs and dodges have been attempted to try and get round the system – such as describing proposed new loft accommodation as 'hobby rooms', 'computer workshops' or 'libraries' – but

Habitable rooms

What exactly is a 'habitable room'? Answer: it's a room that can be used for dwelling purposes, which actually includes kitchens but not bathrooms or utility rooms.

The question arises for a number of reasons. One of the first questions that will be asked at Building Control HQ when your plans plop onto their desk is how many habitable rooms you intend to construct in your loft. As we shall see, a single habitable room (which includes a bedroom with en suite bathroom) can mean you qualify for the use of compact or spiral stairs, if required. Also, most fires originate in habitable rooms, hence the requirement for fire doors to resist the spread of smoke and flames.

Building Control Officers have heard it all before. So even employing Shakespearean linguistic skills will still result in new loft accommodation being defined as a 'habitable rooms', for which the regulations will apply.

In any case, it's a bit daft trying to evade the Building Regulations because they're essentially about ensuring safety – stuff you'd want to get right anyway, like sanitary fittings that don't leak and wiring that doesn't kill. Their objective is simply to enforce minimum standards for such things as fire protection, safe stair access, decent heating, ventilation and drainage, and, above all, to ensure that buildings are structurally sound and weathertight. Increasingly, however, the emphasis is on meeting insulation standards in order to conserve fuel and power. Building Control will also need to be convinced that work is carried out safely, without risking the lives of builders, visitors and passers-by. Which is all pretty sensible really.

For loft converters there are some special concessions, such as the possible use of compact space-saver stairs and reduced headroom requirements, and in some cases reduced insulation requirements may be accepted where it would affect useable floor area. It's very much in your own interest to comply with the Building Regulations so that the resulting structure can be shown to be safe, and your house will therefore be mortgageable and saleable.

Only if the building work has been carried out to the satisfaction of the Building Control Officer will you receive official Building Regulations approval, in the form of a 'final certificate' upon completion of the build. The primary responsibility for making sure your loft complies with the regulations rests with the person doing the building work, so if you're employing a firm of builders it's important to remind them of this at the outset. Be clear about whose job it is to liaise with Building Control.

The approved documents

Practical guidance showing how to comply with the Building Regulations is contained in 'approved documents' issued by the Government. As far as your build is

Cartoon: ODPM licence C2007000130

concerned, these are the bible and are legally enforceable. The full documents can be accessed on the website.

Approved documents
A Structure
B Fire safety
C Site preparation and resistance to moisture
D Toxic substances
E Resistance to the passage of sound
F Ventilation and condensation
G Hygiene
H Drainage and waste disposal
J Heat producing appliances and fuel storage systems
K Stairs, ramps and guards (protection from falling, collision and impact)
L Conservation of fuel and power
M Access and facilities for disabled people
N Glazing – materials and safety
P Electrical safety

Of these, documents A, B, F, K, L, N and P will definitely apply to loft jobs, and in some cases E, H, J and M as well. So you'll be getting to know your Building Control Officer pretty well over the next few months. If you live in Scotland or Northern Ireland, guidance is instead provided

in the form of technical handbooks. However, the nitty-gritty areas of concern are largely the same as those for England and Wales. The main difference is that in Scotland you'll require permission in the form of a 'building warrant' before work can start.

Site inspections
Inspections are carried out by the Building Control Officer at several important stages and spot checks are made to enforce minimum standards. But the Officer does not supervise the works on your behalf. For that you'd need to privately appoint your own surveyor or architect. The builder is required to notify Building Control in advance at key stages, and leave the work exposed for inspection before covering it up and continuing. Should they fail to do this, they may later be required to break open and expose such parts of the structure for inspection.

Key Building Control inspection stages
■ Start on site (commencement)
■ New beams and floor joists installed
■ Insulation to roofs and walls, including checking ventilation spaces
■ Stairs, headroom and handrails
■ Fire doors, smoke detectors, fire insulation and fire escapes
■ Completion

This is just the bare minimum, the stages where you must legally provide a formal invitation notice requesting a visit. More than one inspection may be carried out for each stage, and additional checks are often required. For example, the following works would also normally need to be inspected:

■ All structural alterations including new timbers to roofs and walls such as to dormers
■ Raising the height of any party walls or chimney stacks
■ Rebuilding any missing or defective party walls
■ First and second fix electrics, plumbing, heating and drainage of sanitary fittings
■ Room ventilation and extractor fans

To notify Building Control that work is ready to be inspected, notices usually need to be submitted in writing by your builders. The notice period required is only one day, except for the first and last stages (commencement and completion), when two days' notice is required. If the Officer doesn't arrive within the time limit, don't be tempted to cover up and press on regardless – make contact.

Building Control Officers are busy people, so in reality site inspections often tend to be fairly brief affairs. This is certainly the case where they judge that the works are not too challenging technically, or where they know the builder to be competent, an opinion possibly formed from working on previous projects.

Only when the final inspection has been carried out will the completion certificate be issued, but you'll need to

formally request it. This is a valuable certificate, so keep it safe, along with the planning consent documents, since it will be required when you come to sell or re-mortgage your property.

Policing and penalties

The Building Regulations are law. If you deliberately contravene them or obstruct Building Control Officers from doing their job, then you can be fined (currently up to £5,000) for non-compliance. The ultimate penalty is a short holiday care of HM Prisons.

Officers have the right to enter sites at all reasonable hours to check if the rules have been contravened. Action is normally taken against the main building contractor, but enforcement notices can alternatively be served against owners, demanding the demolition of any work contravening a regulation, or complete rebuilding so that it fully complies. If you refuse, they can employ another firm of builders to take down non-conforming parts of your property at your expense.

Where works have been done illegally it is sometimes possible to legalise them retrospectively, by applying to Building Control for what's known as a 'regularisation certificate'. Such unauthorised works often only come to light when a house comes up for sale and the buyer's surveyor or solicitor spots the problem. In some cases getting the loft to comply may only require fitting a new handrail. On the other hand, the quality of work might be so appalling that it all needs to come down and be rebuilt at great expense. Many house purchases have collapsed at the last minute when illegal works are belatedly detected, so hard-pressed buyers sometimes instead opt for an indemnity insurance policy, but this is a short-term quick fix that may enable the purchase to proceed but will only postpone the problem until the next time the property is sold. More importantly, it won't magically make a dangerous structure safe for the occupants. If, God forbid, your house should burn down or subside into oblivion, the last thing you want is for your insurers to announce that your building insurance is null and void as a result of an illegal loft conversion.

Structural calculations

Converting lofts involves making major structural alterations to floors, and usually also to roofs and walls. So Building Control will ask you to provide structural calculations from a qualified structural engineer in order to prove that the key components, such as floor joists and roof timbers, are tough enough to take the loadings imposed on them. Any other structural alterations you plan to make to the existing house, such as new supporting columns built up from foundation level, will also require calculations. In Scotland a special Structural Design Certificate has to be submitted confirming the stability of the proposed new structure.

Plans are sometimes approved on the condition that some design details and calculations will be passed at a later date (such as for steel beams), so it can be tempting to crack on before the paperwork has all been checked. But if it later becomes horribly clear that the proposed alterations can't be made to work without huge expense you don't want to be sitting in a house with part of the roof missing whilst the engineers argue about it. So it's best not to start building work until all the calculations have been OK'd in advance by Building Control.

Tall buildings

Most loft conversions are carried out to existing two- or three-storey buildings. However, if you happen to be

converting a four-storey or higher house there may be some additional structural issues with cost implications. The kind of properties that fall into this category are typically grander Georgian or Victorian urban terraced houses. The first question is whether basements count as a storey. Most basements are not counted because the storey height normally relates to the position of the final exit door, usually at ground-floor level. Where a site is sloping you might have a 'split level' building with, say, two storeys on one side and three on the other, which will obviously increase by an extra storey once the loft has been converted. For some multi-storey buildings you may also be required to carry out extra structural work fitting anchoring systems, such as restraint straps to the timber floors and main walls throughout the building. (See Chapter 9.)

Smoke alarms

There's no doubt that receiving early warning of fire is a real lifesaver, so there are strict rules on the provision of smoke alarms. You need at least one automatic smoke detection alarm per storey, and these must be wired into the mains and have a battery back-up.

The logical place to fit them is where they can detect smoke at the earliest stages of a fire, *ie* somewhere between the place where fires are most likely to start (kitchens and living rooms) and the sleeping accommodation. So the rules are that they should be sited on ceilings in 'circulation spaces' such as hallways and landings, within 7.5m of habitable rooms but no closer than 3m to bedrooms. See Chapter 11.

Fire!

Adding an extra floor to your home raises serious questions about how you would escape from a raging house-fire. Jumping is normally preferable to being burnt alive, and if you're reasonably fit, escape from a ground- or first-floor window should be possible in most cases without serious injury. But leaping from a second-floor window or higher is a daunting and dangerous prospect – which is why protection from fire is a major concern of the Building Regulations. Everything you need to know is contained in Approved Document B.

Escape from fire

When designing a loft conversion it's very easy to get totally focussed on the new loft room itself and to overlook the impact on the rest of the house. Maybe this is why few things cause more grief than belatedly discovering that a 'protected corridor' needs to be driven straight through your living room, in order to comply with fire regulations. Therefore it's important to consider as early as possible how you could escape from the new loft room in the event of a house-fire.

There are two basic principles when it comes to surviving a fire: early warning and escape. Obviously it's a sensible idea to have some means of being woken from a deep slumber before a fire could become uncontrollable, engulfing the occupants in smoke, flames and toxic fumes

Photo: Charles Grosvenor

– hence the requirement for a linked automatic smoke detector on each storey. Once awake and fully conscious of the imminent danger, you must then be able to escape unassisted, which normally means reaching a 'final exit', such as the front door. Windows don't count as 'final exits', not even special escape windows.

As you'd expect, the requirements for fire protection and escape become ever more demanding the taller the building. Just how severe the fire regulations will be in each case will largely depend on one critical

Main stairs safely protected within entrance hall

Photo: Charles Grosvenor

New full width dormer to rear

Ceiling over landing 30 mins fire resistance

Fire door 20 mins

NEW LOFT ROOM

Protected corridor

Walls — 30 mins fire resistance

Fire door 20 mins

Protected corridor

Ceiling over landing 30 mins fire resistance

Walls — 30 mins fire resistance

Fire door 20 mins

Protected corridor escape route

Above: Existing hallway, stairs and landing should suffice as protected corridor

Below: New landing to loft

Photo: Velux

measurement – the distance between the floor surface in your new loft room and the outdoor ground level on the lowest side of the building. But it's not just the height of your loft above ground that matters. The existing layout of the ground floor rooms can have a major influence on the cost of complying with the fire regulations.

Protected stairways

Basically what you're trying to achieve here is to buy yourself a lifesaving 30 minutes in which to wake up and get the hell out of the building. By far the best solution, and the one that Building Control will really want to see in most cases, is a 'protected escape path' that leads down from the new loft room and out to a 'final exit' door, normally the front door. The attraction of this protected stairway method (also known as 'protected corridor', or 'protected escape route') is that it provides the highest standard of passive safety with a fully protected enclosure that gives 30 minutes' fire resistance all the way from the new loft to the final exit door on the ground floor.

Fortunately, in a great many houses this should not be too hard to achieve. If your existing staircase leads down to the front door via an entrance hall then you already effectively have a protected escape route. Here, the entrance hall is separated by partition walls from the kitchen and reception rooms which are the places where most fires originate. Upstairs, the landing will be similarly separated from the bedrooms.

Hallways and landings are referred to in fire-escape language as 'circulation areas', and the good news is that the existing walls enclosing them should already meet fire-resisting standards – except, of course, for one obvious weak point: the doors. This is why the doors to all habitable rooms along the route will need to be replaced (or possibly upgraded) so that they can resist fire for a minimum of 20 minutes. The only exceptions are cloakroom and bathroom doors (unless there happens to be a boiler in there).

But to be sure that your escape route is fully fire-protected, the performance of your partition walls will need to be assessed. Any weak points such as glass fanlights above bedroom doors will need upgrading. Glazing will comply if it's replaced with thick 'Georgian' wired glass and the beading is modified. Any part of the new loft floor that's directly above the escape route must have 30 minutes' fire resistance, *eg* where your loft room extends over a landing to the stairway enclosure below. The other parts of the loft floor need only meet a reduced performance or 'modified 30 minute' standard of fire resistance. This is a lot easier to achieve, and in most cases the existing ceilings should be satisfactory. (See Chapter 7.)

Open-plan layouts

Many houses, especially those built from the 1960s onwards, don't have traditional entrance halls. Instead, the front door opens directly into an open-plan living room, perhaps via a small entrance lobby. Because there's no hallway to double as a ready-made protected escape route, if a house-fire started in the downstairs rooms the rapid spread of smoke and fire would swiftly block your chances of escape and survival.

So a suitable means of escape must be found, otherwise it simply won't be possible to convert the loft. To comply with the Building Regulations, the optimum solution will depend in each case on the layout of your main staircase. If the bottom of your stairs faces the front door (or any other main door) all that might be required is to construct a new partition wall joining the staircase and the door entrance, thereby creating a separate hallway. The new partition can be built either in timber studwork and plasterboard or blockwork and shouldn't prove too expensive. (See 'instant protected stairway' photo-feature in Chapter 10). The downside is that you stand to lose a sizeable slice of your living room floor space. But it needn't be as bad as it sounds: in some Victorian houses where the original entrance hall walls have been torn down, reinstating the original layout may even improve the property's period charm and value.

If, on the other hand, your stairs run from side to side across the reception room there is a useful alternative solution described below, under 'Other options'.

In some properties (with or without entrance halls) the underside of the stairs may be accessible from the living room or kitchen and will therefore be potentially vulnerable to fire. Imagine how you would react if a house-fire broke

out down below in the kitchen or a reception room one dark night as you snoozed peacefully in your loft bedroom. With nothing to stop the flames rapidly reaching the exposed underside of the stairs, by the time you'd woken to the emergency your chances of escape wouldn't look too healthy: trying to descend the stairs, you discover in horror that they're already engulfed in flames. Such a nightmare could easily occur where your staircase is open-plan or accessible from a room below. The solution is to suitably enclose the exposed sides or underside of the staircase in a layer of pink-coloured fire-resistant plasterboard finished with a defensive coating of skim plaster. (See Chapter 10.).

Loft stairs

When it comes to the new loft stairs, the basic requirement is the same – for the occupants of the loft to be protected for at least 30 minutes from fire. The simplest arrangement is where the loft stairs are run directly above the original main stairs, continuing upwards within the existing stairwell enclosure which is already protected. As we shall see in Chapter 10, this allows the fire door for the new loft room to be fitted at the top of the stairs, to a lobby on the loft landing.

Alternatively, where the new stairs are positioned away from the existing stairwell they'll need to be enclosed in a fire-protecting structure (such as suitably fire-boarded and plastered stud walls) from the first-floor landing upwards, in which case the fire door will normally be located at the bottom of the loft stairs.

Other options

If it turns out to be impossible to provide a protected route to the 'final exit', there are a number of alternatives that may be acceptable, depending on the type of property you're converting:

1 Bungalow conversions

New loft floor *less than* 4.5m above ground level

To convert a bungalow into a two-storey 'chalet bungalow', if it's not possible to create a protected

Photo: Charles Grosvenor

stairway the alternative is to fit escape window(s) to the new loft room. This is still an acceptable arrangement for bungalows, but not for loft conversions to houses. There are a number of other methods listed below for house conversions that may also apply to bungalows, but the escape window alternative should offer a cheaper and easier solution.

2 Two-storey house conversions
New loft floor *more than* 4.5m above ground level (but *less than* 7.5m)

Twin escape routes
In many houses the main stairs run from side to side, across the building, dividing the front and rear ground-floor rooms. Some semi-detached or end terrace properties which have their main entrance door to the side wall have a small lobby at the foot of the stairs serving this 'front' door, which effectively forms a ready-made protected stairway. But in a lot of properties, especially mid-terraces, the stairs lead directly down into a reception room. The problem here of course is that if this room was engulfed by smoke and flame, your escape route would be well and truly scuppered.

Fortunately, there is an ingenious solution, based on the logic that a fire could be raging in one of the ground-floor

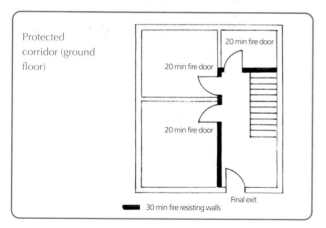

Protected corridor (ground floor)

20 min fire door
20 min fire door
20 min fire door
Final exit
■ 30 min fire resisting walls

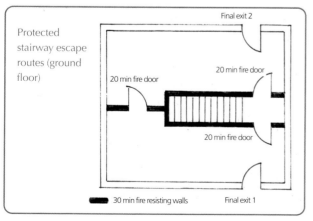

Protected stairway escape routes (ground floor)

Final exit 2
20 min fire door
20 min fire door
20 min fire door
■ 30 min fire resisting walls   Final exit 1

rooms, but not both simultaneously. So when you reach the bottom of the stairs there should be a choice of two doors, each leading into a separate room with its own outer entrance door through which you can then flee safely outdoors. In other words, if a fire occurred in one of the ground floor rooms, escape should be possible through the other, as shown in the diagram. This is likely to require cutting a new door opening from the foot of the stairs to the other room, which could cause a good deal of disruption. Furthermore, the two rooms must be linked to each other by a separate doorway incorporating a fire door, although in most cases there should already be a suitable opening for this purpose. The walls dividing the two rooms must be fire-resisting, and normally the existing walls should meet this requirement. Finally, where the sides or underside of the staircase are open to a room it will of course need to be enclosed within fire-resistant boarding, as described earlier.

Sprinkler protection
Where there's no other option, sprinkler systems are becoming an increasingly common alternative. With a sprinkler detection system installed to open-plan reception areas, Building Control may accept designs that wouldn't otherwise meet the normal fire rules or comply with escape requirements. But for this to be acceptable, the sprinklers need to be installed in conjunction with a fire-resisting partition wall and a fire door (minimum 20 minutes' resistance) separating the ground floor from the first floor. There must also be an escape window accessible from *first-floor* level. Depending on the property's layout, this new partition and fire-door lobby could be either constructed near the base of the stairs or at the top. And if you already have a first-floor window of a suitable size (see below) this may well suffice as an escape window. The thinking behind this arrangement is that in the event of a fire in the ground-floor open-plan area, loft occupants could make a frantic dash down to the first floor where they could then safely bale out of the window. The third requirement with the sprinkler option applies to any cooking facilities or kitchens within the open-plan layout, which must be separated off with a new fire-resisting partition wall.

The main benefit of the sprinkler option is that you don't need to sacrifice a sizeable chunk of your living room by turning it into an entrance hall. The downside is the expense, plus the possible need to partition off any open-plan kitchen. Thankfully, false alarms from errant sprinklers shouldn't be a problem, since they're activated by a metal sensor in the ceiling that needs to reach a high temperature before triggering a downpour. But you might still think twice before letting your sprinkler-protected home to students.

External escape routes
A third alternative could be to devise a more adventurous outdoor solution. If, for example, there's a handy balcony or flat roof nearby that leads conveniently to a place of

safety, then an external escape route may be possible. One example of this is found outside large blocks of flats, in the form of traditional cast iron fire escape stairs, but these are normally only practical for multi-storey buildings and hotels, since the planners and neighbours may not be overjoyed at Bronx-style fire escapes sprouting from conventional suburban houses. At the risk of stating the obvious, external fire escape stairs need to resist fire (otherwise what's the point?), but this can cause unexpected problems: for example, locked plastic (UPVC) double-glazed doors leading to the fire escape could melt under intense heat, barring the escape of trapped occupants.

Photo: G macdonald

buildings, to the extent that any ducts or grilles that lead to a protected stairway (such as those for old warm-air heating systems) may need to be 'fire-stopped'.

Emergency escape windows

Perhaps disappointingly for anyone who relishes the thought of being rescued in the burly arms of a

3 Multi-storey house conversions
New loft floor 7.5m or more above ground level

The taller your property is, the more challenging complying with fire regulations becomes. For example, adding an extra floor to a typical Georgian town house of three or more storeys (plus the loft room) is potentially the most complex type of conversion. Here, not only do you have to create a 'protected stairway', but for each floor higher than 7.5m there needs to be an alternative escape route. As noted above, this is defined as an additional separate stairway leading to a place of safety, which could take the form of either an outside fire escape leading over an adjacent flat roof, or a second independent flight of internal stairs that are fully fire-separated from the main staircase.

Because of the complexity of such solutions, Building Control may be willing to consider alternatives, especially if the combined floor area of all floors in the property is less than 200m². For example, you may find that offering to install 'active fire protection' such as a sprinkler system – the kind of thing required for offices and hotels – means that they could be willing to relax the rules on 'passive fire protection' for escape routes. The risk of fire spreading is taken extremely seriously in taller

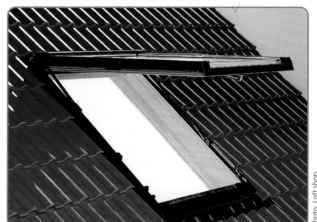
Photo: Loft shop

Emergency egress roof window

Great escape routes
Balconies and flat roofs can form part of an escape route, provided that:

- The flat roof is part of your own building (ie it doesn't belong to the guy next door).
- An escape route across the roof doesn't leave you stranded in thin air – it must lead to a further external escape route, such as stairs.
- The flat roof escape route is itself protected with 30 minutes' fire resistance, so that it's not a case of out of the frying pan into the fire.
- There's a guardrail of minimum 1.1m height along roof edges and balconies to prevent sleepy escapees plunging to their doom.

fireperson (of either sexual persuasion), fitting escape windows in your loft as a primary means of escape is in most cases no longer a popular option. The exception is for bungalows, where you should be permitted to fit escape windows instead of going to the trouble of creating an escape corridor leading down to the front door.

However, for peace of mind's sake it's still well worth installing 'MoE' (means of escape) windows as an additional safety measure, given that there would be no significant additional cost.

Escape windows built into roof slopes need to be accessible from ground level outside so that, in an emergency, occupants can be rescued by ladder-borne firefighters. Any openable window can qualify as an escape window as long as it meets certain criteria, notably the size. It has been calculated that to escape in a hurry, an average curry-consuming UK citizen can successfully squeeze through an opening with a 'clear openable area' of 0.33m^2, as long as neither the height nor the width are less than 450mm. So a window with a clear openable area of 450 x 750mm or larger should do the trick, although the various caches and hinges must be carefully designed so as not to restrict access (or rip your pyjamas). Skylights designed for this purpose often have side-opening casements, rather than a centre pivot arrangement, to maximise the area of clear space. If they're top-hung, they need to be fitted with a device such as gas struts to ensure they can stay open in an emergency without having to be held.

One of the problems with escape windows is the potential conflict between being positioned low enough to allow a swift and safe escape from fire, but high enough to prevent inquisitive children tumbling out of them. The compromise requirement is for the bottom edge of the window's openable area to be no higher than 1.1m above the room's floor level, but no lower than 600mm for skylights or 800mm if it's a dormer. If achieving this minimum height is difficult, placing a fixed step below it may help. Child-resistant release catches are also required, preferably fitted at the top. Child safety can be further enhanced by fitting a small baby-gate in front of them internally. To facilitate rescue by ladder the distance to the roof edge should also be no more than 1.7m, but in reality ladder access is often impeded by conservatories, carports or extensions added at a later date. There's also one other possibility for conflict – that of home security versus safety. Burglar-proof lockable windows are fine, as long as you can still escape quickly in an emergency without fumbling for mislaid keys.

Fire doors

It's not always appreciated that one of the penalties for converting a loft is that you normally have to replace most of the existing internal doors in your house. This is down to a fairly recent change in the Building Regs. Up until April

2007, as long as you fitted suitable escape windows in the loft it was often possible to retain the old doors as long as they were fitted with self-closing devices. But as everyone knows, living with automatically closing doors can be peculiarly irritating. In reality, door-closers usually ended up being binned, or the doors wedged open for all kinds

Self closers are no longer required

of reasons, such as parents not able to hear the cry of babies during the night, children wanting the door left ajar in the dark, pets cooped up unable to roam around the house, and so on. Building Control realised that frustrated occupants frequently removed them, so the decision was taken to dispense with door-closers.

Despite this relaxation of the rules, the doors facing the internal 'escape corridor' (ie to the rooms adjoining your landing and entrance hall/ lobby) must provide a minimum of 20 minutes' fire resistance, whether you fit an escape window in your loft or not. Which normally means having to fit new purpose-made fire doors.

The trouble with conventional internal doors is that even the solid ones have panels that are only a few millimetres thick. Alternatively, you may have hollow doors with a cardboard honeycomb interior, which are terrific for Bonfire Night. Fire doors, as the name suggests, are designed with inbuilt fire resistance. You can tell them apart from normal doors because:

- They're heavy.
- Most have a small round plastic mark, like an RAF roundel, on the side – see below.
- There are no thin door panels.

Fire doors perform a dual lifesaving role, acting as a barrier to smoke and toxic fumes during the early stages of a fire, and then, once the blaze is raging, inhibiting the spread of flames. Delaying the spread of smoke and flames should safeguard the escape route and hopefully buy enough precious time to save the unfortunate occupants' lives. Most house fires start in ground floor rooms, and a firmly closed fire door should contain it long enough for you to escape from upstairs.

Antique doors can sometimes be fire-proofed – see chapter 13

Photo: Envirograf.com

Identifying fire doors: 'core plugs'

Most manufacturers set a plastic plug into the edge of their fire doors, indicating the fire resistance rating (in accordance with BS 478: Part 8: 1972 and BS 8214).

A blue core in a white background means the door should achieve 20 minutes' fire resistance, the minimum standard for protected escape corridors. But this can be increased to 30 minutes by fitting an intumescent seal to the door or frame. A white background means the door can provide minimum 20 minutes' fire resistance, a yellow background 30 minutes, and a blue background a full 60 minutes. Only those with a green inner core come with an intumescent seal already fitted under the lipping.

Fire Resistant ratings	Intumescent seal necessary (red core)	Intumescent seal factory-fitted (green core)
20 minutes (30/20)	◉	◉
30 minutes (30/30)	◉	◉
60 minutes (60/60)	◉	◉

There is a similar coding system from TRADA (the Timber Research and Development Association) featuring a tree image as the centre core.

Essentially there are 2 options when it comes to achieving the required 20 minutes minimum resistance. Fitting a standard 30 minute (FD 30) fire door into a frame without an 'intumescent strip' (see below) will count as a 20 minute (FD 20). Alternatively, the target can be achieved by fitting a FD20 fire door together with an intumescent seal.

Of course, there's no point having immensely strong fireproof doors if all the flames need to do is lick their way around the sides, through the frame. This is where 'intumescent strips' or 'seals' can be a godsend. These special strips of material, typically about 4mm thick by 10mm wide, are fixed into a groove cut into the side of the door or the frame. As soon as the temperature exceeds 200°C, which is usually about ten minutes after the start of a fire, the strip swells up, sealing the gaps between the door and the frame. Today, all fire doors providing 30 minutes' or greater fire resistance come pre-fitted with intumescent seals and may also contain a blade or brush seal for smoke sealing.

It has to be said however that there remains a niggling doubt as to how effective an escape route through a blazing house can really be if the doors, no matter how fireproof, are left open at night. From a survival viewpoint, the only positive side of no longer being required to install door-closers is that the smoke alarms will activate a lot sooner when doors are left open. But, on balance, you might think it worth going the extra mile and fitting rising butt hinges or self-closers. Ask the opinion of your Building Control Officer.

For many homeowners this may all be fine, except for one small thing. The unpalatable prospect of having to sacrifice the existing internal doors. Of course if you've just bought a house that suffers from hideously naff old doors which are crying out for replacement, then this won't be a problem. But what if your property boasts classic four or six panel Georgian or Victorian gems, or iconic 'one over three' 1930s originals. Or perhaps you're the proud owner of a matching set of hand-carved, antique hardwood heirlooms? And what if you live in a Listed Building? Surely the Council Conservation Officer could instigate savage enforcement action if they caught you ripping out old period doors, even though it's for the noble purpose of compliance with Local Authority Building Control?

If homeowners are not conscious of the requirement to replace or upgrade internal doors, there is clearly going to be a risk that the contractors will fit the cheapest and ugliest new fire doors, defacing all the rooms en-route to your new loft room, lending your home the ambience of a grotty warehouse. So it's important to discuss alternatives with Building Control at the design stage, since it should be possible to find decent looking new doors or even to upgrade the existing ones – see Chapter 13.

FIRE KILLS

Submitting your Building Regulations application

Before submitting your application to the Local Authority Building Control Department, you may wish to consider an alternative method that bypasses them in the interests of 'consumer choice'. If you prefer, you're allowed instead to submit your application via an independent 'approved inspector'. Approved inspectors are private firms approved by the Council to do basically the same job as in-house Building Control staff.

With this method, to start the ball rolling, the person carrying out the building work together with the approved inspector must jointly issue an *initial notice* to notify Local Authority Building Control of the intended work. From then on, the approved inspector will independently process your plans, carry out spot checks as the work progresses on site and ultimately produce a final certificate once the works are completed to their satisfaction. In other words, it's all pretty much the same as the Council would do it, but may suit those who prefer a bit of private-sector involvement.

Most applications, however, are still made in the time-honoured manner, direct to the Local Authority, which we'll assume is the case here.

You now have two important choices when it comes to submitting your application: either the 'full plans' method, or a 'building notice'. Both methods cost the same in fees plus VAT, regardless of how many site visits they later need to make.

Building notice

For loft conversions, a 'full plans' application is normally advisable (see below). But there's a useful short-cut. If you have unshakeable faith in the skill and knowledge of your designer and builders, you may wish to save time by instead submitting a simple building notice. Here you're basically making a promise that you'll comply with the Building Regulations on site, rather than submitting detailed drawings to prove it in advance.

You'll still need to complete a form giving a description of the property and the proposed building works, and this should be submitted together with a Site or 'Block' plan (see page 59) showing the position of the building in relation to its boundaries and any relevant drain runs. You'll still need to provide engineer's calculations for all the structural work. Many Local Authorities also insist on plans and section drawings of the whole building to demonstrate compliance with matters such as fire safety and headroom.

The fee is paid in one go when you submit the building notice. Once it's been checked and accepted, the next stage is simply to give the Building Control Officer a minimum of two working days' notice of your intention to start work on site. The Officer will then inspect the work at key stages, just as with a full plans application.

The big risk with this method is that because detailed plans haven't been fully approved in advance, you can't be sure the work will fully comply with the Building Regulations. So a site inspection could uncover something that contravenes the regulations while the job is in full swing. Obviously this could prove highly disruptive, not to say expensive, so this method should only be adopted after first discussing the scheme in detail with Building Control. Work must start within three years, after which time the approval will automatically lapse. Strictly speaking, at the end of the job a Local Authority isn't required to issue a completion certificate under the building notice procedure, but they normally will do so upon request.

Full Plans application

Because loft conversions involve making fairly complex structural alterations, some Local Authorities insist on a full plans application. Here the applicant demonstrates by way of detailed drawings that the construction will comply with the regulations. If you're proposing to build some or all of your loft conversion yourself, it's best to go down this route so that you'll have an approved set of plans to work to. Here the fee is split into two payments – a 'plans fee', paid up front when you submit your application, and an 'inspection fee' paid prior to inspection at the start-on-site.

What drawings to submit

Your Building Regulations application will require the same drawings as for the planning application, modified to provide a lot of additional detail, plus a section plan. These are submitted together with the application form and payment. The drawings must clearly show all the proposed building work and explain the details of construction. To streamline the process, for a small fee some Councils offer a plan-checking service prior to you making a formal application.

Note that your plan and section drawings should show not just the loft but every floor, both existing and proposed. This is

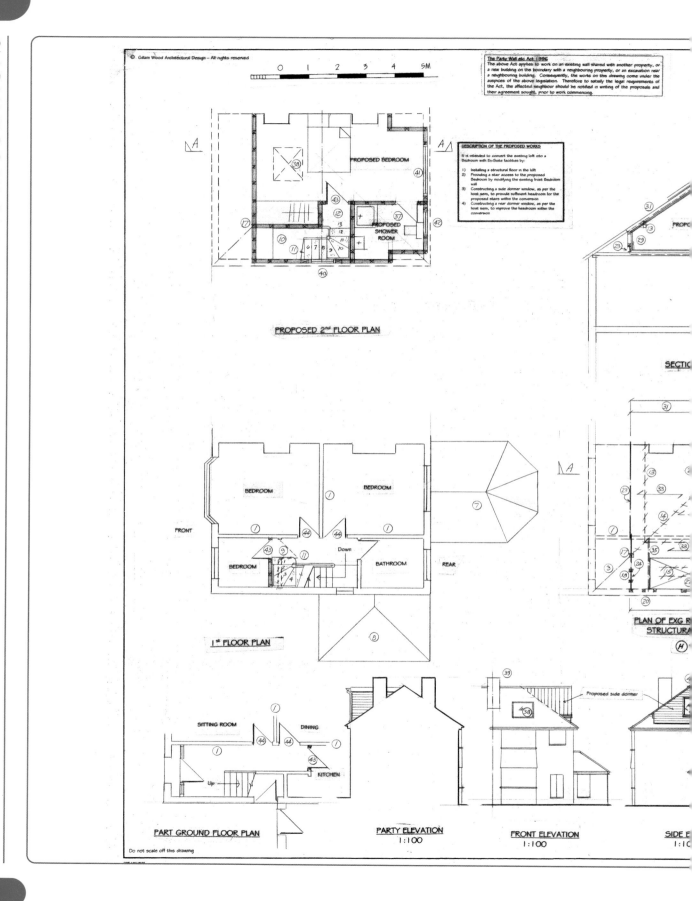

0 1 2 3 4 5M

The Party Wall etc Act 1996
The above Act applies to work on an existing wall shared with another property, or a new building on the boundary with a neighbouring property, or an excavation near a neighbouring building. Consequently, the works on this drawing come under the auspices of the above legislation. Therefore to satisfy the legal requirements of the Act, the affected neighbour should be notified in writing of the proposals and their agreement sought, prior to work commencing.

PROPOSED BEDROOM

DESCRIPTION OF THE PROPOSED WORKS
It is intended to convert the existing loft into a Bedroom with En-Suite facilities by:

1) Installing a structural floor in the loft
2) Providing a stair access to the proposed Bedroom by modifying the existing front Bedroom wall
3) Constructing a side dormer window, as per the host item, to provide sufficient headroom for the proposed stairs within the conversion
4) Constructing a rear dormer window, as per the host item, to improve the headroom within the conversion

PROPOSED SHOWER ROOM

PROPOSED 2nd FLOOR PLAN

SECTIO

BEDROOM

BEDROOM

FRONT

Down

BEDROOM

BATHROOM

REAR

1st FLOOR PLAN

PLAN OF EXG R
STRUCTURA

SITTING ROOM

DINING

KITCHEN

Up

PART GROUND FLOOR PLAN

Proposed side dormer

PARTY ELEVATION
1:100

FRONT ELEVATION
1:100

SIDE E
1:10

Do not scale off this drawing

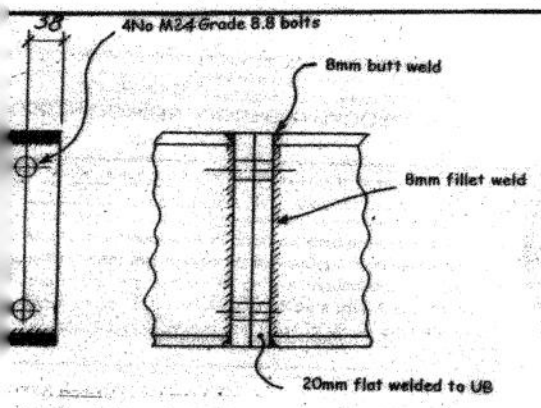
38
4No M24 Grade 8.8 bolts
8mm butt weld
8mm fillet weld
20mm flat welded to UB

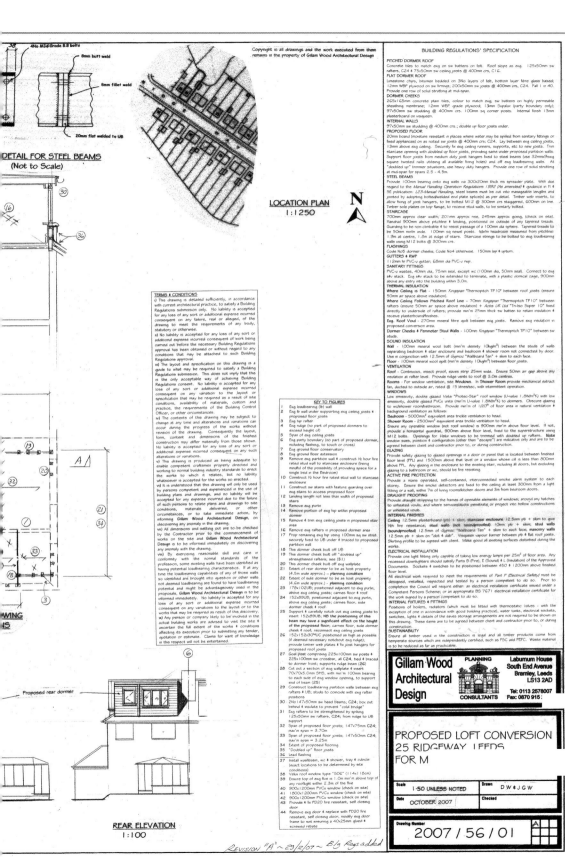

DETAIL FOR STEEL BEAMS
(Not to Scale)

Copyright in all drawings and the work executed from them remains in the property of Gillam Wood Architectural Design

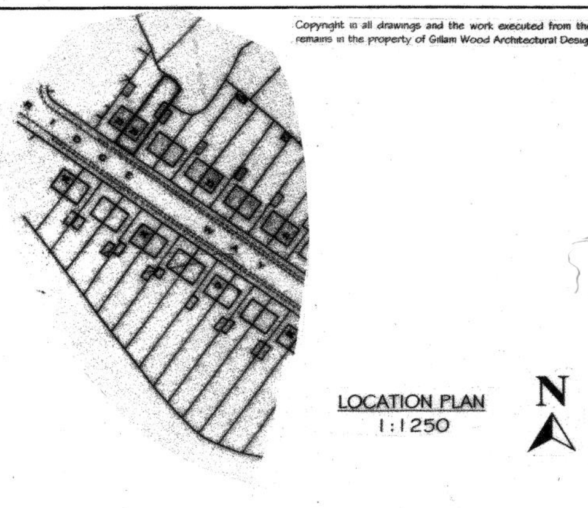
N

LOCATION PLAN
1:1250

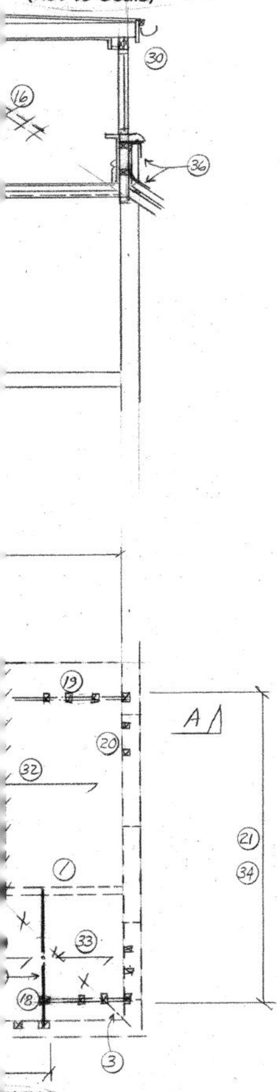
30
16
36
19
20
A
32
21
34
1
33
18
3

WING
NS

TERMS & CONDITIONS

i) This drawing is detailed sufficiently, in accordance with current architectural practice, to satisfy a Building Regulations submission only. No liability is accepted for any loss of any sort or additional expense incurred consequent on any failure, real or alleged, of the drawing to meet the requirements of any body, statutory or otherwise.

ii) No liability is accepted for any loss of any sort or additional expense incurred consequent of work being carried out before the necessary Building Regulations approval has been obtained or without regard to any conditions that may be attached to such Building Regulations approval.

iii) The layout and specification on this drawing is a guide to what may be required to satisfy a Building Regulations submission. This does not imply that this is the only acceptable way of achieving Building Regulations consent. No liability is accepted for any loss of any sort or additional expense incurred consequent on any variation to the layout or specification that may be required as a result of site conditions, availability of materials, custom and practice, the requirements of the Building Control Officer, or other circumstances.

iv) The contents of this drawing may be subject to change at any time and alterations and variations can occur during the progress of the works without revision of the drawing. Consequently the layout, form, content and dimensions of the finished construction may differ materially from those shown. No liability is accepted for any loss of any sort or additional expense incurred consequent on any such alterations or variations.

v) This drawing is produced as being adequate to enable competent craftsmen properly directed and working to normal building industry standards to erect the works to which it relates, but no liability whatsoever is accepted for the works so erected.

vi) It is understood that this drawing will only be used by persons competent and experienced in the use of building plans and drawings, and no liability will be accepted for any expense incurred due to the failure of such persons to relate plans and drawings to site conditions, materials delivered, or other circumstances, or to take immediate action, by informing **Gillam Wood Architectural Design**, on discovering any anomaly in the drawing.

vii) All dimensions and setting out are to be checked by the Contractor prior to the commencement of works on the site and **Gillam Wood Architectural Design** is to be informed immediately on discovering any anomaly with the drawing.

viii) By exercising reasonable skill and care in conformity with the normal standards of the profession, some existing walls have been identified as having potential loadbearing characteristics. If at any time the loadbearing capabilities of any of those walls so identified are brought into question or other walls not deemed loadbearing are found to have loadbearing potential and might be advantageously used in the proposals, **Gillam Wood Architectural Design** is to be informed immediately. No liability is accepted for any loss of any sort or additional expense incurred consequent on any variations to the layout or to the works that may be required as result of this discovery.

ix) Any person or company likely to be involved in the actual building works are advised to visit the site & ascertain the full extent of the works & conditions affecting its execution prior to submitting any tender, quotation or estimate. Claims for want of knowledge in this respect will not be entertained.

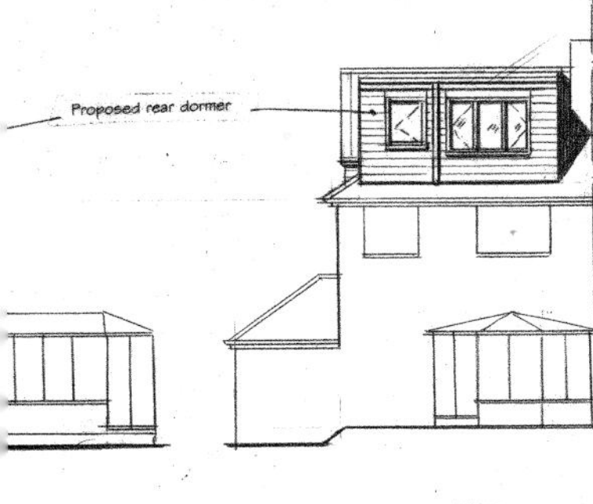
6
Proposed rear dormer

REAR ELEVATION
1:100

KEY TO FIGURES

1	Exg loadbearing (lb) wall
2	Exg lb wall under supporting exg ceiling joists & proposed floor joists
3	Exg hip rafter
4	Exg ridge (no part of proposed dormers to exceed height of)
5	Span of exg ceiling joists
6	Exg party boundary (no part of proposed dormer, including flashing, to touch or cross)
7	Exg ground floor conservatory
8	Exg ground floor extension
9	Remove exg partition wall & construct ½ hour fire rated stud wall to staircase enclosure (being mindful of the possibility of providing space for a single bed in the Bedroom)
10	Construct ½ hour fire rated stud wall to staircase enclosure
11	Construct sw stairs with feature guarding over exg stairs to access proposed floor
12	Landing length not less than width of proposed stairs
13	Remove exg purlin
14	Remove portion of exg hip within proposed dormer
15	Remove & trim exg ceiling joists in proposed stair area
16	Remove exg rafters in proposed dormer area
17	Prop remaining exg hip using 100mm sq sw strut securely fixed to UB under & braced to proposed partition wall
18	This dormer cheek built off UB
19	This dormer cheek built off "doubled up" strengthened rafters; see (31)
20	This dormer cheek built off exg wallplate
21	Extent of rear dormer to be as host property (4.5m wide approx.) – **planning condition**
22	Extent of side dormer to be as host property (4.6m wide approx.) - **planning condition**
23	178x102UB; positioned adjacent to exg purlin, above exg ceiling joists; carries floor & roof
24	152x89UB; positioned adjacent to exg purlin, above exg ceiling joists; carries floor, side dormer cheek & roof
25	Support & carefully notch out exg ceiling joists to insert 152x89UB; **NB the positioning of this beam may have a significant effect on the height of the proposed floor**; carries floor, side dormer cheek & roof; reconnect exg ceiling joists
26	152x152x30kgUC positioned as high as possible (if deemed necessary notchout exg ridge); provide timber web plates & fix joist hangers for proposed roof joists
27	Goal post comprising 225x100mm sw posts & 225x100mm sw crossbar, all C24, tied & braced to dormer front; supports ridge beam (26)
28	Cut out a section of exg wallplate & insert 70x70x5.0mm SHS, with min'm 100mm bearing to each side of exg window opening, to support end of beam (25)
29	Construct loadbearing partition walls between exg rafters & UB; studs to coincide with exg rafter positions
30	2No147x50mm sw head beams; C24; box out behind & insulate to prevent "cold bridge"
31	Exg rafters to be strengthened by spiking 125x50mm sw rafters, C24; from ridge to UB support
32	Span of proposed floor joists; 147x75mm C24; max'm span = 3.70m
33	Span of proposed floor joists; 147x50mm C24; max'm span = 3.25m
34	Extent of proposed flooring
35	"Doubled up" floor joists
36	Lead flashing
37	Install washbasin, wc & shower, tray & cubicle (exact locations to be determined by site conditions)
38	Velux roof window type "S06" (114x118cm)
39	Ensure top of exg flue is 1.0m min'm above top of any rooflight within 2.3m of the flue
40	900x1200mm PVCu window (check on site)
41	1800x1200mm PVCu window (check on site)
42	900x1200mm PVCu window (check on site)
43	Provide & fix FD20 fire resistant, self closing door
44	Remove exg door & replace with FD20 fire resistant, self closing door; modify exg door frame to suit ensuring a 40x25mm glued & screwed rebate

REVISION "A" ~ 29/12/07 ~ B/g Regs added

BUILDING REGULATIONS' SPECIFICATION

PITCHED DORMER ROOF
Concrete tiles to match exg on sw battens on felt. Roof slope as exg. 125x50mm sw rafters, C24 & 75x50mm sw ceiling joists @ 400mm crs, C16.

FLAT DORMER ROOF
Limestone chips, bitumen bedded on 3No layers of felt, bottom layer fibre glass based; 12mm WBP plywood on sw firrings; 200x50mm sw joists @ 400mm crs, C24. Fall 1 in 40. Provide one row of solid strutting at mid-span.

DORMER CHEEKS
265x165mm concrete plain tiles, colour to match exg; sw battens on highly permeable sheathing membrane; 12mm WBP grade plywood; 13mm Supalux (party boundary only); 97x50mm sw studding @ 400mm crs. 100mm sq corner posts. Internal finish 13mm plasterboard on visqueen.

INTERNAL WALLS
97x50mm sw studding @ 400mm crs.; double up floor joists under.

PROPOSED FLOOR
20mm board (moisture resistant in places where water may be spilled from sanitary fittings or fixed appliances) on as noted sw joists @ 400mm crs; C24. Lay between exg ceiling joists, 13mm above exg ceiling. Securely fix exg ceiling runners, supports, etc to new joists. Trim staircase opening with doubled up floor joists, providing same under proposed partition walls. Support floor joists from medium duty joist hangers fixed to steel beams (use 32mmx9swg square twisted nails utilising all available fixing holes) and off exg loadbearing walls. At "doubled up" trimmer situations, use heavy duty hangers. Provide one row of solid strutting at mid-span for spans 2.5 - 4.5m.

STEEL BEAMS
Provide 100mm bearing onto exg walls via 300x20mm thick ms spreader plate. With due regard to the *Manual Handling Operation Regulations 1992 (As amended)* & guidance in H & SE publication: *L23-Manual Handling*, steel beams must be cut into manageable lengths and jointed by adopting bolted/welded end plate splice(s) as per detail. Timber web inserts, to allow fixing of joist hangers, to be bolted M12 @ 300mm crs staggered, 600mm on line. Timber sole plates on top flange, to receive stud walls, to be similarly bolted.

STAIRCASE
700mm approx clear width; 201mm approx rise, 245mm approx going, (check on site). Handrail 900mm above pitchline & landing, positioned on outside of any tapered treads. Guarding to be non-climbable & to resist passage of a 100mm dia sphere. Tapered treads to be 50mm min'm wide. 100mm sq newel posts. Min'm headroom measured from pitchline: 1.9m at centre, 1.8m at edge of stairs. Staircase strings to be bolted to exg loadbearing walls using M12 bolts @ 300mm crs.

FLASHINGS
Code No5 dormer cheeks; Code No4 otherwise. 150mm lap & upturn.

GUTTERS & RWP
112mm hr PVC-u gutter; 68mm dia PVC-u rwp.

SANITARY FITTINGS
PVC-u wastes, 40mm dia, 75mm seal, except wc (100mm dia, 50mm seal). Connect to exg s&v stack. Exg s&v stack to be extended to terminate, with a plastic domical cage, 900mm above any entry into the building within 3.0m.

THERMAL INSULATION
Where Ceiling is Flat - 150mm *Kingspan* "Thermopitch TP10" between roof joists (ensure 50mm air space above insulation).
Where Ceiling Follows Pitched Roof Line – 70mm *Kingspan* "Thermopitch TP10" between rafters (ensure 50mm air space above insulation) + *Actis UK Ltd* "Tri-Iso Super 10" fixed directly to underside of rafters; provide min'm 25mm thick sw batten to retain insulation & receive plasterboard/finishes.
Exg. Roof Void - 270mm mineral fibre quilt between exg joists. Remove exg insulation in proposed conversion area.
Dormer Cheeks & Perimeter Stud Walls - 100mm *Kingspan* "Thermopitch TP10" between sw studs.

SOUND INSULATION
Wall - 100mm mineral wool batt (min'm density 10kg/m³) between the studs of walls separating bedroom & stair enclosure and bedroom & shower room not connected by door. Use in conjunction with 12.5mm of *Gyproc* "Wallboard Ten" + skim to each face.
Floor - 100mm mineral wool quilt (min'm density 10kg/m³) between floor joists.

VENTILATION
Roof - Continuous, insect proof, eaves strip 25mm wide. Ensure 50mm air gap above any insulation at rafter level. Provide ridge vents to roof @ 3.0m centres.
Rooms - For window ventilation, see **Windows**. In **Shower Room** provide mechanical extract fan, ducted to outside air, rated @ 15 litres/sec, with intermittent operation.

WINDOWS
Low emissivity, double glazed *Velux* "Protec-Star" roof window (U-value 1.8W/m²K) with low emissivity, double glazed PVCu units (min'm U-value 1.8W/m²K) to dormers. Obscure glazing to wc/shower room/bathroom. Provide min'm of 1/20th of floor area in natural ventilation & background ventilation as follows:
Bedroom - 5000mm² equivalent area trickle ventilation to head.
Shower Room - 2500mm² equivalent area trickle ventilation to head.
Ensure any openable window (not roof window) is 900mm min'm above floor level. If not, provide a horizontal guardrail, 900mm above floor level, fixed to the superstructure using M12 bolts. Openings for *Velux* windows to be trimmed with doubled up rafters. **Note** window sizes, position & configuration (other than "escape") are indicative only and are to be agreed between client and contractor prior to, or during construction.

GLAZING
Provide safety glazing to glazed openings in a door or panel that is located between finished floor level (FFL) and 1500mm above that level or a window whose cill is less than 800mm above FFL. Any glazing in the enclosure to the existing stair, including all doors, but excluding glazing to a bathroom or wc, should be fire resisting.

ACTIVE FIRE PROTECTION
Provide a mains operated, self-contained, interconnected smoke alarm system to each storey. Ensure the smoke detectors are fixed to the ceiling at least 300mm from a light fitting or a wall, within 7m of living rooms/kitchen doors and 3m from bedroom doors.

DRAUGHT PROOFING
Provide draught stripping to the frames of openable elements of windows; around any hatches to unheated voids; and where services/ducts penetrate or project into hollow constructions or unheated voids.

INTERNAL FINISHES
Ceiling 12.5mm plasterboard (pb) + skim; **staircase enclosure** 12.5mm pb + skim to give ½h fire resistance; **stud walls (not soundproofed)** 10mm pb + skim; **stud walls (soundproofed)** 12.5mm of *Gyproc* "Wallboard Ten" + skim to each face; **masonry walls** 12.5mm pb + skim on "dot & dab". Visqueen vapour barrier between pb & flat roof joists. Skirting profile to be agreed with client. Make good all existing surfaces disturbed during the works.

ELECTRICAL INSTALLATION
Provide one light fitting only capable of taking low energy lamps per 25m² of floor area. Any recessed downlighters should satisfy Parts B (Fire), E (Sound) & L (Insulation) of the Approved Documents. Sockets & switches to be positioned between 450 & 1200mm above finished floor level.
All electrical work required to meet the requirements of *Part P (Electrical Safety)* must be designed, installed, inspected and tested by a person competent to do so. Prior to completion the Council will require either: an electrical installation certificate issued under a Competent Persons Scheme; or an appropriate BS 7671 electrical installation certificate for the work signed by a person competent to do so.

INTERNAL FIXTURES & FITTINGS
Positions of boilers, radiators (which must be fitted with thermostatic valves - with the exception of one in accordance with good building practice), water tanks, electrical sockets, switches, lights & details of the eaves storage arrangements are not required to be shown on this drawing. These items are to be agreed between client and contractor prior to, or during construction.

SUSTAINABILITY
Ensure all timber used in the construction is legal and all timber products come from temperate sources which are independently certified, such as FSC and PEFC. Waste material is to be reduced as far as practicable.

Gillam Wood Architectural Design
PLANNING CONSULTANTS
Laburnum House
South End Avenue
Bramley, Leeds
LS13 2AD
Tel: 0113 2578007
Fax: 0870 915

PROPOSED LOFT CONVERSION
25 RIDGEWAY LEEDS
FOR M

Scale	1:50 UNLESS NOTED	Drawn	D W & J G W
Date	OCTOBER 2007	Checked	

Drawing Number
2007 / 56 / 01 A

Photo: Charles Grosvenor

because the structure and room layout of the other floors can have a big impact on your design's feasibility, especially when it comes to fire protection and structural stability.

■ **Location plan** – showing the property size relative to boundaries, neighbouring streets and houses. This, or a similar 1:1250 Site plan or 'Block' plan, can help assess potential for rescue in the event of fire.

■ **Section plan** – showing a cross-section 'sliced through' the proposed new extension (typically drawn to 1:20 or 1:25 scale, but no greater than 1:50). These are the most informative of building plans since they expose the details of the new building's construction, showing materials and thicknesses as well as heights and dimensions. This is often the drawing that has most of the specification written on it.

■ **Plan and elevation drawings** – featuring technical notes that fully describe the proposed works. Preferably 1:50 scale (or not smaller than 1:100), showing every floor, existing and proposed.

■ **Engineer's structural calculations** – in a typical loft conversion, calculations are needed for new or altered load-bearing elements such as the new floor structure, new roof beams, and trimmers to roof rafters or floor joists. Where they need to support extra loadings, calculations will also be needed for lintels over windows and doors, and for existing internal walls.

You normally need to print at least four copies of your drawings to submit, plus a few more for the builders. Don't be surprised if you ultimately get through as many as 20 copies.

Having submitted your full plans application, Building Control should write confirming who will be dealing with your case. Your application should normally be passed or rejected within five weeks, although this can be extended for up to two months. Ultimately you should receive a 'plans approved' notice to confirm that the plans comply with Building Regulations. Work must then start within three years, or the notice will expire and a new application will have to be made. This is not the same as a final certificate (otherwise known as the 'completion certificate'), which should be issued once all the work is satisfactorily completed.

What information to write on the plans

On the Section drawing and the elevation plans you need to show:

The specification

The types and thicknesses of materials should be clearly stated, including:

■ The dimensions of all the main components (floors, windows, roofs, walls etc), explaining their type and their position in the building.

■ The type and size of insulation to be used (in walls, roofs etc).

Levels

■ Clearly show the floor levels of new loft rooms.

■ Show outside ground levels, and those of any new drains.

Approval or rejection

There are basically three possible outcomes to your Building Regulations application:

Approval

If you receive a 'plans approved' notice, congratulations. But it's unlikely that you'd get everything 100 per cent right first time if you submit your own plans. Even drawings submitted by professional designers are rarely perfect. So unless you're already familiar with current Building Regulations don't be shy of asking for guidance here.

It's more likely that Building Control will first write to you with an 'amendments letter' asking for clarification on various points or requiring additional information. This may seem like they're being unnecessarily pedantic, but if the experts at Building Control aren't clear what your plans mean then it's a fair bet that your builders won't know what you're on about either. It's a whole lot easier sorting out problems on paper at this stage than it would be trying to alter roof structures on site. If you haven't got a clue what they're asking, just phone, email or visit and they should normally be pleased to explain things in plain English.

Conditional approval

As the name suggest, conditional approvals normally have conditions listed as an attached document, stating any required modifications. Or they may simply request further plans to be submitted.

Sometimes Building Control will add their own notes to your plans before they're 'approved with endorsements'. It's important that your designer resolves any conditions in good time before the start-on-site date.

Rejection

A rejection notice needn't be as bad as it sounds. It can usually be overcome by resubmitting amended plans, for which no additional fee should be charged. Fees should also not apply for providing advice and for work that benefits people with disabilities. Common reasons for refusal include:

■ Fire safety details are unclear, especially failure to show adequately protected escape routes.

■ Insufficient detail shown for new loft stairs and landings, especially the amount of headroom.

■ Dimensions of floor and roof beams are not clearly written, or do not have supporting calculations.

■ Insufficient information is given about thermal insulation.

■ Details of the electrical work are missing.

When can I start work?

Cartoon: ODPM licence C2007000130

5 PICKING YOUR TEAM

Assuming that the local Council have smiled favourably upon your proposals, you'll now need to pick the best team for the job. If there's one thing you have to get right above all else, this is it. A dodgy builder can, at a stroke, turn your lofty dreams into an expensive nightmare. But first, you need to decide how much building work you want to personally contribute – which could be anything from none at all with the 'full package-deal' option, right through to doing the whole job yourself.

Loft conversions have the potential for massive intrusion into your private life if the works aren't carefully programmed at the outset, so another important issue to consider at this stage is how to prevent the project driving everyone in the house absolutely bananas. If you don't want building supplies carted up and down the stairs every hour of the day by lots of tea-guzzling geezers, now's the time to plan ahead.

The impact of loft works in your home often revolves around the stage at which the new stairs are fitted. Because this can be one of the more difficult parts of the job to get right, traditionally stairs were installed quite early on. This makes access easier for the following trades and for supplies of materials, and can also save on scaffolding costs. But unless the family have been dispatched on a world cruise for a couple of months, or you plan to do most of the work yourself, it's now

generally considered a better option to postpone fitting the stairs until as late as possible.

The best plan is to get all the heavy and messy work completed before finally breaking through the ceiling and installing the loft stairs. Of course, there's always the potential for an Ealing Comedy situation if the stairs don't fit, but we'll assume that all the necessary measurements have been taken correctly in advance. (See Chapter 10.)

Many specialist loft firms now routinely programme jobs to minimise inconvenience to the occupants, by entering the roof space from scaffolding via a new roof window opening. If this isn't possible, a compromise solution might be to access an existing upstairs window from the scaffolding, which will at least spare your entrance hall and stairs from major upheaval.

Building options

As noted earlier, there are basically four ways you can get your loft converted:

- Employ a specialist loft firm to do the full design-and-build job.
- Employ a specialist loft firm to design it but only build the shell, leaving some finishing work for yourself.
- Employ an experienced building contractor, and independently employ an architect for the design and project management.
- Employ specialist trades direct, project managing and doing some work yourself.

The fifth option, self-building the whole thing, is really only advisable if you have good experience doing this type of work, plus a small coalition of willing helpers. The major structural alterations normally required will in many cases put such projects beyond DIY capabilities. It's better to cherry-pick the tasks you feel confident about doing yourself, and subcontract the rest.

Design and build: specialist loft firms

Most conversions are carried out by specialist firms who do nothing else but lofts. Here the contractor and designer are effectively one and the same, and the whole job is done as a package deal. You'll probably want at least three firms to quote for the job, and the process should proceed more or less as follows:

Feasibility

The first step is an initial inspection to assess the potential of your loft. This will form the basis of the firm's quote and is carried out by a salesman/surveyor. They may have seen a million lofts before, but you would still expect them to take a peak inside the loft space, because otherwise the job can't be accurately priced. There could be all kinds of hidden nasties up there that will add to the cost, such as missing party walls, asbestos water tanks, leaking flashings or unstable chimney breasts.

The price quoted will depend on whether a planning application is needed. So the firm should check whether you're in a Conservation Area or if the building is Listed, as

Photo: South London Lofts

planning is normally required in such cases. The salesman should take the time to ask you exactly what you want from your new accommodation, and ascertain whether you have any special requirements, such as an en suite wet room, extra sound insulation, or special cabling for a multimedia system?

The quotation

In a few days you'll receive the quotation, perhaps embellished with lots of seductive glamour photos of ecstatic customers luxuriating in their new loft rooms. Most firms know the going rate for jobs in a specific area, so the rival prices probably won't be a million miles apart. The problem for you is trying to interpret all the half-baked technical blurb that's mixed in with a few bits of the Building Regulations to make it all look convincing. Often it's what's left *out* that really matters. Many quotations will exclude decoration and the supply of en suite fittings, which can add up to a significant sum. Smaller details such as the number of electrical sockets can vary dramatically. So it's worth asking them specifically what's *not* included in the price.

If there's no mention of Planning and Building Regulations being fully complied with, forget it. There are plenty of dodgy operators who'll be in and out within a few days, happy to take your money and leave you to sort out potentially dangerous structural alterations with Building Control later.

Accepting a quotation should always be put in writing, and your acceptance should be subject to:

- Works being carried out in full compliance with the Building Regulations, and Planning consent being obtained if needed. Receipt of a completion certificate from Building Control at the end of the job is essential.
- The contractor being responsible for all necessary drawings and calculations and all liaison with Planning and Building Control, as well as making all necessary payments to them (unless you choose to be directly responsible for these fees).
- Payments being made at agreed stages, if possible paying for completed work only.
- Confirmation of agreed start and completion dates.
- The site being left clean and tidy at completion, with all materials and waste removed.
- The contractor being responsible for the requirements of the Party Wall Act, unless you've agreed to do this yourself. This means giving neighbours two months' advance notice.

You'll also need to consider what penalty should be applied if the job isn't completed on time. Ideally a 5 per cent retention should be kept back from eacy payment until all the work is complete and the snagging done. And what happens if defects start to appear several months after the job's finished? Keeping half the 5 per cent

retention for a further three-month period after the completion date is a reasonable proposition – see 'Picking the right builder' on page 80.

The survey
The loft firm will next need to carry out a detailed survey to provide the raw measurements for drawing up the plans and for the specification. Key factors such as roof dimensions, the thickness of party walls, the location of plumbing for bathrooms and the position of stairs will be noted. The overall structure of the building will determine how the new loadings are to be supported.

Plans, calculations and specifications
The contractor will now have plans professionally drawn up for the Building Control application and, when necessary, for Planning. You should first be given an opportunity to review them and make any amendments. Normally the specification takes the form of notes written on the drawings rather than a pukka separate document of the type normally produced for larger construction jobs. Structural calculations must be produced by a qualified engineer.

Building Regulations and Planning
The contractor should now submit the Local Authority applications and pay for them. You should be informed how long this is likely to take, and be kept updated on progress. In some cases this can be very swift indeed. If the Building Control application can be done via a 'Building Notice' and if you don't need Planning it may be possible to start work in a couple of days.

The programme
Before work starts, it's a good idea to agree a rough list of works to be completed each week. The contractor should also explain how they plan to minimise disturbance. As noted earlier, disruption can be reduced by fitting the stairs as late as possible, so all the dust and mess from breaking

through is postponed. Issues such as delivery of materials, hours of work and shared use of WCs should be discussed in advance.

Work commences
The builders arrive and materials are delivered. A supervisor should be at hand most of the time, or at least easily contactable. A brief weekly meeting is advisable to deal with any issues that arise. Payments should be made at previously agreed stages. Work progresses and Building Control carry out key stage inspections.

Completion
The job is completed to the satisfaction of Building Control, from whom the contractor obtains a completion certificate. After minor snagging works are finished, final payment can be made.

The 'shell only' option
A shell conversion is a good way to cut costs by doing some of the lighter work yourself; but it's obviously essential to be very clear about the stage at which you'll be taking over the job. Normally the contractor will complete all the structural work, such as the new floor joists, beams, roof work, dormer windows and stairs. You might want to consider tasks such as fitting the floorboards, internal walls and joinery, installing the insulation, plasterboarding the walls and ceilings, installing bathroom fittings, and fitting fire doors. Or perhaps you just want to do some decorating.

The procedure is pretty much as described above for the full works, except that before you make your final payment when the contractor hands the incomplete project over you must first confirm with Building Control that the work to date fully complies with the regulations. From then on you'll be personally responsible for liaising with Building Control, arranging the remaining inspections, and obtaining the completion certificate at the end of the job.

Employing a building contractor

This approach gives you more control, and should work out cheaper. By employing an architect or surveyor to independently draw up the plans and submit the applications, as well as perhaps project managing the job, you'll have the professionals on your side. This way you're telling the builders what you want, rather than a loft firm dictating to you what gets done. If you want something more than a standard product bolted onto your house, this may be the best approach. Of course, you're still free to project manage if you wish, or to cherry-pick a few easier jobs where your skills are strongest, although the precise extent of your involvement should be agreed with the contractor at the outset.

Employing subcontractors and part self-building

This is a good option for experienced home-improvers. It offers the maximum freedom to get the conversion you really want at the cheapest price – because you're spending your time and skill doing much of the work – plus there are legitimate potential extra savings from VAT that may not necessarily be chargeable on direct labour.

This option means you're free to employ a professional designer, but to run the project yourself, bringing in specific trades for key tasks and doing much of the work yourself. See 'Employing your own subcontractors' on page 87.

Picking the right builder

Whichever method you ultimately decide to go with, there are some useful guidelines for making sure you don't get stuck with a cowboy contractor. Of course it doesn't help that anyone with zero qualifications, lacking even the most rudimentary experience, is perfectly entitled to set up in business calling themselves 'loft conversion specialists'. But despite TV schedules packed with 'Builders from Hell', the plain fact is that the cowboys are in the minority. Most builders will try and do a difficult job well. However, the builder is only one part of the equation. It greatly helps when clients are clear about what they require from the outset and stick to agreed deadlines, especially when it comes to paying!

Fortunately there are some useful golden rules for running a successful building project and avoiding vexed relationships on site. These are explained later in the chapter. But first, how do you go about choosing decent contractors to convert your loft? What you *don't* do is pick the first nice-looking advertisement you come across in *Yellow Pages* or the local paper. A glossy, professional looking ad doesn't mean that the firm being advertised is professional. Neither is it true that 'the posher the van, the better the builder' – it simply means he's good at spending money on vans.

The best place to start is with a personal recommendation, or by speaking to previous customers.

From a shortlist of four or five firms you should be able to find one that fits the bill in terms of experience, price, quality, and availability to start the job within a reasonable timescale.

The criteria for selecting a good builder

Recommendations

Ask people you know locally if they can recommend someone good. Architects and surveyors are particularly well placed to make recommendations. Best placed of all to provide sensible advice are Building Control Officers, but regrettably they may not be at liberty to make recommendations. Citizens Advice Bureaux often keep lists of local contractors such as those with a good track record working for senior citizens, and The Office of Fair Trading produces leaflets to help you locate builders.

Trade association membership

Builders sometimes belong to trade federations, but these exist primarily to represent the interests of their members, not the customers, and the requirements for joining are not always terribly demanding. It is not unknown for unscrupulous builders to 'borrow' logos to make their ads look nicer, or even to make up their own 'guilds', 'leagues' and 'federations', of which they're the only member! So proceed with caution and check that your chosen firm's membership is still current.

Membership of 'proper' trade associations with their own codes of practice can, however, be a useful way to identify good firms. And there may be additional benefits, such as dispute resolution services and complaints procedures, or even insurance-backed warranties. But don't automatically reject a builder because of their lack of 'badges' – many excellent individual tradesmen may work entirely from local references and feel that they don't need to belong to any organisation.

Membership of trade bodies is no guarantee of site quality, but federations that offer additional insurance if you employ one of their members are a definite bonus. To be of any real value however, insurance needs to cover you for a period of up to ten years after completion, for defects caused by poor workmanship or materials or if the builder goes bust during the job.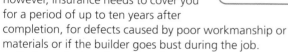

Perhaps the best-known trade association is the Federation of Master Builders, but each trade has its own professional body. There are also Government-funded schemes such as 'TrustMark' that claim to be able to provide consumers with a list of reliable firms. Thousands of 'pre-qualified' contractors, including many sole traders and small specialist firms, are registered with www.constructionline.co.uk.

Quality Assurance

Do ISO 9001/2 or BS 5750 sound familiar? These are widely held Quality Assurance accreditations, but they can be misleading. Although they might appear to be some kind of guarantee of quality for site work, they aren't. They simply prove that a firm is able to reproduce the same

standard of work time and time again. And some builders have absolutely no problem faithfully reproducing poor work! Nonetheless, they do indicate the general aspiration of a firm to deliver a good quality job.

Previous work

It's essential that your contractors have good experience specifically of loft conversions. This is where doing a little detective work can really pay off. Although you should always obtain written references, bear in mind that they may sometimes be of limited value. A builder who's a crook will have written them himself, and the referee will turn out to be his mum or one of his mates! All decent contractors should be able to easily provide a list of recently completed jobs, and a list of customers (such as Housing Associations) to whom you can write.

Go and take a look at the work, and ideally speak to the homeowners – most people will be happy to help. Asking some fairly detailed questions will help ensure they're genuine, for example:

- Did the builders turn up when agreed?
- Did they clear away their rubbish and use dust sheets to protect furniture?
- What was the quality of work like?
- How was their attention to detail with finishing work?
- Did they price any extra work reasonably?
- Did the job start and finish on time?
- Were they helpful and considerate?
- Would you employ them again?

If all the referees sound the same and can't give much detail except to say the firm is 'really great', forget it.

If you can visit one of the builders' current loft conversion sites to see work in progress, it's well worth doing. Note how tidy it is, and whether materials are protected and stored neatly, or just chaotically littered about. Is it a rushed or badly planned job? Running the name of your chosen firm past Trading Standards isn't a bad idea either.

Bankers' references

Ask for a bankers' reference. A firm without sufficient funds to finance the work without demanding a large cash deposit for materials up front will be trouble.

Insurance

Suppose your contractor accidentally drops some roof tiles off the scaffolding, injuring or killing a passer-by. If it turns out the builder isn't fully insured you could be held jointly liable to pay compensation as the owner of the property. More likely some irritating minor damage will occur, like next door's fence getting broken or their roof tiles dislodged. So it's important to cover yourself by asking the builder to produce his current certificate of public liability insurance, which must provide cover to a minimum of £1 million. This is a normal and reasonable request, and any bona fide builder will have no trouble co-operating. Your designer should also have full professional indemnity liability insurance.

However, if you employ subcontractors directly, you are deemed to be an employer, at least from an insurance angle. This means you will need two policies – public liability covering risks to the public, and employers' liability which covers you should someone working for you have a nasty accident and promptly sue you. Most employers' policies now cover you up to £10 million, and public liability for £2 million. It might also be advisable to arrange 'all risks' insurance to cover theft of plant and materials from the site, as well as the risk of fire and structural damage to the property. But first check whether it would be cheaper to extend your existing buildings and contents insurance temporarily to include these risks.

VAT registered?

Unfortunately, VAT is chargeable on labour and materials for loft conversions. Even if a main contractor only does a few loft jobs in a year, his turnover will almost certainly place him above the registration threshold, so he'll need to be VAT registered. Cash deals are best avoided. It's wise to assume that tax has to be added to the quotation, unless it's clearly shown. You should obtain proper receipts for all payments, so check the builder has a valid VAT number and isn't just pocketing it. However, many one-man-band subbies won't need to be VAT registered – one reason why employing trades direct can be a cheaper option (see below).

Guarantees

Major defects in loft works, such as to roofs, dormers, floors and double glazing, can take several years to manifest themselves. For extensions and loft conversions there's no direct equivalent to the NHBC warranty for new houses, but standard contracts such as the JCT Minor Works (see opposite) fortunately include six-year warranties. Guarantees, however, are only as good as the firms offering them, so to have any meaning they need to be insurance-backed.

QUOTATION

Telephone (020) 831 8311
Facsimile (020) 888 8888
E-mail
Website

Date		Number
To		
Address		

A LOFT CONVERSION WITH A DORMER EXTENSION

01. To constructing one major room and a shower-room
02. Approximate size of conversion including the new stairs is 285 sq ft .
03. Timber framed tile-hung dormer with an approximate width of 15 ft with two double glazed PVCu windows plus two double glazed Velux roof windows (one in shower-room).
04. Tongue and groove suspended floor.
05. Traditional staircase rising over the existing stairs to match existing stairs as closely as possible.
06. Walls and ceiling studded and plaster-boarded.
07. Insulation to the new ceiling and all external walls. Soundproof new floor as required by the Building Control Officer.
08. Half hour fire-check doors to the loft rooms.
09. Recessed ceiling lights to the main and shower-rooms (if permitted by the Building Control Officer), two-way light over the stairs and four double 13 amp sockets in the room.
10. Board the eaves space floor and provide a light and access door.
11. Supply and fit a radiator to each room— from the existing system if technically possible or provide an alternative if not.
12. Supply & fit shower tray (stone resin not plastic) cubicle, WC and hand-basin with taps and either a pedestal or vanity unit (clients choice) and a shower system and provide water services from the existing combination boiler if powerful enough. If not, then supply and fit a Triton T80 (or equivalent) shower system and water heater..
13. Remove Loft Hatch and make good.
14. Plaster skim finish all round.
15. All rubbish removed from site.
16. Survey, plans and all Local Authority fees.
17. We estimate the above work will take 10 -12 weeks.
18. ANY WORK NECESSARY TO COMPLY WITH BUILDING REGULATIONS. WHICH INCLUDES FITTING HEAT RESISTANT GLASS.
10. When completed the conversion should be ready for decorating.

Quotation or estimate?

Quotations and estimates are two very different things. A quotation is a firm price which is legally binding. It's a fixed sum for a fixed amount of work. An estimate, on the other hand, is the builder's best guess at what the cost might eventually be. It is not legally binding, and allows the builder to present a higher (or lower) final bill, and is far too risky for a big project like a loft conversion.

If you insist on a firm quotation you will need to provide sufficient information for the builder to understand exactly what you want built. To judge how good a quotation is, consider the amount of care and detail that's gone into it, and whether the contractor actually went to the trouble of inspecting your loft before quoting.

This is important, because having provided a quotation your builder must stick to it. If you're presented with a larger final bill, you're only obliged to pay the agreed quotation price unless you've requested 'extras' or agreed to 'changes' (see page 89). Contractors will include in their price a sum to cover the risk that the job could turn out to be more complicated than it seems.

You'll need to obtain three or four quotations in writing. Quotations can either be written in terms of a firm price for the completed job, *ie* the total amount you are expected to pay, or alternatively as a 'metreage rate' known as 'pricework'. This is where you're given a price for certain works expressed either per square metre (tiling, brickwork, plasterwork etc) or per metre run (for laying pipes etc). Quotations based on a price per day ('day rate') are best avoided because of the obvious temptation to sit around and string the job out indefinitely.

The information you need to send out to contractors for pricing can be in the form of a covering letter and a set of plans. It's worth explaining how far you've got with the Planning and Building Control applications so that it's clear this is a serious undertaking. On larger projects, the best way to get a job priced is to tender it. A tender is a sort of super-detailed competitive quotation based on a detailed specification of works that you've provided. For most loft conversion jobs, however, quotations based on detailed plans should be sufficient, although providing an additional written specification along with the plans can help clarify exactly what you want (see 'the specification' below).

Small builders

A smaller firm of builders will have less labour available to share between competing jobs, so you should stand a better chance of getting their undivided attention for the full project. If you're very lucky indeed they may even finish one job at a time rather than juggling resources between different jobs, as larger firms invariably do. But as noted earlier it's best to avoid small firms that don't have enough funding to pay for materials up front.

Contingency sums

The chances are that as you lovingly watch your new loft rooms take shape something will occur to you (or your partner) that 'would look nice'. Something that you wish you'd included in the specification but didn't. You are not alone. It is by no means unknown for property professionals to omit items from specifications. Of course you're not expected to get everything right first time, so to allow for the inevitable human error factor it's wise to budget at least 5 per cent more than the quoted cost as a contingency sum.

The contract

A building contract is simply an agreement between you and your builder for them to undertake an amount of work, to a certain standard, for an agreed sum of money. Although, strictly speaking, accepting a verbal offer can form a contract in law, to run the job properly it's advisable to use a written contract, signed by both parties.

Dodgy builders have been known to keep postponing starting a job they've quoted for and then to try claim compensation when your patience is finally exhausted and you tell them to sling their hook. They may claim that you entered into a verbal contract with them. So if you do accept a builder's offer to do a job without a formal contract, always make your acceptance conditional upon them confirming in writing that they agree to a specific start date and completion date. It's worth noting that where a contract can be proved to exist, one of the key implied conditions is that 'the work shall be performed within a reasonable time'.

Using a written contract is always advisable because it shows that both sides are serious, and gives you both certain rights and duties that are enforceable in court. If things later all go horribly wrong, it allows you (the innocent party) to seek compensation, known as 'damages', for any losses incurred. You're also able to terminate the contract and employ someone else.

But which contract to use? There's nothing to stop you writing your own if you want, but it's a lot easier to use a ready-made 'off the shelf' contract, such as a suitable JCT (Joint Contracts Tribunal) contract. The JCT 'Building Contract for a Home Owner/Occupier' can be used for straightforward, lower-price jobs (costing below about £25,000). Or for more complex or expensive projects the JCT 'Minor Works' contract. Alternatively, the Federation of Master Builders have a free one you can download from the website. If you're employing an architect or surveyor, ask their advice.

Don't be too gobsmacked when you first read the contract. It's basically a collection of all the things that could ever go wrong with any property development, based on other people's bad experiences over many years. It clarifies who's responsible for what, thereby reducing the risk of a major dispute messing up the job. All the important stuff is there, including how frequently you agree to pay the builders, and whose responsibility it is if the job is only half finished by the completion date.

There's nothing to stop you adding your own specific conditions if you wish. For example, you might want the builder not to start work until after 7.30 am, not to work at weekends, and not to entertain the neighbours by blasting out The Arctic Monkey's greatest hits all day long. Before you sign the contract, remember that this is your last chance to ensure that you'll be getting exactly what you want; any changes from now could cost you extra money.

The specification

Most disputes with builders are (surprise, surprise) about money. This is often down to misunderstandings about exactly what work was meant to be done for the quoted price. Fortunately many loft conversions tend to follow a similar pattern, so for an experienced local firm there shouldn't be too many surprises. But builders aren't psychic, so the key to a smoothly run job is to clearly

specify what's required. This takes the form of a shopping list or 'specification' describing all the small jobs that go to make up the entire project, so that nothing gets overlooked. Known as 'the spec' (pronounced 'spess'), this is based on information gleaned during the survey, back in Chapter 2. It's sometimes also referred to as a 'schedule of works'. Normally the architect or surveyor producing your plans will write out a basic specification in the form of notes written on the Building Control drawings. If this is sufficiently detailed, the plans alone may be satisfactory for the builders to
price from.

However, the process of writing out a detailed list of your requirements is important in itself, because it helps

focus on exactly what you want, reducing the risk of misunderstandings later. Spending time planning the project at this stage can save hours of frustration later. The real danger is that if you rush writing the specification, some items will inevitably get left out. This in turn will result in quotations or tenders that omit these items, and you'll later end up paying for them as expensive 'extras'. Bad feeling on site and poor workmanship can also result. The trick is to be precise, leaving nothing to question.

Briefs

Writing a loft specification requires good technical knowledge, so if it's your first time it might be better to write the draft version for someone else with good construction knowledge, such as a chartered surveyor, to finalise. If you want to produce your own specification, it may be better to instead refer to it as a 'detailed brief' when you submit it to the contractor. Whereas a spec is regarded as a definitive list, a brief is simply your 'best attempt' to convey your requirements. A brief doesn't exempt the contractor from his responsibility to use his expertise to interpret your desires, and to employ suitable methods and materials. In the event of a later dispute, a brief can be a little more forgiving.

Start by writing down a general outline of the work required and then list specific requirements, explaining what you want and the standards you expect. Together with information taken from manufacturers' specifications this can form the basis of your brief. You'll need to research the available sizes and quality of materials such as tiles and roof windows etc. One other tip: using the phrase *'allow for all necessary work in connection with…'* covers a multitude of sins and will reduce the risk of the contractor trying to charge extra for something which is obviously needed but which you might have forgotten to include in the brief.

Workmanship

So much for accurately describing the job and precisely defining the required materials. But there's one thing that's a lot harder to nail down, and that's the standard of workmanship. Under the terms of the contract, the builder will normally be required to 'use reasonable care and skill', which is obviously open to some interpretation. One solution is to specify 'British Standard BS 8000' on the plans, and to make sure the plans are included as contract documents so that, if push comes to shove, they're legally enforceable (so staple a set of plans to the contract and have each party jointly sign all pages and drawings). Then if the workmanship becomes unsatisfactory at any stage, your builder will be in breach of contract and you'll be able to give him notice to correct the defective work, or terminate the contract. It helps to include advisory phrases such as *'Provide temporary support to floors and ceilings as necessary'* and *'All new structure to be in place before cutting or removal of existing roof members and ceiling joists'*.

Photo: Wooden Hill

Design detail – choosing materials

Never assume that the builder will automatically do everything just the way you like it. This may sound obvious but many disputes grow out of misunderstandings over tiny details – for example, the type of skirting or architraves. You might have visualised a Victorian ogee style to beautifully complement your new en suite fittings, but unless instructed otherwise the builder may be justified in sticking on the cheapest bit of timber he can find. Unless you clearly specify the *'Italian, stone resin, one-piece, bow-fronted shower cubicle'* that you've long dreamed of the contractor may simply install a cheapo acrylic one he found on E-bay, and you won't have a leg to stand on. So think carefully about the details, such as the kind of light switches, sockets, taps and basins that you want, or you will inevitably discover that they've fitted some bargain ones left over from the last job.

On the other hand, your builders may well come up with bright ideas as the job progresses, which can sometimes reduce the cost. Most builders know their stuff and have seen it all before. So don't be too proud or suspicious and reject all their ideas out of hand. But be aware that some suggestions come with a price tag. If your friendly builder suggests that something 'might as well be done', don't assume he'll do it out of the goodness of his heart.

This is the time to do your homework. There'll be less room for mistakes if you quote details and catalogue numbers. If you intend to supply some fittings or materials yourself make sure that your specification or brief states that the contractor is to 'allow for fitting only'. This means that you're solely responsible for ensuring that these items are available on site exactly when the fitter needs them. If they're delivered too soon there'll be a greater risk of damage – too late, and the plumber or chippie may not appear on site again for another month.

Even with package-deal loft jobs the client is often expected to supply bathroom sanitary fittings such as baths, showers, basins and WCs. Wall tiling is also often excluded. There may be some grey areas, such as who pays for associated items such as loo seats, waste traps and pipework. So the responsibility for supplying materials and fittings must be made very clear at the start, otherwise it can very easily flare up into a major issue. Rather than supplying stuff yourself, it's usually simpler to specify exactly what materials you want by writing 'allow price of £X to supply 1 no. pair B&Q basin taps ref: ABC123' (*ie* quote the product reference number). This will save a whole lot of your time fetching and delivering things.

The materials used to build your new loft room obviously need to be safe and fit for purpose. Your designer and builders should be familiar with the materials available, and the specification document will normally state the quality required (*eg* 'plywood shall be in accordance with BS 1455').

Products should normally carry a recognised quality branding such as the BSI (British Standard Institute) kitemark or BBA (British Board of Agreement) approval. Products with 'CE' marks are also acceptable, as it means they comply with European standards. If in doubt, ask Building Control what they'll accept. The biggest problems with materials usually relate to the way they've been installed. If a dispute arises with the builders, the manufacturers normally have product advisers available who should be able to clarify matters.

Preliminaries

The 'prelims' are your way of explaining to the contractor the arrangements for all those important little things that

make a job run smoothly – such as the provision of toilets for the workers, rubbish collection, site security, temporary power and water supplies and arrangements for storage of materials. If such things aren't spelled out clearly you may find yourself temporarily entombed in your home one fine day by mountains of insulation boards deposited outside your front door.

Designers have a legal duty to minimise risks on site, so it's a good idea to specify some wise site safety advice in the prelims and to encourage the builder to keep the site (ie your home and garden) as tidy as possible. For example, 240-volt power supplies are prohibited on building sites so contractors must only use 110-volt power tools, and it wouldn't do any harm to include this in the documentation as a reminder.

Comparing quotations

Having received three or four quotations for your loft job the process of picking the best one can begin. Unfortunately this isn't as simple as just choosing the lowest price. This is where you need to get smart and read between the lines and be sure you're comparing like with like.

It's possible that one firm may have undercut the others because he's just totally inept at estimating and has under-priced the job. Or an unscrupulous firm may be skilled in spotting loopholes in your specification, knowing that they can later charge you premium prices for lots of 'extras'. So it's worth spending some time comparing all your tenders, section by section, since this may reveal surprising differences in quoted prices for the same works. If one is absurdly cheap compared to the others, they may have forgotten to include some materials or labour. This means they'll later need to find ways of recovering that loss by cutting corners. Unless the firm has been highly recommended, it may be cheaper in the long run to select

another, rather than risk them skimping on materials and labour to recoup losses.

Then there's the important matter of the start date. It's unlikely that a really good small firm would be so in need of work that it could start tomorrow. But on the other hand, a firm that can't begin for another year is hardly ideal either.

Finally, use a little intuition about the people themselves. Talk to the contractor. There may be something about their attitude that makes you feel uneasy. Someone swaying from the effects of lunchtime binge drinking should make you think twice about doing business with them.

And the winner is...

Having made your choice, you'll then need to set up a meeting to go through your drawings (and specification) in some detail prior to signing the contract. If you're independently employing a designer, they should also be present so that any complex parts of the drawings can be discussed in detail.

Run through key things like the positions of new beams, the sizes of roof timbers, work to party walls, and types of fire doors. If the builder's face turns a peculiar shade of ghostly white at any stage it means he's just realised that something's been seriously underpriced. If so, it's always better to agree a revised price at this stage than to have a dispute later on.

Although as a rule they don't like doing this, ask the contractors to provide a week by week programme so that you'll be able to monitor progress. Even a simple 'milestone programme' would be useful, showing the dates by which key stages will be completed.

This is the honeymoon stage. Everything is sweetness and light, as the contractors rejoice in the warm afterglow of winning your business. So it's as well to bring them sharply down to earth and run through all the important issues – the agreed start date and completion date, arrangements for storage of materials, and the welfare facilities (loos etc).

If you've opted for a package deal with a loft firm, they'll normally have their own form of contract which, needless to say, will be skewed in their favour. You can, of course, agree modifications, but basically you'll have very little flexibility.

As far as the agreed timescales are concerned, it's not unknown for contractors to be prone to bouts of over-optimism at this stage, which will only cause problems later. So it may be worth asking them to think twice about the projected time to finish the job. If necessary they might want to agree an extra couple of weeks, just in case. They are, of course, perfectly at liberty to finish the job earlier (but they won't). All contract documents, including the drawings and specification, now need to be signed by both parties and stapled together with the contract itself. Be sure to personally retain the originals.

Alternatively, if you're not using a contract form you can instead seal the deal by writing to the contractor to formally accept his offer. Your 'letter of acceptance' is a legally binding contract document and should include a list of the drawings and documents on which he based his quotation, together with confirmation of the agreed price (the 'contract sum'), the agreed start and completion dates, and the stages of payment etc. You must also request that the builder formally replies and acknowledges receipt of your letter.

Employing your own subcontractors

If you've opted to employ trades direct, now's your chance to manage your own team. Of course, you can't expect to instantly become the Sir Alex Ferguson of the loft conversion world, so only take on this role if you know your Flitch beams from your RSJs.

Strictly speaking, subcontractors are trades employed by a main contractor. If they work directly for you then they aren't actually subbies at all, just plain old contractors, but everyone still calls them subbies. They tend to operate as one man bands or as small firms. It's important to note that if you officially become the 'main contractor' then you could suddenly be responsible for policing your subbies' tax affairs. This will only happen if the taxman somehow defines your loft project as 'running a business or trade', and deems you to be a 'professional developer', in which case you'd also get lumbered with all the main contractor insurance liabilities.

In this case however, you are acting as a 'domestic client' who's chosen to do some of the building work himself, and to employ some trades direct. But you will still need to adopt some of the responsibilities of a main contractor, and to budget for increased overheads, such as phone bills and mileage.

With subbies, the work is normally described with reference to the plans, rather than signing contracts. But the clearer and more specific you are about what you want, the less chance there is of expensive misunderstandings. Your mission now is to achieve nothing less than the smooth running of the project, which means having to co-ordinate all the various materials and trades on site at each stage of the build. Easy to say, harder to deliver.

It's normally best to either appoint a main contractor or to employ trades direct, rather than attempting to combine both methods. For example, it's sometimes tempting to cut costs by arranging for a friend of a friend to undertake jobs such as electrics or plastering. The problem is that friends of friends inevitably turn out to be incredibly busy on those crucial weekends when they promised to finish your job. So just when the main contractor needs to press ahead he can't, because an important piece of work hasn't been done. This is one reason why some loft projects never get completed.

The team

Like any team, yours will only be as strong as its weakest link. Select only those who you know to be skilled and experienced at their particular trade. You need to ensure that each subbie knows exactly what's expected of them, or the job will be done the way that is easiest for them, rather than the way you want it. As client and main contractor rolled into one, you'll need to get a quotation from each trade in turn, and to be clear about what exactly

is included in each subbie's price. Normally this is done in the same way as larger projects as 'pricework', with one quotation for the whole job. Alternatively, if they come highly recommended you could perhaps agree a day rate, with a price for each full day worked. Trades who supply materials as well as labour ('supply and fix') typically include roofers, plumbers and electricians. Part of their profit margin comes from the mark-up made on the materials they purchase on your behalf.

According to urban folklore, the legendary 'Polish builder' will do a good job for a very fair price. But employing non-English-speaking trades means that, with the best will in the world, communication problems can arise (not unlike Fabio Capello and the England football team). For example, a roofer who's just arrived from, say, Bulgaria may have a totally different way of working that doesn't take account of UK Building Regulations. Plus there's a tendency for illegal immigrant workers to grab their tools and leg it out the back door as soon as the Building Control Officer makes an appearance! So for the more complex parts of the job, it's normally safer to stick with experienced, home-grown trades folk.

Each trade has its own quirks and particular ways of working:

- **Carpenters** or 'chippies' work as one-man-bands or in pairs, and don't supply materials. Prices normally include building dormer roof structures (except for the battens, which are fixed by the roofers), cutting and fixing timbers to form valleys, fitting fascias and soffits, and stripping the existing tiles from the old roof where the new roof will join it or for new valleys to join it. The carpenter may also be the best person to fit the guttering, but this won't be included unless specified.
- **Roofers** may be hired in gangs of two or more. Roof tilers will either quote to 'supply and fix' or as 'labour only' and will sometimes also organise scaffolding. If you opt for 'labour only' you'll need to be pretty confident that all the roof tiles, valley tiles, battens and underlay etc will be delivered to the right place at the right time. The price should include laying all felt, battens and tiles, forming valleys and bedding ridge tiles and verges. Most will also do small amounts of leadwork such as fixing valley linings and lead flashings, but leadwork to flat roofs and large valleys is a specialist roofing trade.

- **Felt roofers'** quotations are usually calculated per square metre, but dormer roofs can be very labour intensive and may be priced individually. Check that the price includes fitting any necessary lead flashings.
- **Plasterers, plumbers and electricians** are usually sole traders or very small firms who supply and fix.

Overseeing the works

A typical loft conversion might take roughly 8 to12 weeks to complete. If you've opted to employ subcontractors directly, or even a main contractor with an independent designer, someone will need to manage the project during this period. A surveyor or architect could be appointed or alternatively you may want to take on the role of Project Manager yourself.

Payments and retentions

The stages at which you pay your builder should be agreed in advance. For a typical loft job 'interim payments' are made, perhaps every four weeks or fortnightly. It is obviously important to keep clear records of each payment you make. It's customary on all but the smallest jobs for the client to hold back a small retention sum during the works, which must be agreed at the outset. The main purpose of this is to provide an incentive that will encourage the builders to return at later stages to fix any minor defects. Normally the contract permits the deduction of a small retention (say 5 per cent) from each payment. Half the retained money is released to the builder at the end of the build, at 'practical completion', and the remaining half paid after a further three months, known as the 'defects liability period'.

If you insist on keeping too large a retention, the contractor will simply price the job higher. But if the retention is too small they might find it easier to lose the money rather than to physically come back and carry out any minor finishing tasks. If you're dealing with a trusted local firm you may not need to keep any retention at all.

There are 2 golden rules when it comes to payments:

Pay contractors promptly

Failure to pay is a breach of contract. You're normally obliged to pay within 14 days of the due date (or within 30 days of practical completion). No one is going to do their best work if they're not paid on time, and paying promptly is an easy way to create a positive atmosphere of trust and co-operation.

Avoid paying for work in advance

If the builder goes bust halfway through the job, or if he's a rubbish builder and you want to terminate the contract, you'll be in a far stronger position if you haven't pre-paid. Also, if you pay for work that's not yet been done it removes much incentive for good quality workmanship to be completed on time. However, specialist loft firms usually have standard contract terms, often requiring part payment in advance. This should be negotiable, especially if you offer to make more frequent payments instead of paying up front.

Extras and changes

In an ideal world the need to vary the work as it progresses shouldn't occur. But in reality there are four situations where this sometimes becomes necessary:

You request additional work

Something occurs to you that you really wish had been included but wasn't – perhaps a small roof window to the bathroom. Some builders make nearly half their profits from clients requesting extra works, because clients often forget to check the cost implications. So always be sure to get a price for any additional work before it's carried out.

The builders suggest extra work

Most builders have considerable experience of similar projects to yours, and as a result may have some genuinely smart ideas about how to improve the design, even saving you money by doing it another way. On the other hand, many are also highly skilled at the art of 'soft selling'. Friendly, casual suggestions, such as 'While we're at it, we may as well replace those old ceilings', or 'It's no problem to just replaster the walls', may be perfectly pitched to illicit the required client response. But it's fatal to assume that there'll be no charge. Always ask how much it will cost.

Unforeseen circumstances

The builders stumble across something unexpected – perhaps a rotten old timber lintel hidden in the walls. This

Photo: Boundary Bathrooms

requires extra work, but who will stump up the additional cash? It depends on whether such work was reasonably foreseeable and should have been built into the contractor's price. Or perhaps it should have been clearly specified by the client. One important issue with lofts is who pays for any damage to perfectly good existing bedroom ceilings. It's hard to avoid a lot of banging and vibration during works in a loft, which may loosen old lath and plaster ceilings. Responsibility is best agreed at the outset as a 'what if' situation, perhaps by settling on a 50:50 arrangement.

Items not specified

You expect to get what you've asked for. If you specified 'guttering' but didn't specifically mention the extruded aluminium ogee style that you really wanted, the contractor will price for fitting cheaper standard half-round black plastic guttering. If your architect leaves 'holes' in the specification that end up costing you extra cash, you may be entitled to claim a proportionate reduction in their fees.

Ordering materials

The most bulky materials for loft conversions tend to be steel beams, timber floor joists, sheets of plasterboard and lots of giant insulation boards.

Managing the logistics of getting the right materials delivered to the right place at the right time can be a demanding task, one that clients using main contractors often take for granted.

So if you decide to source your own stuff, start by writing out a detailed shopping list of all your materials (known as a 'bill of quantities'). This is based on your specification and plans, from which all the areas and volumes can be calculated with the help of a scale rule.

You need to be clear about whether you want the trades to provide their own materials or supply 'labour only'. As noted above, some trades such as electricians and plumbers normally expect to 'supply and fix' their own materials unless requested otherwise.

When ordering materials you often have to accept the nearest pack quantity size. And don't forget to add an allowance for the materials that get wasted, or are surplus, perhaps to the tune of around 10 per cent. Ordering more than you need may be expensive, but buying too little is probably more so.

Having worked out exactly how much of what you need to order, next select two or three major suppliers (usually builders' merchants) and give them your shopping list together with a copy of your drawings. For a large order you'd normally expect to be able to negotiate a sizeable discount, first by registering for a trade account and then negotiating a bit more. Most small builders expect to pay at least 15 per cent less than the list prices shown in catalogues. With a trade account you should qualify for at least a month's credit, as well as keener prices. Haggling is standard practice at builders' merchants, but not of course at the big DIY sheds like Wickes and B&Q, where some prices for some products can be as competitive as trade prices elsewhere.

Builders' merchants are normally most competitive on price when supplying timber, mass-produced joinery and plastering materials. However, some components, such as windows and bathroom fittings, may need to be ordered from specialist suppliers well in advance.

Deliveries

Delivery dates are crucial, but it's an unfortunate fact of life that materials sometimes arrive later than promised. Get this wrong and you could end up paying trades to sit around idly on site, and then have trouble getting them to turn up again next time. So never leave things to chance – it's best to double-check with a quick call to your supplier a day or so in advance to confirm the delivery date. When deliveries do arrive, always check the materials for damage before signing them off. If in doubt write 'unchecked' next to your signature. Don't dump materials down where they're going to invade the clear workspace that the builders need to do the job. A tidy site is a safe site.

To keep control of things, it's useful to write a chart showing what's supposed to be happening at each stage in the project, week by week. It's essential to co-ordinate the delivery of materials with the scheduled arrival of different trades on site. Allow some flexibility, as these dates and times are only your best guess – they're not set in stone, and you may need to fine-tune things a little as the project develops.

Plant hire

Just when you're starting to appreciate how much the main contractor does for his money, there's a third

per metre run for each 'lift' or storey.

Site safety

Approximately half of all construction fatalities are due to falls, which makes loft jobs especially sensitive. Hence the 'Working at Height Regulations' which, amongst other things, restrict the use of ladders. But ladders aren't the only worry. The risks from such routine objects as power tools, sharp blades, tiles dropped from scaffolding, flame guns, toxic or flammable sprays and live electric cables are very real and need to be treated with respect. Combine these with kids, pets and unwary adults living in the property and you've got a potentially lethal cocktail – an injury compensation lawyer's dream.

dimension to add to the equation. The curious world of plant hire. Just about everything can be hired, from scaffold towers to angle grinders and tarpaulins, normally on a daily or weekly basis. Be clear about whose job it is to arrange plant hire, since there's a limit to how many bolt-firing nail guns you can usefully employ at one time. There is normally scope for price negotiation, especially when ordering associated materials (nails, cartridges, sanding discs etc).

When employing subbies it's a good idea to discuss each trade's requirements beforehand. Whereas some subbies tend to arrive fully tooled up (*eg* electricians, plumbers and carpenters) others may not. Scaffolding is normally priced for a hire period of 8 to 10 weeks, with a small surcharge levied for each extra week. Prices are quoted in terms of £X

Cleanliness and protection

Never underestimate the amount of dust and mess that loft works can potentially create. Power sanders and angle grinders can swiftly create an unpleasant swirl of gritty smog that rapidly engulfs your living space, clothes, food, children etc. For many homeowners this is the most disheartening part of the whole process. This is why the importance of carefully programming the works was stressed earlier – leaving the knocking through and fitting of the new stairs until as late as possible. Come to think of it, now might be a good time to stock up on bargain-size packs of wipes and furniture polish!

6 GETTING STARTED

Photo: South London Lofts

You don't have to be a genius to realise that a loft full of builders armed with power tools isn't going to do a lot for the soothing feng shui ambience of your home. So be prepared for normal life to be disrupted by a lot of hammering, drilling, and materials being dumped in the front garden. If you have a family, be sure to brief them fully before the forces of Armageddon strike. You may also need to be prepared for a short-term loss of power or heating towards the end of the job, if the existing services need to be extended upstairs. But before works can start in earnest the loft must first be cleared, and access must be provided to the front of the property for the delivery of materials and the arrival of the scaffolding.

The greatest upheaval indoors will occur in those rare cases where the engineer has concluded there's a need for additional support for the new loft loadings from foundation level. This is more likely to be required in older period properties, where the party walls may be of dubious character and the main walls are already looking a bit structurally challenged. In which case you may find your living room playing host to some interesting excavations.

The order of works

The precise order of works will vary according to the way different firms are used to organising their work, and the extent to which you need to minimise disturbance to occupants. From a contractor's viewpoint it's often simpler to access the loft from inside the main house. But to minimise the upheaval this would cause, the first job is often to provide suitable access arrangements externally. So once the scaffolding is erected, an opening can be cut through the roof into the loft. This may be carried out to the rear roof slope where a large box dormer may later be scheduled to take shape. But in terraced houses without side access, a temporary opening that's larger than any intended roof window may need to be cut in the front roof slope.

Once the access arrangements are in place, any necessary structural upgrading can be carried out, such as

building up missing firebreak party walls in lofts, beefing up lintels over windows and doors, or supporting loose masonry above any removed chimney breasts. But normally the first major task is to construct a strong new floor in the loft, which serves as a platform for all the following work. (See Chapter 7.)

Relocating the existing services

If it hasn't been done already, one of the first jobs is to clear the loft so that you can see exactly what you're dealing with. At this point, to avoid the possibility of an embarrassing mishap such as a leg poking through the ceiling, planks or boarding can be laid across the old ceiling joists, which will also help to spread the load. A lot

of dusty old insulation will also need to be stripped out, to locate any hidden pipes and cables. If anything, this is an even more unpleasant job than laying it in the first place, so it's important to don dust masks and goggles to protect your lungs and eyes.

Most lofts will contain a large cold-water tank and also a smaller 'feed and expansion' or header tank serving the hot water cylinder. These will need to be relocated, unless they happen to already be conveniently sited at the edge of the loft, which is the zone destined to become eaves cupboards (see Chapter 13).

If your heating system is on its last legs anyway this may be a good opportunity to replace it, ideally with a new pressurised system fed direct from the mains. Combination boilers or an unvented Megaflow system (which has a pressure expansion vessel on top of the hot water cylinder) don't require tanks in the loft.

Normally the only serious pipework found in lofts is that serving the tanks, which will include plastic overflow pipes leading out to the eaves. Very occasionally boilers or hot-water cylinders are also located in lofts, a significantly more expensive obstacle to deal with. Hot-water cylinders can be relocated to a more conventional place, such as a cupboard to a landing or bedroom. Modern room-sealed boilers can operate from a variety of locations, but are normally best relocated to kitchens, utility rooms or garages. But to keep costs as low as possible, a better option – if they're not positioned smack in the middle of the loft – may be to work around them by neatly boxing them in, always remembering to allow access for maintenance.

Electric cables found in lofts tend to be those supplying the lights to bedrooms below. Where cables are run parallel to the ceiling joists it may be possible to leave some in place, but a certain amount of rerouting is likely to be needed to make way for the new floor joists.

The final part of the jungle of pipes and cables may be encountered in the form of flexible 'concertina' plastic ducts serving bathroom extractor fans, meandering their way up to vented ridge tiles at the apex of the roof, or to gable wall vents. It shouldn't be too hard to redirect these around the perimeter of the new loft room where they won't be seen.

Preparing the loft

Out of site is out of mind. No one's going to get too bothered about the occasional mouse camping out in their draughty old loft. And who's going to notice if a little damp has leached through the brickwork of chimney breasts hidden away up in the roof? Such formerly trivial matters can suddenly become a serious issue as soon as you want to occupy the loft as living space. Unless action is taken now, the subsequent appearance of ugly stains and damp smells, or nests harbouring angry wasps or vermin, could ruin that idyllic loft-living experience.

It's not really surprising that chimneys can harbour a lot

of moisture. Big open chimney pots provide an open invitation for rain to enter. Condensation is another common source of damp in flues.

To protect active flues from deterioration and condensation it should be a fairly easy job to insert flue-liners whilst the scaffolding's in place. More importantly, flue-liners should also seal any gaps in old chimney masonry that could otherwise allow invisible, odourless, toxic fumes to enter your new loft room with potentially deadly consequences. To protect chimney pots from driving rain, special cowlings can be fitted that allow smoke to escape whilst acting as small umbrellas. Even if your fireplaces are disused, flues should still be capped-off and vented, in order to deter damp from condensation.

Any botched structural alterations from years gone by will now need to be rectified, typically where chimney breasts have been removed from the bedrooms below but the remaining chimney masonry in the loft wasn't properly supported. Because the loft conversion will most likely involve installation of new steel beams for the new floor structure, providing some extra support to any old chimney breasts at the same time shouldn't add greatly to the cost.

Erecting scaffolding

Definitely not a DIY job, scaffolding must be erected by a licensed specialist firm with plenty of insurance cover. Arranging this is normally the responsibility of the main contractor, but if you're employing trades direct this task may be down to you. Your scaffolding needs to be ordered well in advance, so that it can be erected in good time. You may decide to wait until the roof work begins in earnest, but ideally it should be erected prior to any work starting, so that materials such as giant steel beams don't have to be carted through your hallway.

A high proportion of building site accidents and fatalities arise from poor erection and dismantling of scaffolding or temporary work platforms, and spectacular collapses have occurred from time to time. Scaffolding has to support a considerable weight, not just of loads of burly builders but also from lots of heavy roof tiles and materials being stacked up on it, making the possibility of overloading a real danger.

Because of the real risk of serious injury, scaffolding is the subject of much health and safety legislation. To help weed out cowboy scaffolding firms, it's worth quoting this phrase when confirming instructions in writing: *'the scaffolding shall be erected and maintained in accordance with BS 5973 and 5974 "Access & working scaffolds and special scaffold structures in steel" and The Construction (Health, Safety & Welfare) Regulations 1996.'*

This should at least cover you in the event of an accident. Also, request a handover certificate once the scaffolding is all in place, to confirm that it's been erected properly. Any platform over 2m high must have metal edge-guarding fixed to the sides, and if people are likely to be passing underneath there should be protective netting to catch falling debris.

During the course of the works, check from time to time that the scaffolding hasn't sunk into soft ground, and that ladders are securely tied and set at an angle of about 75°. The vertical tubular scaffold poles ('standards') must rest on substantial base plates, and care must be taken that the horizontal poles ('putlogs') don't damage the walls.

Starting the build

Start-on-site is usually a fairly harmonious occasion. Everyone is full of the best intentions and wants to crack on and make it happen. The good news is that all the trouble you've taken so far preparing for the works should now really start to pay off. You're about to avoid all those expensive mistakes, nasty conflicts and hidden dangers lying in wait to trap the unwary.

At least two days before work begins, you must formally notify Building Control. True, they may sometimes choose not to visit at this stage, but that's their call, not yours. Failure to notify them is an offence for which you can be prosecuted, which wouldn't be the best start.

Opening it up
As described above, to get access a portion of the roof slope will be cut open, which will at a later stage probably be used to install a dormer window or skylight. But first, a word of

caution. As soon as you decide to remove a part of your roof, the skies will inevitably rumble and darken, threatening a downpour of biblical proportions. So be prepared with tarpaulins. The procedure is as follows:

- ■ Strip off and set side the roof tiles in the areas where the new dormer or roof window is to be located. Cut and remove underfelt and battens to the immediate area. (In the rare cases where roofs have been sprayed on the inside with a layer of polyurethane foam, this can prove considerably harder because the tiles will be 'glued solid').
- ■ Where necessary, build a temporary support structure with timber props inside before cutting the opening of the correct size. Trussed rafter roofs are highly sensitive and shouldn't be cut until the structure has been reinforced.
- ■ In most roofs, small openings up to about a metre wide can be made in the roof by cutting a single rafter. This typically involves sawing out one or two rafters, doubling up the remaining rafters on either side and then trimming across the top and bottom of the new opening, as described in Chapter 9. In modern roofs the trussed rafters are typically spaced at wider 600mm centres and this width of opening may be adequate for temporary access purposes without cutting any rafters.

Storing materials

There's an art to managing incoming materials. The key is to plan ahead. Consider which materials are going to need protection from the weather with covers, and avoid dumping materials where they could block access routes. Then there's the question of security for higher value items, and of course the logistics of timing deliveries to fit with the work programme, and minimising time spent stored on site.

Loft conversions are mainly built using dry but bulky materials, such as timber and plasterboard. So without careful planning, it may come as a shock when a ten-tonne builders' merchant's truck pulls up and starts

craning giant sheets of boarding onto your prized dahlias.

Things such as roof tiles can be stored outdoors, but still need some protection from the weather. Other materials, such as plaster, need to be delivered fresh, just prior to use.

Timber is especially vulnerable to distortion and warping, especially if it's allowed to get damp. Timber products should therefore be stacked off the ground, on bearers. It's not unusual for structural 'caracassing timber' to arrive on site damp, in which case it should really be returned to the timber yard or at least given time to dry out. Perhaps surprisingly, the Building Regulations don't require structural timbers to be preservative treated, with the exception of those used for flat roof construction.

Only if you're having the entire roof replaced is it likely that giant prefabricated roof trusses will be required. Despite their size, these are fairly delicate and require careful treatment to prevent them warping and distorting – they must be stacked on a level base, kept clear of the ground, and covered.

Staggering the delivery times can help avoid overcrowding the site with mountains of materials all arriving at once, so that industrial quantities of roof tiles aren't suddenly dumped in the middle of the neighbours' lawn. Try to get materials swiftly distributed to where they'll be needed, or covered up and stored away safely. Make full use of lockable garages and garden sheds. If you're one of the few people who actually use their garage to park a vehicle, alternative parking arrangements may need to be considered.

Finally, there's the question of skips. You're going to need quite a few, especially later in the job with loads of surplus bulky insulation to dispose of. So it's important to be clear that the cost is fully included in the price, or else to budget accordingly. Also consider where they can be safely deposited without causing maximum annoyance.

The new structure

In terms of enhanced life expectancy, messing about with roof structures is the building world's equivalent to dangerous sports. Hence the importance of obtaining detailed guidance from a qualified structural engineer, well in advance. This is the 'smart bit' of a loft conversion – figuring out how to safely transfer the new heavier loads down to the existing foundations, without the building cracking, subsiding or collapsing from under you. Get this wrong and lives will be at risk.

The general idea is to channel the additional loads from your new loft rooms onto the existing walls. This is achieved by running new beams (or joists) resting in these walls.

In the majority of loft conversions the new beams are supported by the side or party walls, but in some cases the existing internal load-bearing walls can also be used to shoulder some of the burden.

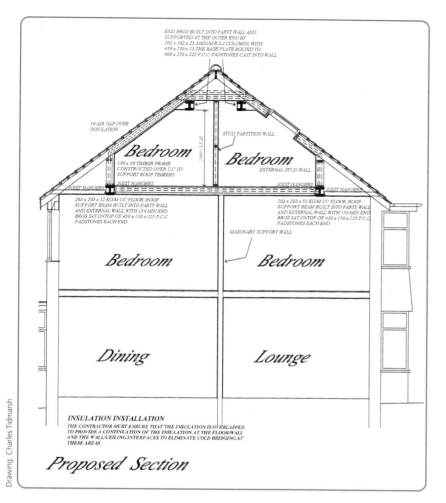

END BRGS BUILT INTO PARTY WALL AND
SUPPORTED AT THE OUTER END BY
203 x 102 x 25.33KGM R.S.J COLUMNS WITH
450 x 250 x 15 THK BASE PLATE BOLTED TO
600 x 250 x 225 P.C.C PADSTONES CAST INTO WALL

50 AIR GAP OVER
INSULATION

STUD PARTITION WALL

Bedroom

150 x 50 TIMBER FRAME
CONSTRUCTED OVER U.C TO
SUPPORT ROOF TIMBERS

Bedroom

EXTERNAL STUD WALL

JOIST HANGERS   JOIST HANGERS   JOIST HANGERS   JOIST HANGERS

203 x 203 x 52 KGM UC FLOOR /ROOF
SUPPORT BEAM BUILT INTO PARTY WALL
AND EXTERNAL WALL WITH 150 MIN END
BRGS SAT ONTOP OF 450 x 150 x 225 P.C.C
PADSTONES EACH END

203 x 203 x 52 KGM UC FLOOR /ROOF
SUPPORT BEAM BUILT INTO PARTY WALL
AND EXTERNAL WALL WITH 150 MIN END
BRGS SAT ONTOP OF 450 x 150 x 225 P.C.C
PADSTONES EACH END

MASONARY SUPPORT WALL

Bedroom   *Bedroom*

Dining   *Lounge*

INSULATION INSTALLATION
*THE CONTRACTOR MUST ENSURE THAT THE INSULATION IS OVERLAPPED
TO PROVIDE A CONTINUATION OF THE INSULATION AT THE FLOOR/WALL
AND THE WALL/CEILING INTERFACES TO ELIMINATE COLD BRIDGING AT
THESE AREAS*

Proposed Section

Drawing: Charles Tidmarsh

botched in single thickness 115mm brick. The new wall can be built from lightweight concrete blocks built right up to meet the underside of the roof coverings. Any remaining small gaps at this joint are then normally filled with inert mineral wool used as 'fire-stopping'.

Because it's common in loft conversions for the party walls to have to support major loadings from new steel beams, a structural engineer's guidance will be needed before selecting the materials for a new wall. Sometimes existing roof timbers such as purlins will also need to be incorporated in, and continued through, a new party wall.

Mortgage lenders have long required that missing firebreak party walls are reinstated where originally omitted, so in many Victorian terraces it may be found that the loft walls are of relatively recent origin, perhaps built only 100mm thick – either of blockwork or plasterboarded timber studwork. This is unlikely to provide adequate support for heavy new floor and roof beams, and won't be much cop for sound or thermal insulation either. Replacement with a suitable new blockwork structure may be the best solution.

As noted earlier, party walls are not always of brilliant quality. Indeed, in some 19th-century and older properties they were notoriously jerry-built, using cheap under-burnt bricks laid by unskilled apprentices. Or they may have been omitted in the roof space altogether, in which case they will now need to be constructed (see 'Party walls' in Chapter 3). This can be done by building a new dividing wall to the full 229mm thickness – assuming, of course, that the original construction of the wall below wasn't also

When it comes to the main walls in older properties, they may also be structurally weak. It's not only Victorian cottages that can pose problems, exhibiting suspicious bulges and worrying cracks. A large number of houses dating from the 1940s to the 1970s were built without lintels over windows and doors. Despite such defects, these buildings have managed to stay more or less upright over the years, until, that is, someone decides to add a whole load of extra stress – which could be the final straw!

This should have all been considered in detail at the design stage, and Building Control will have requested engineer's calculations to justify how the new loft rooms are

to be supported. In cases where the engineer believed the existing structure could not be guaranteed to safely support the new conversion, the solution would normally be for new vertical posts to be built up through the house from new foundations.

One option here is to install timber posts or steel universal beams (or columns) running up your walls. These 'goal posts' are bolted at their base to a concrete pad foundation – *ie* a hole excavated under your ground floor and filled with concrete. These posts are relatively slim compared to the alternative of building new 330mm square brick columns or 'piers', which is some consolation since in most houses internal room space will be at a premium.

Foundation work

If you're one of the lucky majority, you can skip this bit. Very few properties will be required to upgrade their existing foundations or construct new independent pad foundations inside the house.

Concrete pad foundations may be circular, square or rectangular. They're not a new idea – massive masonry piers supported on pad foundations were used by Sir Christopher Wren for St Paul's Cathedral. But obviously excavating a narrow hole to a depth of more than 1m in a confined living space isn't going to be easy. The process is similar to underpinning, but thankfully not as extensive (or expensive). Nonetheless, you will need to temporarily vacate the rooms in question, or at least remove your collection of fine bone china from the immediate vicinity: slicing through concrete ground floors with angle grinders

will inevitably spew out massive clouds of dust. Suspended timber floors will obviously need to have their floorboards raised, and any inconvenient joists temporarily set aside. Excavation by hand and spade can then proceed, taking care not to cut through any hidden gas, electricity, phone, water or waste pipes or cables in the immediate vicinity.

Once excavation is complete, it's essential that Building Control are invited to carry out an inspection before the concrete is poured to check whether the holes have been dug to the appropriate depth.

A typical foundation concrete mix would be 1:3:6 Portland cement/sand/gravel (sand premixed with gravel is known as ballast). Because access to awkward indoor excavations will be restricted, the concrete will probably have to be wheelbarrowed to the foundation hole. So it may be necessary to add some retarder to the mix to delay the drying out time a couple of hours. Once the pad and post structure has been constructed, the floors can then be reinstated.

All about beams

At the heart of every loft conversion lies a major decision concerning the correct type of beams. Get this wrong and your loft dreams could literally come crashing down. Steel beams are very popular because of their small size relative to their strength, which gives them an advantage within existing buildings where space is in short supply. At least,

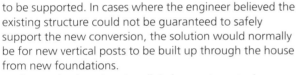

that's what architects tell you. Anyone who's actually done the job will know what a back-breaking task it can be,

trying to install extremely heavy steel beams in a cramped loft.

Alternatively, timber composite and laminated beams may be worth considering, although their relative size can make them impractical for some jobs. Of course, timber and steel are often used together, such as where a new steel ridge beam at high level is supported at its end by a vertical timber post.

The real trick with structural alterations to old buildings is to minimise the amount of disturbance, by carrying out as little new work as possible. A good loft conversion design will therefore employ each beam so that it serves more than one purpose. As we shall see, it's common for new steel floor beams to also provide support for the roof.

Steels

Today, it's hard to imagine doing a loft job without steels. The truth is, however, that a lot of conversions are over-engineered, using steel beams where timber would have done nicely. But steels are readily accepted by Building Control, and aren't particularly expensive, as well as being readily available.

The most widely used type of steel beams in lofts are probably 'universal beams' ('UBs'). But how do you go about ordering them? Steel beams are described in

terms of depth x width x strength. For example '203 x 133 UB30' means it's a 203mm high x 133mm wide universal beam with a weight of 30kg per metre.

As everyone knows, steel beams are normally 'I' shaped. The top and bottom faces of the 'I' are known as the 'flanges', and these provide most of the beam's strength. The tall centre part is called the 'web', which forms the beam's recessed sides. The web doesn't actually do much work, its main job being to separate the top and bottom flanges. The deeper a beam is, the stronger it becomes, so its strength increases the greater the distance between the flanges.

There are four common types of steels:

RSJ – rolled steel joist

'RSJ' is often used as a general term to describe any type of steel beam, but RSJs are have their own quirks. They are always taller than they are wide, but unlike similar-looking universal beams, the flanges on RSJs are tapered, with the inner parts nearest the web being thicker, and this can make them less convenient for inserting square timber joist ends.

Common sizes range from 152 x 127mm x 37kg up to 203 x 152mm x 52kg.

UB – universal beam

Like RSJs, universal beams are always taller than they are wide, but their top and bottom flanges are flat and parallel and hence easier to fit timber joists into. They're produced in a variety of standard sizes ranging from 127 x 76mm x 13kg up to 457 x 191mm x 74kg.

UC – universal column

Universal columns are similar to universal beams but are distinctively square in section, with the same depth and width. Despite the name, their purpose in life is not constricted to use as vertical columns. Because of their shorter depth, they're widely used as compact horizontal floor beams where it's necessary to accommodate the beam

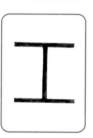

within the floor structure. As with UBs, the flanges are flat and parallel. Common sizes range from 152 x 152mm x 23kg up to 254 x 254mm x 89kg.

PFC – parallel flange channel

Looking rather like a UB with one side of the flanges sawn off, these are '[' shaped rather than 'I' shaped beams, which can be useful in tight spaces, such as when replacing timber roof purlins. Common size ranges from 100 x 50mm x 10kg up to 430 x 100mm x 64kg.

Timber beams

Ordinary timber floor joists are typically limited to spans of about 4m unsupported, which can limit their usefulness for loft conversions. So, not to be outdone by the steel industry, the timber research boffins came up with a new generation of super strong 'engineered timber beams'.

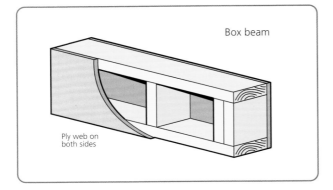

Box beam

Ply web on both sides

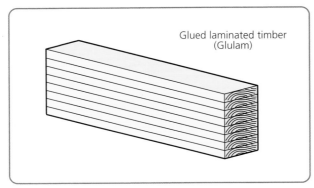

Glued laminated timber (Glulam)

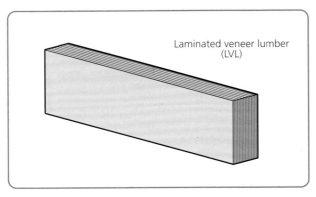

Laminated veneer lumber (LVL)

'I' beams

Factory-made timber 'I' beams are a fairly recent innovation. These are similar to steel beams and work in exactly the same way. By discarding the part that does the least work – the middle section – and replacing it with a central web made from composite timber, 'I' beams can be engineered to span greater distances than ordinary solid softwood joists. The web is usually made from manufactured OSB

('oriented strand board'). Despite their slender appearance they're actually incredibly strong as well as light, making construction considerably easier on site. They're now almost universally used as floor joists in new housing developments since they can span larger distances without support, typically to 6m or more.

Unlike ordinary timber, 'I' joists don't suffer from shrinkage, which therefore helps to eradicate creaks and squeaks in floors. However, apart from their expense the main drawback is that they're somewhat sensitive. Most of their strength is derived from the top and bottom flanges, so although beams can be cut to length, the flanges cannot otherwise be cut or drilled. Instead they have factory pre-prepared 'knockout' holes in the web to accommodate pipe and cable runs. See also 'Eco-joists' page 117.

Laminated timber beams

Special man-made timber purlins can span up to a massive 9m unassisted. The main types are LVL (laminated veneer lumber), Glulam (glued laminated timber), box beams, and trussed purlins made from 'ply web'. Like 'I' beams, these are factory-made, and Glulam or LVL beams can be cut to length without damaging their structural performance. Their main drawback is their size. With relatively deep sections they can be awkward to fit into lofts, where every millimetre of extra headroom is valuable.

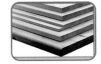

Flitch beams

Also known as 'sandwich beams', for the very good reason

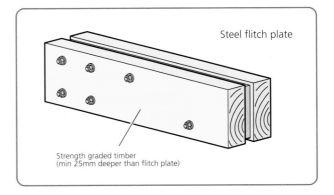

Steel flitch plate

Strength graded timber (min 25mm deeper than flitch plate)

that they comprise a steel plate filling sandwiched between two outer strips of timber. Flitch beams can be made up on site and are widely used in loft conversions, often as floor trimmers (see next chapter). As with steel beams they need support underneath from padstones or steel plates where their ends rest in walls.

Installing beams

This is the big one, the job that above all others demands the most careful measuring and planning before even attempting lifting. In some cases cranes or winching equipment will be required. Or it may be possible for three or four blokes to manhandle the beams into place. Because of the sheer physical challenge of lifting and manoeuvring these monsters, it's essential that the precise positioning of the beams must be considered in detail well in advance.

It may seem hard to believe as you look at a steel beam, but once safely installed, you need to allow for them moving. A 5m length of steel can expand by several millimetres as the temperature changes by a few degrees. This may not sound much but it can be enough to push out and loosen adjoining brickwork. So it's important to leave a small expansion space rather than butting the ends tightly up against a wall. Over a large span steel also 'deflects' or bends slightly, up to around 5mm over a length of about 6m, which is why a small gap also needs to be left underneath beams, in floors for example.

Padstones and plates

Where the ends of beams are supported in walls the loadings are highly concentrated. The danger is that old walls might struggle to cope with intense pressures suddenly being imposed on them. The structural engineer must therefore carefully consider how easily crushed the bricks, stone or blockwork is likely to be, by calculating the wall's crushability or 'compressive strength'. Old Victorian brick walls built with lime mortar may be quite weak, with a low compressive strength of only around 0.21 Newtons per mm^2. So to help spread the load, a 'padstone' or steel plate is normally required under the end of the beam where it rests in the wall. Obviously, the area that takes

most of the loading and stress will be directly under the end of a beam, but engineers know that this danger zone extends downwards, fanning out in the shape of a pyramid, and the padstone has to be large enough to absorb this.

In most cases a minimum of 100mm at the end of the beam must be supported. In a cavity wall this 100mm 'end bearing' will coincide with the thickness of the inner leaf, which is the main load-bearing skin of the wall. But in older properties you're more likely to have solid walls,

typically about 229mm (9in) thick. Here a 100mm deep recess is cut out, which is roughly the width of one brick.

Special pre-cast concrete padstones are produced in sizes to fit with standard bricks and blocks, typically 215 x 140 x 102mm. Engineering bricks are sometimes used instead on account of their strength. Once a recess has been cut into the wall, the padstone can be conventionally laid with mortar. But the steel beams must bear directly on the padstone itself, without any mortar. Given the choice, however, builders may prefer to fit steel plates rather than padstones under the ends because there's less need for awkward cutting out of masonry. As with padstones, these steel 'bearing plates' are bedded in mortar but the beam end itself should rest directly onto the plate.

Beams in party walls

A solid brick or block party wall should be the same width as traditional solid main walls – *ie* about 229mm thick. This means that the end of the beam need not, in theory, extend beyond the halfway 'centre line'.

But what if there's a chimney breast right where you want to rest a beam? The answer is that it's not advisable to use a chimney breast to support beams. This is because the brickwork will be extremely thin and cheaply built and further down there may be large fireplace openings, which will not provide a tremendously reliable foundation. Even if there appears to be no chimney breast running up the wall, there are instances where people have started cutting into the brickwork only to discover next door's flue staring them in the face!

This can cause difficulties, where there's an inconveniently placed chimney breast precisely where you

want to install the end of a new beam, such as high up at ridge level. In such a situation, a useful alternative is to support the end of the ridge beam on a new timber post (say 100 x 100mm) fixed top and bottom in steel shoes. The upper shoe can be bolted to the underside of the new steel ridge beam. The lower shoe is supported at its base on a secondary steel beam at floor level running parallel to the chimney breast and ceiling joists. Or a 'tripled-up' timber floor joist may be sufficient. Because this sort of dilemma is more likely to occur in older properties with internal load-

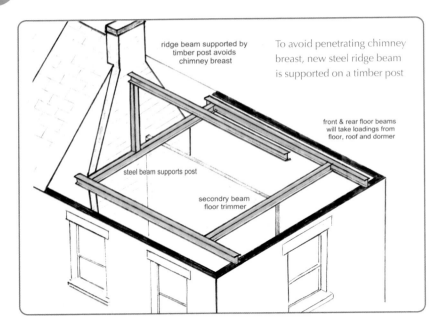

ridge beam supported by
timber post avoids
chimney breast

To avoid penetrating chimney
breast, new steel ridge beam
is supported on a timber post

front & rear floor beams
will take loadings from
floor, roof and dormer

steel beam supports post

secondry beam
floor trimmer

bearing walls, it may actually be possible to support the lower shoe directly from the internal spine wall instead.

Note that combustible material, such as a timber post, should be separated from a brick or blockwork chimney breast by at least 40mm from the outer surface of the chimney (and 200mm from the flue itself). Metal fixings such as joist hangers that contain combustible materials (*eg* timber joists) need to be positioned at least 50mm from a flue.

Splicing steels

It's all very well for engineers sitting in air-conditioned offices to specify enormously heavy steel beams of sufficient dimension to support the Empire State Building. They haven't got to manoeuvre them into position inside a sweltering, confined roof space.

So here we come to a classic dilemma. In order to provide a sufficient bearing of 100mm at either end (*ie* where it will slot into the walls) a beam will obviously need to be specified at least 200mm longer than the gap it has to span. Which means unless you can feed it through a

small opening cut in a side gable wall or roof hip, you have a potential logistical nightmare on your hands. Even if you're lucky enough to have a handy side gable wall, there may not be enough space outside to allow the safe manoeuvring of massive steel beams at high level. If you're converting a mid-terraced house then your options are definitely limited, putting it mildly. The temptation might be to cut a hole in the party wall and drive the beam through, before reversing out again. With the neighbour's permission this might be a useful option, subject to repairing the wall afterwards.

But what you really need is two or three smaller beams that can first be easily transported into position, and then, once in place, joined together to make one full length beam. Fortunately someone has already come up with this idea, and there are three methods of doing it:

Flange and web plates

The simplest and most common method of joining the ends of two beams together lengthways is by bolting

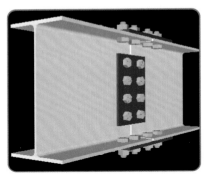

thick steel plates across the join. The top and bottom flanges are each covered with a steel plate bolted in place, with additional plates similarly fixed either side of the web.

End plates

Here the beams are specially manufactured with thick, flat

upturned ends. This allows them to simply butt up against each other and be bolted together. This is a more expensive option that requires the use of special bolts, known as HSFG bolts (high-strength friction-grip). The drawback of this method can be the beams' bulkiness. Some have upturned end plates projecting beyond the edges of the beams, so their increased width makes them relatively fat and can reduce valuable ceiling or floor clearance.

PFC bearing

The most ingenious, and expensive, solution utilises beams that can telescopically extend once they're in place. These employ special parallel flange channels (PFCs) at each end, which can slide out, extending the beam to the required length. So the main beam itself doesn't penetrate the wall, just the projecting PFC. Once extended and installed, they can be bolted together.

The weakest link – bolts and connectors

Even the strongest beams are only as good as their weakest link, so you can't just use any old bolts to connect these structural components.

Steel to steel

In some loft designs you may need to join a pair of steel beams together at a T-junction.

Beams can be joined at right angles using cleat connections. Cleats are L-shaped thick metal brackets ('angle plates') that are bolted or welded to the web sides of the secondary beam, where the main beam is going to join it. The brackets are then bolted into the web of the main beam. The precise type of cleats will be specified by your structural engineer, who'll also need to advise which bolts should be used. Special high-strength bolts made from high tensile steel must be used for steel-to-steel applications. It's essential to get this right, as some ordinary bolts can sheer, with potentially disastrous consequences. As noted earlier, where two beams are spliced together special high-strength friction-grip bolts are needed. These should not be confused with conventional high-strength bolts – HSFG bolt heads are wider. Sometimes special load-indicating washers are also employed to ensure the minimum specified tension has been achieved.

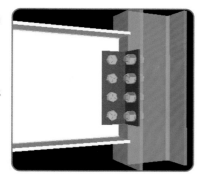

Timber to timber

For structural timber-to-timber connections, such as where two parallel floor joists are doubled up and bolted together, toothed plate connectors (a.k.a. 'timber plate connectors') are used. These improve the stress distribution, reducing the tendency of timber to shear along its grain when loaded. They're also commonly used for trimming floor joists, or doubling rafters.

Where one joist butts up against another at a 'T' junction, special steel joist connecting hangers are used.

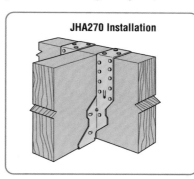

JHA270 Installation

Timber to steel

There are several ways of fixing timber joists to steel. Joist ends can be shaped to fit directly into the side web of a beam, or they can be hung from metal joist hangers wrapped over the beam. Hangers can't be fixed directly to steel, so strips of timber ('bearers') are first fixed along the top

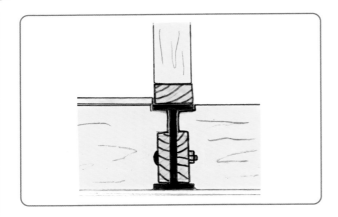

masonry, as long as the masonry is in good condition. After drilling a hole in the wall the bolt is then hammered in. Tightening the bolt anchors it firmly into the masonry. Problems arise where old bricks are soft or crumbling, plus expansion bolts can't be used close to the edges of masonry, as the expansion process can cause weak masonry to fail.

flange of the steel beam, or packing timbers are set into the side web. Traditionally these would be bolted in place or fixed with self-drilling screws, but a relatively recent US import is the use of shot-firing bolt guns. As the name suggests, these fire special rivet-like nail connectors that punch clean through the timber to become embedded in the steel beam. It's obviously essential to wear eye and ear protectors as well as gloves. Also be aware that extensive use of bolt guns can cause HAVS (hand arm vibration syndrome), more commonly known as 'Vibration White Finger', which must be taken into account when planning such jobs.

Timber to masonry connections

It's often necessary to fix new timbers such as wall plates to existing masonry walls. There are several methods of anchoring timber to masonry:

Restraint straps

Made from galvanised steel, typically 5mm thick with a standard width of 30mm, straps are available in lengths varying from an unambitious 100mm up to a whopping 3.6m. Restraint straps (a.k.a. 'tension straps') are used vertically in new-build projects for holding wall plates to the tops of walls. In a loft conversion, using them at wall plate level means that the legs of the straps extend down through the ceiling into the room below, damaging wall finishes.

Expansion bolts

Expansion bolts are an effective way of fixing timber to

Chemical anchoring

Instead of relying on expansion, epoxy resin anchoring systems provide a strong, glued connection. These are very useful where fixings are needed near edges of walls. A hole is drilled and cleared of dust, and the resin introduced before a threaded steel bar anchor is inserted to create a stud.

Fire resistance

As always with loft conversions, the threat of fire has to be safely designed away where possible. Fortunately, in most cases the new floor beams will be position above the existing ceiling, which should provide the required 30 minutes' fire protection. The only situation where this is likely to be a concern is where steel beams support the new loft floor from underneath. In such cases, exposed beams are normally boxed-in with a 12.5mm layer of pink fire resistant plasterboard with a skim plaster finish. The alternative, painting them with special intumescent paint, is a specialist job and may not be acceptable to Building Control. Such paints work by forming a protective fire-barrier at high temperature, so the paint needs space in which to char and form the defensive layer. But this process may not be effective if it's impeded where timbers are butted right up against the beam. So you normally need to box-in exposed beams.

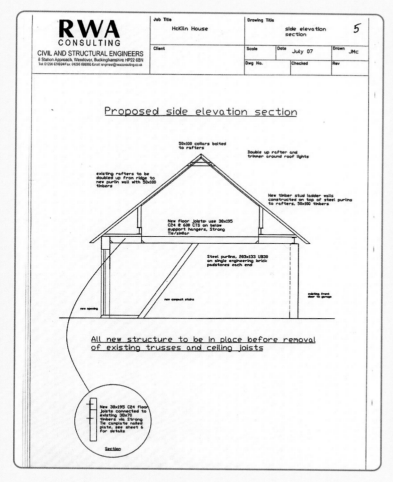

RWA CONSULTING

CIVIL AND STRUCTURAL ENGINEERS
8 Station Approach, Wendover, Buckinghamshire HP22 6BN
Tel 01296 624994 Fax 01296 696996 Email: engineer@rwaconsulting.co.uk

Job Title HcKiln House	Drawing Title side elevation section	5
Client	Scale	Date July 07	Drawn JMc
	Dwg No.	Checked	Rev

Proposed side elevation section

50x100 collars bolted to rafters

Double up rafter and trimmer around roof lights

existing rafters to be doubled up from ridge to new purlin wall with 50x100 timbers

New timber stud ladder walls constructed on top of steel purlins to rafters, 50x100 timbers

New floor joists: use 38x195 C24 @ 600 CTS on below support hangers, Strong Tie/similar

Steel purlins, 203x133 UB30 on single engineering brick padstones each end

existing front door to garage

new compact stairs

new opening

All new structure to be in place before removal of existing trusses and ceiling joists

New 38x195 C24 Floor Joists connected to existing 38x70 timbers via Strong Tie complate nailed plate, see sheet 6 for details

Section

Case study

The structural engineers came up with a neat design solution for this loft conversion to a modern double garage. The building has a trussed rafter roof, and the walls are of relatively good quality 270mm rendered blockwork cavity construction. Planning restrictions limited the external changes to just a couple of new roof windows, rather than dormers.

The main problem was the limited height inside the roof space. So the decision was taken to lower the floor by construcing a new one under the original ceiling, stealing some headroom from the garage below. At the heart of the loft design are two new steel beams inserted through the side gable wall just above floor level, each positioned approximately 1 metre in from the front and from the rear.

The beams are installed so they run across the tops of the existing ceiling joists (leaving a space of about 25mm between the underside of the beams and the existing joists). The beams are supported at each end on padstones set into the 100mm thick inner leaves of the side gable walls. Once in place, a timber stud 'purlin wall' is constructed on top up of each beam, rising up to the underside of the rafters. These will act as new purlins supporting each roof slope.

To gain additional headroom, the new 38 x 195mm floor joists are installed approximately 50mm below the existing ceiling joists (which still leaves 2.1m headroom in the garage). The new floor joists are spaced at 600mm centres, the same as the existing trussed rafter ceiling joists above them, and are supported at either end in joist hangers to the front and rear walls.

But there's a potential problem. The span of the new joists is nearly 5 metres, and consulting the span tables reveals some bad news. Even if thicker joists were spaced closer together, at say 400mm centres, the span would still be too long even for this size and quality of timber. One solution would be to use 'I' beams which can cope with longer spans without extra support. Or you could perhaps run a new support beam underneath – except there is no spare headroom to accommodate it.

Fortunately, extra support can easily be provided from the new steel beams running across the floor joists upstairs. By fitting long-legged joist hangers, which hang down from the steel beams, the joists can be supported at 1m in from either end, effectively reducing the clear span of the joists to only 3m. This way, each beam helps supports the new floor as well as supporting the rafters above via the stud wall built on top. The clever thing about this design is that because each steel beam is made to perform a dual task, only two new beams in total are needed.

The structural work is completed by 'doubling up' the existing trussed rafters with new 100 x 50 rafters fixed alongside, from ridge level down to the purlin wall. Finally, for extra strength, short timber collars are bolted across the remaining rafter tops. Once the new structure is in place, the old trussed rafters can be cut out, including the old ceiling joists. But the outermost sections of the original trussed rafters are left intact, *ie* the area behind the new studwork purlin walls, that will eventually accommodate the new eaves cupboards. Here, the remaining old ceiling joists are nailed to the new floor joists below using large nail plates. This helps maintain the rigidity and 'triangulation' of the original roof.

7 THE FLOOR STRUCTURE

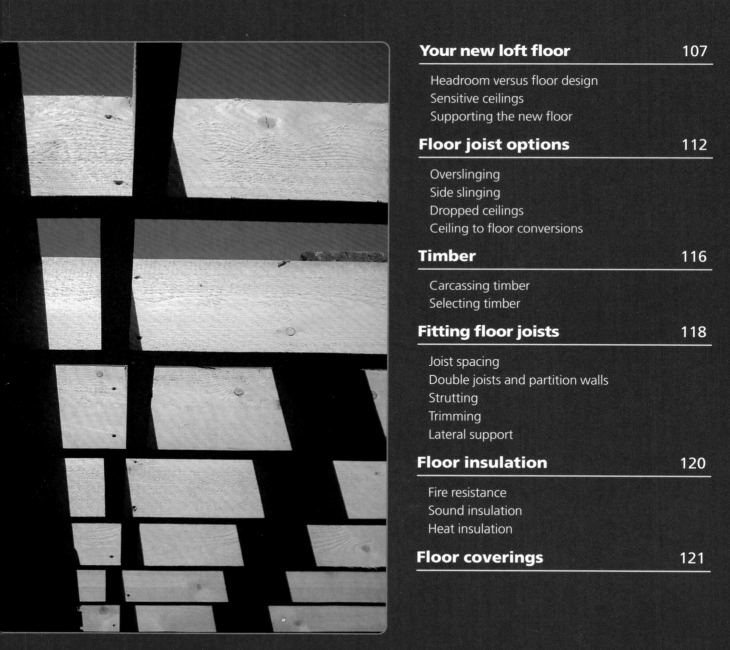

View to rear from landing to new loft floors above

The first big disappointment when you consider converting your roof space is the realisation that the ceiling joists upon which you're standing in the loft are actually pretty feeble. They might be able to cope with a few old suitcases and discarded exercise bikes, but when it comes to supporting a whole new generation of double beds, jacuzzis, and occupants excitedly romping about, forget it. So to successfully create a new living space in the loft it's normally necessary to construct an entirely new floor structure.

Your new loft floor

This is a critical part of the design. Loft floors are more complex than ordinary floors, as they have considerably more to support than their own weight and stuff in the room. Many loft designs employ short purlin walls built around the edges of the room, which play an important structural role by transferring roof loads down to the floor. These, together with the loadings from new dormer windows and internal walls, are known as 'dead loads', since they're static and don't change.

The new structure will also have to take the strain of all the various 'live loads' imposed when it's in use, such as from people and furniture. But there's another highly destructive force that has caused roofs to collapse with fatal results on the rare occasions when designers have omitted to factor it in: the additional stresses caused by periodically severe gales and snowstorms. As if that wasn't enough, your new floor may actually be required to lend a little help to the main walls, in the form of lateral support. In older period properties where the side walls may have

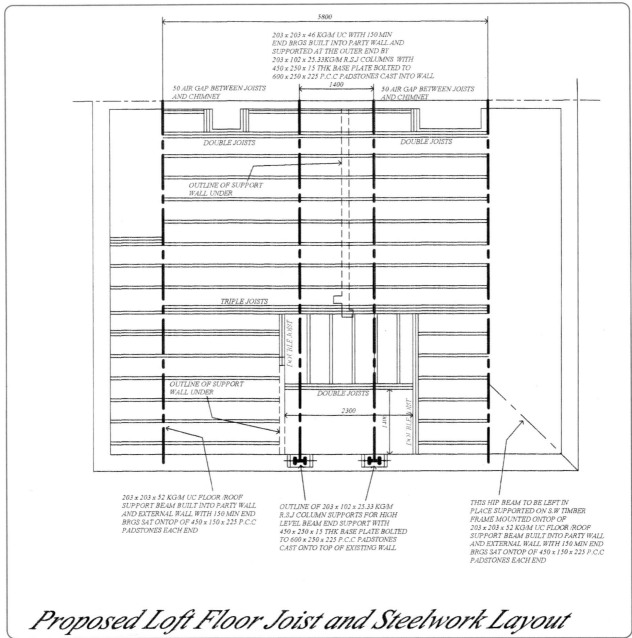

5800

203 x 203 x 46 KG/M UC WITH 150 MIN
END BRGS BUILT INTO PARTY WALL AND
SUPPORTED AT THE OUTER END BY
203 x 102 x 25.33KG/M R.S.J COLUMNS WITH
450 x 250 x 15 THK BASE PLATE BOLTED TO
600 x 250 x 225 P.C.C PADSTONES CAST INTO WALL

50 AIR GAP BETWEEN JOISTS
AND CHIMNEY

1400

50 AIR GAP BETWEEN JOISTS
AND CHIMNEY

DOUBLE JOISTS

DOUBLE JOISTS

OUTLINE OF SUPPORT
WALL UNDER

TRIPLE JOISTS

DOUBLE JOIST

DOUBLE JOISTS

2300

OUTLINE OF SUPPORT
WALL UNDER

DOUBLE JOIST

203 x 203 x 52 KG/M UC FLOOR /ROOF
SUPPORT BEAM BUILT INTO PARTY WALL
AND EXTERNAL WALL WITH 150 MIN END
BRGS SAT ONTOP OF 450 x 150 x 225 P.C.C
PADSTONES EACH END

OUTLINE OF 203 x 102 x 25.33 KG/M
R.S.J COLUMN SUPPORTS FOR HIGH
LEVEL BEAM END SUPPORT WITH
450 x 250 x 15 THK BASE PLATE BOLTED
TO 600 x 250 x 225 P.C.C PADSTONES
CAST ONTO TOP OF EXISTING WALL

THIS HIP BEAM TO BE LEFT IN
PLACE SUPPORTED ON S.W TIMBER
FRAME MOUNTED ONTOP OF
203 x 203 x 52 KG/M UC FLOOR /ROOF
SUPPORT BEAM BUILT INTO PARTY WALL
AND EXTERNAL WALL WITH 150 MIN END
BRGS SAT ONTOP OF 450 x 150 x 225 P.C.C
PADSTONES EACH END

Proposed Loft Floor Joist and Steelwork Layout

moved and bulged out, the new loft floor structure can help tie them in, preventing further movement. Indeed strengthening of such walls is essential before any significant extra loadings can be safely imposed.

Headroom versus floor design

The available headroom in lofts is often a bit tight, so the new floor normally needs to be built as low as possible. Keeping the floor joists reasonably slim will help maximise room height. The problem is that thinner floor joists may not be strong enough to span too far without some extra support along the way. There are a number of possible

solutions to this dilemma, which are described in detail below. These include keeping new floor joists as low as possible by placing them alongside the existing ceiling joists. Or you might prefer the 'nuclear option' – totally demolishing the existing ceilings to the rooms below and replacing them with an entirely new floor/ceiling structure. But before doing anything too drastic, there may be a simpler solution:

The longer the joist, the thicker it needs to be, so by keep them reasonably slim you will probably be limited to a maximum span of only 3 or 4m between supports. As most buildings are considerably deeper than this from wall to wall, the solution is to add extra support to the joists near the middle. This can be provided either by an existing internal wall or via new beams.

The size of your new joists will also depend on how closely they're spaced, and the quality of the timber. Spans can be calculated using official loading tables (see website). For example, a very substantial 47 x 220mm floor joist made from superior quality C24 timber and spaced at 400mm centres can span a maximum of 4.84m. (The span tables assume that the maximum loadings your floor will have to support will be no more than $1.25kN$ per m^2 for dead loads and $1.5kN$ per m^2 for live or imposed loads.)

Sensitive ceilings

Installing new floor joists without damaging the ceilings below can be something of a challenge. In period houses, old lath and plaster ceilings can be fragile at the best of times, so a lot of hammering nearby could easily encourage the odd lump to tumble earthwards. It would therefore be a wise precaution to banish all unauthorised personnel from the danger zone below while this work is in progress.

Ceiling joists were often traditionally built with flat strips of timber running across their tops, providing extra bracing to strengthen the structure. In some properties the main motivation for fitting these timber 'binders' was to save money, because they made it possible to use thinner, cheaper ceiling joists. The problem is that the binders will now have to be stripped out to make space for the new floor joists, and removing them will temporarily weaken the old ceiling. In older properties this means some temporary support to the ceilings from timber props may first be required.

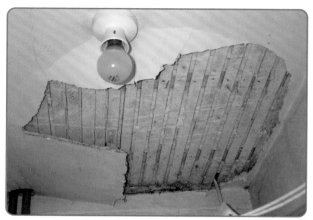

Supporting the new floor

Many new loft rooms are too large for the new floor joists to span the full distance unsupported. So a little extra help will normally be required, either directly from a load-bearing wall below, or indirectly from new beams.

Direct support – from internal walls

Today, it seems that many designers automatically specify enormous steel beams for loft conversions as a kind of universal panacea. However, in some properties the existing structure may be perfectly adequate to support the new floor without any major extra structural help. Most pre-1960s houses have solid internal spine walls located at roughly the halfway point, between the front and rear reception rooms, which are already taking some of the roof loading. These may be perfectly positioned to support your new loft floor.

But before relying on such load-bearing walls, a structural engineer will need to confirm that they're fit for purpose and in good enough nick to take the extra weight – *ie* that they were built with proper foundations and haven't since been structurally altered.

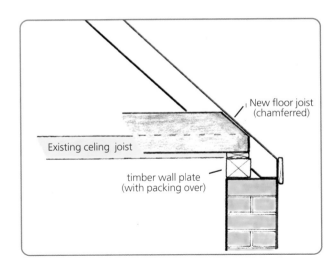

New floor joist (chamferred)

Existing celing joist

timber wall plate (with packing over)

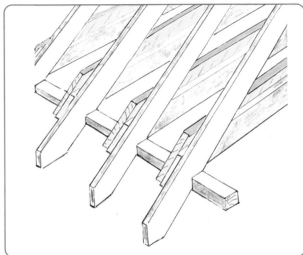

If all's well, internal walls can serve as staging posts, with the ends of one set of new floor joists overlapping with the beginning of the next set. The joists shouldn't be cut to end precisely on top of the wall, but should be continued straight over so that they overlap, overhanging either side by about 100mm. This ensures that the whole wall is fully supporting the joists. To get them perfectly level, a small amount of packing, such as slates, can be eased underneath.

To the front and rear, the outer ends of the new floor joists can be slotted on top of the existing timber wall plates, on top of the main walls (at the bottom of the rafters). To do this you need to be sure that the existing wall plates are in reasonable condition and securely fixed in place. To make it easier to slide them into place next to the old ceiling joists the tops of the joist ends need to be cut at an angle to match the slope of the roof rafters. Again some thin packing may be needed between the old wall plate and the new floor joists to get them level.

So in this design, all the new loadings are being taken by the existing walls. This means that the condition of main external walls must also be assessed for their load-bearing potential. If any lintels over window and door openings in the main walls look a bit dubious it may be possible to trim the joists around them, a useful method to direct the loads to either side and away from possible weak-points.

In reality, lofts employing the direct support method are very rare. This is not just because it's largely restricted to older properties; it's because the new floor structure may also need to take additional loadings from the roof making it impractical. Direct support may still be possible in rare cases where the original purlins can be retained, such as in conversions without dormers, and where there are no projecting purlin struts to be removed. Of course you could always insert new beams independently at purlin level. So the floor doesn't have to absorb any roof loading, but if you're going to the trouble of doing this, you may as well install new floor beams in the first place.

Indirect support – from new beams

In most loft conversions new steel beams need to be installed in order to transfer the new loadings to the walls. This method is used in modern houses that don't have internal structural walls and is also a widely adopted

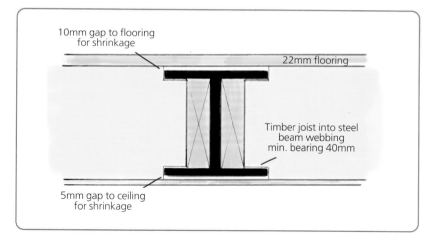

10mm gap to flooring for shrinkage

22mm flooring

Timber joist into steel beam webbing min. bearing 40mm

5mm gap to ceiling for shrinkage

solution for many older properties where the internal walls can't be trusted to take much extra weight.

The beams are normally run from one side of the house to the other, across the tops of the ceiling joists, which in a typical mid-terrace house would mean from one party wall to the other. The new steel beams should actually be positioned about 25mm higher than the tops of the old ceiling joists in order to allow clearance for any unevenness and movement in the old ceiling structure below. Obviously you can't just plonk these enormous beams down anywhere. The drawings should show precisely where they need to be positioned, so that they can successfully perform their essential structural role without becoming a major tripping hazard to future occupants. This normally means placing them towards the edges of the room, marking the area that's destined to become eaves cupboards. Here the roof slopes are so low that no

one will be able to stand, and so would otherwise be wasted space.

This may all be very neat and tidy, but you have to wonder whether the beams will be of much use structurally, tucked away near the edges. Fortunately, this is a question that your engineer will have already grappled with at some length. The fact is, even if they're only set a metre or so in from the main front and rear walls, they will be able to reduce the unsupported span of new floor joists by a very useful 2m in total. For example, an otherwise impossible 6m long joist span would be transformed to an easily achievable 4m span.

Having installed the beams, the next question is how the new floor joists are to be fixed to them. These can either be installed directly into the sides of the new steels, or supported from hangers as described in the previous chapter. But in many lofts you need to retain the absolute maximum headroom by keeping the new floor as compact as possible, so the big question is 'how low can the joists go?'

Floor joist options

There are basically four main methods when it comes to installing the new floor joists. Most are space-saving designs that maximise your available headroom. But if space isn't an issue, then the first option will probably be the most straightforward.

1. Overslinging

Where headroom isn't in short supply, the new floor joists can simply be run above the existing ceiling joists which are left undisturbed. With new steel beams installed across

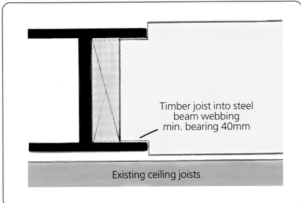

Timber joist into steel beam webbing min. bearing 40mm

Existing ceiling joists

the top of the old ceiling joists (towards the front and rear) the ends of the floor joists can be slotted into the side web of each beam, resting on the bottom flange. The joist ends are shaved both top and bottom, so the main body of the joist actually projects about 10mm above and below the steel. When the floorboards are later laid on top, this will provide a small shrinkage gap over the steel beam. The type of steel beams used here are often universal columns, which are relatively compact.

2. Sideslinging

To keep the amount of upheaval to a minimum, the old ceiling joists are once again left in place. But instead of building the new floor directly above them, to gain valuable headroom the new joists are normally placed at a lower level and run alongside the ceiling joists.

In cases where the new floor is to be supported from the walls, rather than from new beams, the new joist ends can be packed off the existing wall plates on top of the main walls, along with the old ceiling joists. But in most loft conversions new steel beams are first inserted across the tops of the ceiling joists. The new floor joists can then be supported from the

beams by being 'underslung' below them. There are two main ways of doing this, using special joist hangers or fixing joists directly into the beam:

'Long-legged' joist hangers

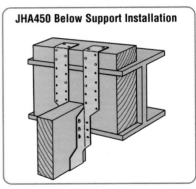

JHA450 Below Support Installation

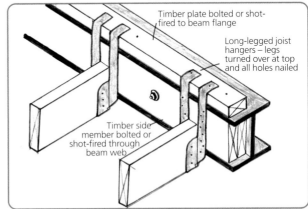

Timber plate bolted or shot-fired to beam flange

Long-legged joist hangers – legs turned over at top and all holes nailed

Timber side member bolted or shot-fired through beam web

These are special joist hangers that drop down below the beam – for example, Simpson strong-tie JHA450 hangers, which are basically cradles with straps that wrap over the beam. The hangers are normally nailed onto timber bearers that have been fixed into the beam.

Direct timber to beam

Here, the ends of the new floor joists are cut so that the upper half is fixed into the web of a steel beam, so the lower part of the joist dips underneath the beam. Clearly with this method there's a limited amount that the joist can 'drop' compared to using hangers, but it should be sufficient in many cases. The maximum amount the joists can hang down below the beam – the 'downstand' – is generally about 75 to 100mm.

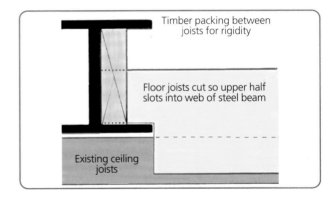

Timber packing between joists for rigidity

Floor joists cut so upper half slots into web of steel beam

Existing ceiling joists

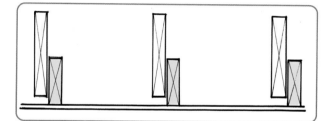

In order not to damage the old ceiling below, a gap of about 25mm should be left underneath the new floor joists, so they won't actually sit quite as low as the ceiling joists. In effect, the new structure 'floats' next to the existing ceiling joists to allow for any unevenness and deflection in the old ceilings.

At this point, it might come as mildly disappointing news to learn that your new space-saving floor may not actually be as low as you'd hoped, despite going to all this trouble. The reason for this is simply that floor joists are always going to be deeper than weedy old ceiling joists. This means that the floor height in your new loft room, including floorboards, could end up being 150 to 175mm higher than in the old unconverted loft.

There is some controversy about the next stage in the process. This revolves around the question of whether you should physically connect the old and new joists together. Some conservationists say that they're best kept apart and not connected, for the sake of preserving old ceilings. Even with a strong new floor structure, some slight movement is still likely to occur. With the old and new structures wedded together, the vibration from say, *Strictly Come Dancing* or other such activities upstairs, could be transmitted down to the highly sensitive old lath and plaster ceilings underneath. On the other hand, where old ceiling structures have already been weakened by the removal of binders, it may not be wise to leave them entirely unsupported. Plus the new floor should be designed as a highly robust structure that should absorb all but the most wild activities without complaint. So in most cases the new and old joists will be screwed, strapped or bolted together. Nailing is *not* advisable, as the vibration really can damage fragile antique ceilings. Where possible the ends of the new floor joists should also be fixed to the rafters.

3. Dropped ceilings

If lack of headroom is a major problem and your existing bedrooms have generous ceiling heights, it can make sense to borrow some of that valuable space to boost the height of your loft room. To do this the new floor structure can be constructed *below* the old ceiling, which will later be removed. On the plus side, you get a nice smooth new ceiling to your existing bedrooms. On the debit side, this will obviously cause an immense amount of disruption; also, sacrificing historic ceiling plasterwork in a period house isn't normally a good idea. It's important to be aware that the old ceiling joists are also performing an important

structural role, acting as collars holding the opposing main walls together. So before they're finally removed the new floor structure will have to take over this task. So the joists must be well tied-in to the main walls to eliminate outward thrust from the roof slopes.

Building a new 'dropped ceiling'

New beams and floor joists

One of the toughest parts of many loft conversions is physically inserting new steel beams. In this conversion only two beams were required, with good access at fairly low level through the gable wall. But it's still not a job for the faint-hearted!

1 Cut a small opening with an angle grinder.

2 Use a power breaker to loosen masonry.

3 Cut some more.

4 The outer leaf neatly cut.

5 A small opening is cut through the inner leaf.

6 Lining up the universal beam (4.8m long).

7 In she goes, heading towards a prepared opening to the inner leaf of the far wall.

8 Resting on a padstone.

13 No one will ever know – the render base coat.

9 and 10: Location: approximately 25mm above the old ceiling joists.

14 and 15 New floor joists fixed into wall hangers, below the existing ceiling joists.

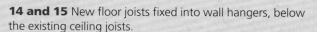

16 The first 1m of each new floor joist is bonded to the remaining existing joists using large nail plates with packing in between .

Remaining section of old joist

Packing timber

New joist

11 and 12 Opening made good and bricked in.

17 Long-legged joist hangers help support the new floor joists (shown after original ceiling joists have been removed to room area).

4. Ceiling to floor conversions

In some ways this is the most obvious solution. Instead of going to all the trouble of building a new floor structure, you can simply beef up the existing bedroom ceilings, making them strong enough to act as the new loft floor. This can be done by running new beams underneath, rather like a country cottage ceiling. The beams are run at right angles across the ceiling joists to provide support and reduce their effective span.

But if this method is so obvious, how come it isn't used all the time? The first reason is that not all properties have sufficiently generous ceiling heights that can easily accommodate large new beams which will substantially reduce headroom in the bedrooms. And second, the job requires strips of the old plasterboard or lath and plaster

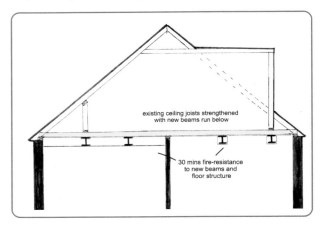

existing ceiling joists strengthened
with new beams run below

30 mins fire-resistance
to new beams and
floor structure

ceiling to be cut away, so there is direct contact between the tops of the new beams and the old ceiling joists. Which means major disruption. Whereas with most other methods the disruptive structural work can normally be contained within the loft, sealed off from the house occupants, here your private space will be overwhelmed by an onslaught of dust and noise. Also, trying to manoeuvre enormous steel beams around bedrooms can prove something of a challenge, not least because internal walls have an awkward habit of getting in the way.

It's also worth bearing in mind that in a lot of Georgian and Victorian houses the ceiling joists were built undersized, and the old connections to wall plates can be

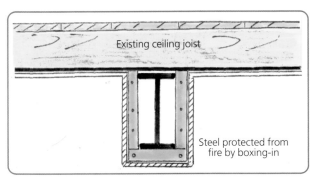

Existing ceiling joist

Steel protected from
fire by boxing-in

weak. This may necessitate a larger number of closely spaced new beams under the ceiling which may obstruct access for the new staircase. Despite these concerns this can still be a useful solution.

Timber

Timber is the most versatile building material of all, but treat it badly and it will exact slow revenge, finding ingenious ways to retaliate over the years by splitting, twisting, buckling and warping.

Internally, a lot of modern houses have suffered from extreme shrinkage cracking, due to the speed of their construction. Timber that's still green can continue to season after the house is occupied, causing it to shrink and bow, especially with the central heating on full blast. This can be a particular problem with floors, where floor joists may start to shrink back from walls, leaving gaps at staircase walls and at the edges of

ceilings. To minimise the risk of shrivelling and buckling, timber used for structural purposes such as joists and rafters should be kiln-dried. But in reality Builder's Merchant's rarely go out of their way to store or deliver timber in perfectly dry condition. So it's always advisable to allow new timber to adapt to the low moisture content of a room before cutting and fixing it, by opening up packs and letting the contents become conditioned. This way, any severe shrinkage will hopefully occur before it can do any harm.

Carcassing timber

Most construction grade carcassing timber is spruce (also known as deal or whitewood). Wood for joinery is usually pine (known as redwood) and is actually more durable than spruce. Pine with a planed finish is widely used for floorboards, windows and skirtings.

Softwood comes from conifers including spruce, Scots pine, firs and yew, whereas hardwood comes from broadleaf trees such as oak, birch and beech. Hardwoods are inherently more durable. However, despite the name it's said that these classifications have very little to do with hardness, although hardwoods such as mahogany, oak, and teak are usually tougher to cut. Hardwood is not only significantly more expensive, but in some cases tropical rainforests are being sacrificed to provide an unsustainable, non-renewable product. It's therefore often better to pick a good quality softwood, such as Douglas fir, which can perform as well as many hardwoods and at a lower price.

Structural timber, such as for softwood floor joists, is supplied 'dry-graded'. Under the Building Regulations, the permitted moisture content is restricted to a maximum of 24 per cent (much higher than this and timber can become attractive to wood boring beetle and fungus). Low moisture content timber is defined as 'below 20 per cent', but the final moisture level in modern houses can be as low as about 10 per cent, so shrinkage problems are still a real possibility.

New structural timber is normally kiln-dried and factory-treated with preservative to protect against rot and beetle attack and to prevent twisting or warping, the curse of much cheaper timber. Here, the timber undergoes 'vacuum impregnation' treatment by being immersed in a vacuum pressure tank, and is either 'tanilised', a water-based treatment that lends the wood a faint green or brown shade; or 'protimised', a spirit-based process that leaves the wood uncoloured (or sometimes dyed red).

Selecting timber

As you pore through the leftover lengths of timber at your local DIY store, the pieces you select should ideally have straight grain and be free of knots or drying splits ('shakes') – which is precisely why all the old knotty and warped bits are left on the shelf. To save builders having to waste time judging every single piece of wood they use, timber should come ready strength-graded, the supplier having already assessed these features. For structural purposes new timber is supplied in strength classes that determine the allowable working stresses:

Timber strength class

C14	C16	C18	C22	C24	C27
weaker					*stronger*

The majority of softwood carcassing timber is kiln-dried and graded at the sawmills to BS 4978 strength classes C16 and C24. C24 costs more than C16 as it is stronger and can be used over larger spans. In all there are 16 strength classes

ranging from C14, the lowest softwood strength, through to D70, the strongest hardwood strength. Softwoods are more difficult to assess than hardwoods, and there are two overall visual strength grades used as guidance for structural use: GS (general stress grade) and the stronger SS (special stress grade). Mechanised grading is referred to as MS (machine stress grade).

What this all basically boils down to is that you need to check that the material is stamped with its grading, and make sure that you purchase the type that's specified in the approved plans. Sizing can be checked using timber tables (see 'Span tables' on the website).

Although caracassing timber is traditionally unplaned, with a rough finish, it's now sometimes supplied sawn on all four sides ('S4S') and planed all round. This helps minimise variations as well as looking better. As a result of this additional machining, timber joist thicknesses have decreased slightly. Traditionally '2-inch' joists were sized 50mm and 47mm, whereas now most are slightly thinner at 47mm or 44mm.

Despite heroic attempts to grade and classify timber, in reality it's rarely perfectly straight. Whereas a slight bow over the length of a joist isn't necessarily a problem, any badly twisted material should automatically be rejected, since it will only tend to get worse over time. Additional guidance is sometimes provided where studwork and joist timbers display the following quality classifications:

- **Regularised (R):** Timber has been checked for consistency, which should help keep floors and ceilings level.
- **Graded (G):** Softwood joist sizes are graded to strength classes, most commonly C16, C24 or C27 and to BS EN 338.
- **Treated (T):** Timber has been treated to a defined hazard class.
- **Dried (D):** Joists and studwork are kiln-dried.

Eco-joists

As noted earlier, the problem with ordinary softwood is that it can be prone to shrinkage. And when softwood joists are combined with chipboard flooring there's a tendency for creaks and squeaks to develop. Factory-made joists such as

Photo: BSW timber

Timber joists – points to check
- Stress grade is as specified.
- Free from bowing, twisting, rot and woodworm.
- Depth and width are as specified.
- Tops of joists are level.
- Joists are correctly spaced.
- Joists are doubled up where supporting upstairs walls.
- Inner wall joist ends are securely fixed into joist hangers or built tightly into brick/blockwork with no gaps.
- Outer wall joist ends are securely fixed into joist hangers fixed tightly to wall.

'I' beams can solve such problems, but the downside is their expense, plus they can't have holes bored in them. Also, to joint two together requires special connectors. They are ideal for building new houses where components are custom manufactured and all fit neatly together like a giant Lego set, but arguably are not so great for loft conversions, where you're normally working with all kinds of peculiar sizes and quirks found in old buildings.

However, it might be worth considering Eco-joists (or 'Posi-joists'), which also have advantages over the traditional solid timber variety, such as the ability to span greater distances unsupported. Eco-joists comprise top and bottom timber flanges with a centre web made from a thin, wavy band of lightweight steel that allows access for pipes and cables.

Although they have to be made to measure, they're about 40 per cent lighter than solid joists, making them easier to handle and quicker to install on site. They suffer virtually no shrinkage and are compatible with solid timber joist depths, but are, of course, more expensive.

Fitting floor joists

Joist spacing
Softwood floor joists were traditionally made from 8 x 2in timbers, the equivalent modern standard size being 195 x 48mm. In most pre-1970s houses the floor joists were spaced apart by 14in (356mm) or 18in (457mm), although in many older buildings the spacings can be fairly haphazard.

Today joists are normally spaced at 400mm, 450mm or 600mm centres, depending on the span. Note that 'centre' measurements are actually taken from the centre of one joist to the centre of the next.

Where joists are supported at their ends, such as on a wall plate to the main walls or over an internal wall, they should ideally have at least 75mm end bearing support from the wall (40mm absolute minimum). This compares to 100mm or even 150mm for a steel beam.

Having taken the trouble to select good-quality timber to construct a nice strong floor, you don't want the structure to later be weakened by plumbers and electricians cutting massive holes in it. So it's important that the rules about running pipes and cables in floor joists are followed. The critical points in joists structurally are at the centre and the ends, so the safe cutting zone starts after the first quarter of the span. Roof timbers such as rafters and purlins must not be cut or drilled for services. (See Chapter 11.)

Also, floor joists and rafters should not be placed in direct contact with any chimney breasts that pass through the loft. The Building Regulations stipulate that a gap of at least 40mm must be left between the brick face and the timber floor or roof structure. It's OK for floorboards, skirting or even roof battens to touch the brickwork, but not structural timbers.

Floor joists (C16) – permissible clear spans		
Joist size (mm)	Joist spacing (mm)	Clear span (m)
47 x 97	400	1.67
47 x 147	400	2.70
47 x 170	400	3.12
47 x 195	400	3.54
47 x 220	400	3.95
75 x 147	400	3.22
75 x 170	400	3.71
75 x 220	400	4.74
(TRADA span tables)		

Floor joists (C24) – permissible clear spans		
Joist size (mm)	Joist spacing (mm)	Clear span (m)
47 x 97	400	1.80
47 x 147	400	2.92
47 x 170	400	3.31
47 x 195	400	3.79
47 x 220	400	4.26
75 x 147	400	3.34
75 x 170	400	3.86
75 x 220	400	4.88
(TRADA span tables)		

Double joists and partition walls

If you read the small print in the official 'span tables' it will state the maximum load that timber joists of each size can tolerate without warping, sagging or collapsing. But there may well be some parts of your new loft floor that need to cope with greater stresses. This isn't necessarily due to occupants furnishing loft rooms with heavy weight-training apparatus. Floor joists normally need to be strengthened where they support partition walls, such as those separating bedrooms from en suites. They may also need to support areas of intense 'point loadings' such as from bath feet, especially enormously heavy Victorian cast iron specimens. The usual solution is to double-up the floor joists underneath by bolting a pair together using 51mm double-sided connectors (the round tooth-plate variety) and M12 bolts at 600mm centres.

When building stud partition walls, the bottom soleplate should be fixed right through the floorboards into the joists below. However, there are limits to the loadings that even doubled joists can support. Where more substantial forces are at work, such as where purlin walls transfer heavy roof loadings down to the floor, steel beams are normally specified by the engineer.

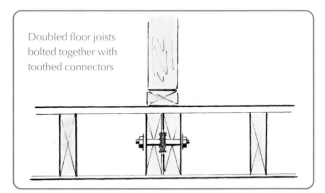

Doubled floor joists bolted together with toothed connectors

Strutting

No matter how carefully you select your new floor joists, there's always a risk that slight twisting and shrinkage will occur. This can lead to distortion of the floorboards and can even damage the ceilings below. To minimise this, and to reduce the risk of vibration and 'bounce' in floors, some form of additional bracing is often needed between the joists. To improve the floor's rigidity, small timber struts are fixed between the joists in an 'X' pattern, known as 'herringbone strutting'. For spans from 2.5m to 4.5m one line of strutting fitted at mid-span should be adequate, but for spans greater than 4.5m you need two rows, one each at about one-third distance. For every additional 1.5m span further struts are needed.

Struts needn't necessarily be made from timber. Today, ready-made, lightweight steel herringbone straps are widely available to fit standard joist spacings. Traditionally, small timber offcuts called 'noggins' (also known as 'noggings', 'nogs' or 'dwangs') were jammed between the joists to strengthen floors, and this method can still be used today, using simple blocks of solid wood, provided they're at least 38mm thick. Noggins in new underslung loft floors shouldn't stick out below the bottom of the new joists, in case they interfere with the old ceiling. Their tops should also be left slightly recessed so that there's a small space under the floorboards. Where floor joists rest on internal walls, additional strengthening between them with noggins is recommended, to prevent any risk of 'rotation'.

Trimming

Where the new staircase is intended to enter the loft room, or where there's a large obstacle such as a chimney breast, the floor structure will need to be built around it. This is done by trimming around the opening. Here, the joists that would otherwise be in the way of the stairs are cut short and their ends trimmed and butted up against a 'trimmer joist'. Trimmer joists actually comprise pairs of doubled-up joists bolted together and fixed at right angles across the ends of the shortened main joists. The various joints at this T-junction are made using special steel joist hangers or fixing plates.

The floor joist that runs along the side of the opening will then need to be strengthened by being doubled-up with another of the same size,

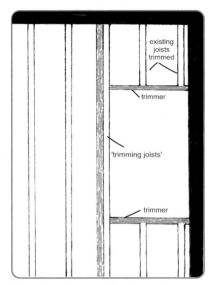

Floor trimming around stair opening

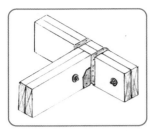
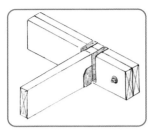

Trimming joists with double trimmer (left) and single trimmer (right)

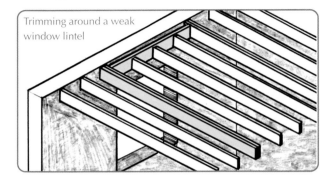

Trimming around a weak window lintel

fixed together with bolts and toothed plate connectors.

Because most new floor structures in loft conversions are built with steel beams, it's fairly common to use steels instead of timber joists for trimming around openings. For example, a steel beam might be used to trim around the front of a chimney breast at floor level. This can then form a useful base for a timber post or steel column, which in turn can support the end of a ridge beam above (ridge beams should not be supported directly into chimney breasts). The only other situation where you may encounter a need for trimming to floors is where the new loadings are to be taken by a main wall with lintels of unknown strength. Diverting the loadings around the opening can avoid over-stressing weak points in a wall.

Lateral support

In some loft designs the side walls of the house are built up, such as where a new gable end wall replaces a hipped roof, or where the sides of a new full-width dormer are constructed. In such cases the new walls will need to be tied into the floor structure. This is done by fitting metal restraint straps horizontally to provide lateral support to walls. Even if you're not extending the walls, the new loft floor structure can provide some very welcome support to strengthen old buildings. Many Victorian and other period properties

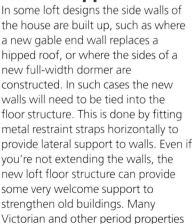

suffer from side walls that are prone to bowing outwards. This is because the walls weren't built with much restraint from the floor and ceiling joists that run parallel to them. So this is a good opportunity to prevent future problems arising in older buildings, by tying the new floor structure into the side wall.

Floor insulation

Fire resistance

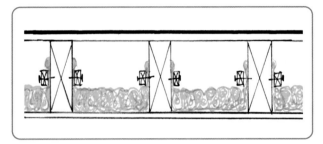

When your old loft space was empty and unloved, fire resistance was never an issue. But as soon as you create living accommodation up there, the potential risk to human life from fire becomes very real. As well as being warm and eco-friendly, your new loft needs to be constructed as a capsule that will protect the occupants. So the new floor and the ceiling below must together provide a minimum of 30 minutes' fire resistance, at least where it's above the landing/'circulation area' below.

In most cases the original ceiling will be retained and this should already provide a good degree of protection. The Building Regulations assume that an existing old lath and plaster of between 15 and 22mm thickness, in good condition, should provide at least 20 minutes' fire resistance. So how can this be upgraded to meet the full 30 minutes' protection standard? Modifying the ceiling itself is not always possible, at least for older properties. Apart from being incredibly messy it can damage delicate historic plasterwork. On post-war houses it's normally acceptable to fix new sheets of plasterboard over the existing ceiling surface, screwed into the ceiling joists. However, the simplest method is to fireproof the new floor structure from above, by firmly packing mineral wool loft insulation between the joists. This might be an opportunity to save some money by recycling some of that dusty mineral wool you removed from the loft at the start.

Note that fitting concealed lighting recessed within the ceiling below isn't going to do a lot for a floor's sound and fire resistance, although lighting with integral fire hoods may provide a partial solution.

Sound insulation

Before the floorboards are laid, there's one other consideration – how to minimise noise. If your new loft

room is scheduled to be used as a kids' den or for teenage gatherings, it might be worth adding some extra sound-deadening material. Living in harmony with family members is always easier when there's a healthy layer of sound insulation between you and them. Laying a 100mm depth of mineral wool loft insulation between the joists should significantly improve the floor's soundproofing qualities.

Sound transmitted through floors falls into two categories: airborne sound (voices and music etc) and impact sound (footsteps). Impact sound can be greatly reduced by a soft floor covering such as carpet on thick underlay, but this won't do much to resist airborne sound. In flat conversions, independent suspended ceilings are constructed below the existing ceilings and packed with mineral wool to provide about 10dB improvement in insulation – roughly halving the loudness.

If you're really serious about blotting out sound, there are special acoustic flooring sheets that can be laid as 'floating floors'. Such a system might comprise a layer of 18mm thick acoustic boards with tongued and grooved edges bonded to a base of 19mm plasterboard on top of the floorboards. Some other systems employ acoustic strips that are fixed along the tops of the joists before the boards are fixed. But if headroom is at a premium, you'll not want to raise the floor any higher than necessary. In which case laying traditional carpets over underlay will provide better insulation than, for example, laminate flooring.

Heat insulation

If your new loft room happens to be above somewhere cold such as a garage or passageway, the floor will need to be well insulated to meet Building Regulations U-values. A 100mm thickness of rigid polyurethane PUR insulation boards can be easily cut to friction-fit snugly between joists and should provide an acceptable U-value of 0.23.

Floor coverings

With your new floor structure in place, the only thing stopping you from stepping through the ceiling may be some makeshift plywood decking. The floorboards aren't normally fixed in place until any first fix electrics and plumbing are done. Also, Building Control will need to pay a visit to check and approve the floor structure before it's covered up. In the meantime, thick sheets of plywood can be temporarily fitted to provide a good solid platform to work from (perhaps to be recycled later for use as flooring in eaves cupboards). Now might also be a good time to mull over the relative merits of ordering chipboard floor panels, which are relatively cheap, or pine floorboards. Because chipboard will later be covered (e.g. by carpet or laminate etc.) it can be fitted now if required. Traditional floorboards can look the business when sealed as a natural wood floor and are therefore best installed towards the end of the project. All will be revealed in Chapter 13.

8 CONVERTING THE ROOF STRUCTURE

We have now arrived at the epicentre of a loft conversion project, the stage at which the very roof over your head will be at stake. The task now is to structurally modify the roof and redirect the loadings so that all the old struts and webbing can be removed to create a clear, open living space. If there is one Golden Rule to remember it is this: before cutting out any existing components, the new structure must first be in place – or at least some substantial temporary supports.

By definition, a loft conversion will involve alterations to the roof, but much of this will concern the internal structure rather than the coverings. Externally, you may get away with simply inserting a couple of rooflights, although most conversions will require new dormer windows. These

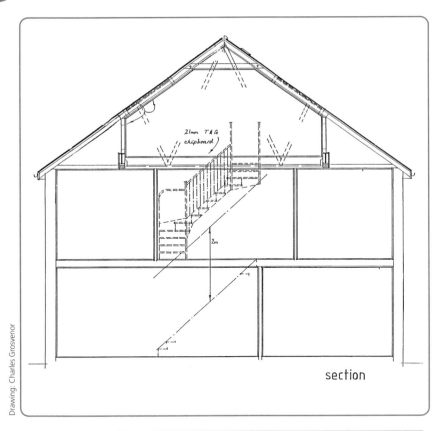

Drawing: Charles Grosvenor

21mm T&G chipboard

2m

section

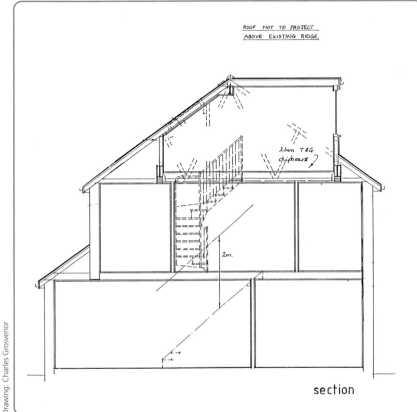

ROOF NOT TO PROJECT
ABOVE EXISTING RIDGE.

21mm T&G chipboard

2m.

section

Drawing: Charles Grosvenor

can sometimes be constructed quite early in the project, but it's probably easier to wait until the roof has been strengthened and the loft space opened up, allowing you to move around freely within the loft. The subject of dormers and roof windows is covered in detail in the next chapter.

Roof Structure

Back in Chapter 2 we surveyed the property to identify the type of roof

construction. So before reaching for a hacksaw, let's take a fresh look at the key components that go to make up the roof structure.

Wall plates

These are the strips of timber that run along the tops of main walls. They perform a crucial role, supporting the ends of the ceiling joists and rafter feet, or the roof trusses. Wall plates are normally of 100 x 50mm softwood (trussed rafter roofs require a minimum 75mm width) and are traditionally bedded in mortar and fixed in line with the inner surface of the wall (the inner leaf on a cavity wall). In modern

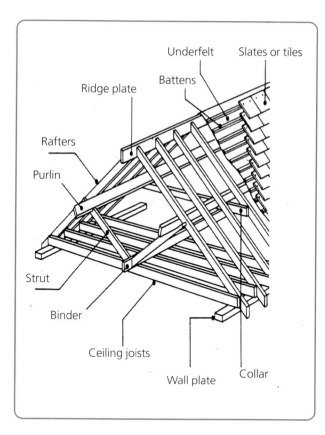

Rafters

Unless you're planning to install a giant dormer which will largely replace one of the roof slopes, the original rafters can often remain largely undisturbed, other than to accommodate a few small window openings. (See Chapter 9.)

Sometimes however structural engineers will specify that the existing rafters should be strengthened, especially on modern trussed rafter roofs. This is done in a similar way to floors, by doubling-up with new rafters fixed alongside the old ones. Where new roof windows are installed, the rafters framing the sides of the opening will need to be doubled up, and those above and below reinforced by trimming. (See Chapter 9.)

50 x 100mm rafters – maximum clear spans		
(TRADA span tables)		
Joist spacing (mm)	C16 clear span (m)	C24 clear span (m)
400	2.38	2.49
450	2.30	2.40
600	2.09	2.18
(NB assumes roof pitch between 30–45°)		

Ridge boards

Traditional timber roofs have a ridge board running along the top of the roof at the apex. The heads of the rafters are nailed to the ridge board, which is typically 25mm to 32mm wide, projecting about 25mm above the top of the rafters. However, modern trussed rafter roofs don't have ridge boards. Instead, the tops of the rafters are joined directly to each other with nail plates.

Purlins

Traditional timber roofs normally have thick timber purlins running across the undersides of the rafters. These provide essential support, effectively allowing the use of thinner rafters to span longer distances. Whereas on modern trussed roofs each rafter receives individual

roofs, wall plates are held down by long vertical steel straps every 2m or so. Without such measures to secure roofs, severe gales have been known to cause 'wind uplift', literally raising the roof off the house.

Ceiling joists and collars

The ends of the ceiling joists are fixed to the wall plates on the main walls of the building (usually the front and rear). This is a crucial three-way tie with the rafter feet. In houses where the connections at wall plates have failed roofs can push the walls out, a phenomenon known as 'roof thrust'.

In older properties with large bedrooms, two or more lengths of ceiling joists would often be needed to span the full distance across the house, the first joist overlapping with the next one at an internal structural wall, where they'd be nailed together. Additional horizontal timber collars are sometimes provided at a higher level in the loft to add strength.

support from its own strut (part of the W-shaped webbing), a purlin does the same job communally to all the rafters, without a large number of struts cluttering up the loft and getting in the way. There is often a single strut supporting each purlin, transmitting the load down to the spine wall below.

Occasionally horizontal collars may be used in addition to, or in place of, struts. In some post-war TDA roofs, support to the rafters is instead provided from a vertical timber studwork 'ladder wall' or truss clad in plywood.

Traditionally, rafters may be skew-nailed direct to purlins, or notched with a small V-shaped birdsmouth cut in the rafter. Or more likely they won't be connected at all, simply resting on top of the purlin.

In older houses the purlin ends are often built into gable or party walls or supported on projecting brick corbels. But in some properties the purlins were originally built undersized, or wrongly positioned thereby giving little support.

It's always advisable to design loft rooms so they cause minimum disruption to the existing structure. The position of the supporting purlins is a prime factor here, and if you can leave them in place so much the better. However, in many loft conversions there'll be no alternative to removing at least one purlin. This will immediately have the effect of doubling the unsupported span of the rafters, and must not be done until alternative support has been provided to the roof slope.

Hipped roofs

From a loft conversion point of view, having a roof slope to the side of your house, rather than a gable wall, needn't be a problem as long as the roof is sufficiently large and

Photo: London & Kent

spacious, which, happily, is the case with many pre-1960s properties. But in smaller houses hipped roof slopes can consume a lot of valuable loft

space. As noted earlier, because hips are located on the sides of houses they often coincide with the position where you want to install the new staircase – which is all highly inconvenient. One solution is to build a dormer window at this point to boost the headroom. Alternatively it's now fairly common to carry out 'hip-to-gable conversions', where the side roof is replaced by building up the wall below. (See Chapter 9.)

Lean-to roofs

As the name suggests, these are simple secondary roofs propped up against the wall of the main house, the kind of thing Ray Mears could erect from a few branches in no time.

Conversions of 'monopitched' roofs (as they're technically known) are one of the easiest type you're ever likely to encounter. Unless, of course, they're constructed using modern trussed rafters, in which case normal trussed rafter rules apply (see below). A conventional lean-to roof is constructed by first bolting a horizontal strip of timber to the wall of the existing house. Onto this the tops of all the lean-to rafters are secured, whilst at the bottom the rafters are fixed to the timber wall plate.

Subsidiary lean-to roofs are often to be found over an attached garage or above a ground-floor extension to the side or rear. Because such lofts adjoin an upper floor of the main house, you may only need to knock a new doorway through an internal wall, without any need for a new staircase. The amount of useable floor area can be massively boosted by adding a large dormer. Lean-to conversions often work best where the rooms were built with generous ceiling heights, such as in Victorian or Georgian houses.

Common conversion works – all roof types

The three main roof types all have their own quirks. So below we take a look at each in turn to see what special treatment they require. But despite these differences, the task of conversion is fundamentally the same for all – to create a clear living space by rerouting and resupporting the loads.

But to see just how much re-routing will be required the big question to ask in any roof is whether the purlins will need to be removed or altered – which they normally will. Structurally, the general idea is to keep the original 'triangulation' of the roof as intact as possible. As we've seen in previous chapters, what this boils down to is strengthening the outer roof structure to compensate for the removal of the original inner supports, and installing new beams at key points.

There are basically three levels where new beams may need to be installed:

■ Floor level

As per the previous chapter, it's very common for a pair of new beams to be installed above the existing ceiling joists (or sometimes below them) to provide support for the new floor. The beams would normally run from one side wall to the other, at roughly a quarter-span in from the front and rear walls.

■ Purlin level

As soon as you remove old purlins or webbing, bang goes the support to the roof slopes with their heavy loadings of tiles. So you need to provide some other means of support. To minimise the amount of new steel going into a house, it makes sense if possible to use the new floor beams for a twin purpose, by designing them to take the roof loadings too. This is commonly achieved by constructing a timber stud 'purlin wall' on top of

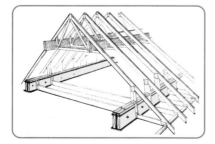

each floor beam which supports the rafters in place of the original purlin.

However, in some conversions, the engineer may consider it necessary for new beams to be installed directly as purlins. These may be placed quite high, near the new ceiling level, dispensing with the need for an extra beam at ridge level. As well as strengthening the remaining rafters, the new beams may also support the new dormer flat roof joists.

■ Ridge level

Where the roof remains largely unchanged, perhaps just with roof windows fitted between the existing rafters, no additional support at ridge level may be required. But in conversions where a large dormer is constructed ('large' meaning more than about 1.2m wide) a new roof beam will be installed under the ridge, spanning from wall to wall. Installing a full-width dormer to your loft effectively means losing an entire roof slope, which is clearly a drastic alteration. So in addition to strengthening the remaining rafters, the primary purpose of the new beam is to support the new dormer flat roof joists. Depending on the precise design of your loft, there are several alternative positions where the new beam can be installed near the apex of the roof. (see Chapter 9).

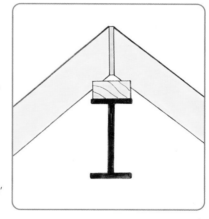

The engineers may have specified steel beams that comprise two or three separate lengths that can be bolted together once safely installed in the loft. This not only saves on hiring cranes, but also minimises damage to gable or party walls by cutting holes through which to pass the beams.

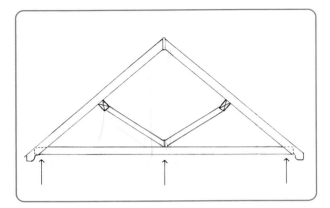

Converting the three main roof types

Traditional cut roof conversions

You're off to a great start with traditional cut timber roof. Unless it's hipped (see below) there should be walls on both sides which can support the new beams. You may even be able to walk through the loft already, unless there are struts or collars barring the way. The following modifications are commonly required:

Removal of purlins and collars

If the purlins need to be removed or altered, an alternative means of support will be needed. But if you're not planning to add a large dormer to your loft, the purlins may not be a problem, unless they happen to be inconveniently located over the new stairs, limiting headroom. Where purlins aren't too intrusive, you can save a lot of trouble by retaining them in place, perhaps leaving them exposed as 'original features'. Unfortunately, in many cases their support struts will be sticking out, obstructing the loft, and will need to be removed. Timber collars always need to be removed in order to create a clear living space. Like struts, collars are there for a purpose, so the structural engineer will have specified another means of support (such as strengthening the rafters by doubling them).

Many roofs are finely-balanced structures, and unless properly supported during the works they may sag or even collapse. Normally new steel beams will provide the required purlin level support, either directly or via a timber studwork purlin wall,

which can transfer roof loadings down to the new floor.

As any chartered surveyor will tell you, in many older houses the roofs have sagged or 'dished' slightly as the roof structures have settled over many years. This isn't necessarily a problem, with the roof having reached a comfortable 'position of repose'. But where alterations are carried out on old roofs it can destabilise them, for example where original Victorian slate roofs have been reclad with heavy concrete tiles, overloading the structure.

Where an old roof has sagged, the new internal support will need to be designed to fit with it. Normally a certain amount of bowing or 'deflection' to a roof slope can be accommodated by a new timber-frame ladder wall. But it's essential when carrying out these works to not let the roof sag any more, as even a small amount of sagging to an existing roof caused by alterations is almost impossible to recover once it's occurred – which could mean the having to rebuild the whole roof.

If your designer has specified manufactured timber 'super-purlins' instead of steel (*eg* Glulam, PlyBox or Prefabricated trussed purlins), these beams should be bedded dry onto a DPC in their support walls, any defective brickwork in the walls around them having first been made good.

Building purlin walls

When purlins are removed, the roof slope will need some other means of support. This can be provided by constructing new timber stud walls under the rafters, also known as 'ladder walls' or 'knee walls'.

These are built from timber studwork, and may literally be only knee-height, but are more commonly about a metre high. First, a timber soleplate is fixed across the top of the new floor joists, or shot-fired to the top flange of a steel floor beam. The timber stud framework is then built up with

New purlin stud wall before supporting truss webbing is removed

Purlin stud wall after webbing cut out

New steel ridge beam resting on padstone, supporting new dormer roof joists

a horizontal top plate ('bearing plate') nailed across the underside of the rafters. Alternatively, where old roofs have bowed each vertical stud can instead be bolted directly to each individual rafter. Obviously here the timber studs would need to be spaced so as to line up with the existing rafters. The space behind the new purlin wall will later form eaves cupboards, accessed via small cupboard doors.

Purlin walls are sometimes positioned a little further out, closer into the eaves than the existing purlin, in order to maximise the floor area of the new room. But there's no point building purlin walls any shorter than about 600mm because the space you gain in the room isn't really useable. Of course their precise position is largely dictated by what's acceptable structurally, as shown on the approved drawings. This can't be changed without getting fresh structural calculations and it being passed all over again by Building Control. The structural engineer will calculate this based on how far the existing rafters can be allowed to span unsupported. This in turn depends on their size and spacing, how strong the timber is, and the weight of the tiles (or slates which are relatively light). The calculation is also affected by the steepness of the roof pitch, since shallower roofs tend to impose greater loadings. This isn't necessarily as difficult as it sounds, because TRADA span tables show maximum spans for all common rafter sizes and pitches (see website).

Of course the precise position of the floor beams under the purlin walls will also depend on these calculations. Alternatively, you can dispense with purlin walls and eaves cupboards altogether if you simply replace the old purlins with new beams at the same height, or if your design simply requires the existing rafters to be strengthened so that they don't need any extra support. This way the roof loadings won't need to be transferred down to floor level.

Fitting a new ridge beam

In addition to any new floor beams it's often necessary to install a new steel ridge beam at the top of the loft, near the apex, as noted earlier. This is typically required where a new dormer is being constructed (see Chapter 9). This new beam provides support at the critical point where the old

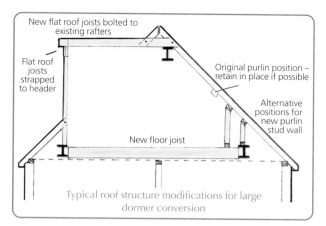

Typical roof structure modifications for large dormer conversion

rafters have been cut out, and the incoming flat roof joists overlap the remaining tops of the old rafters.

Ridge beams are normally supported at each end in the party walls, or side walls, unless the presence of a chimney breast or roof hip means you need to build a timber post or steel column from below to support one end.

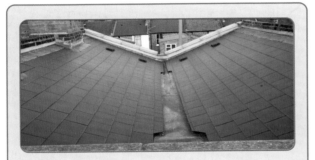

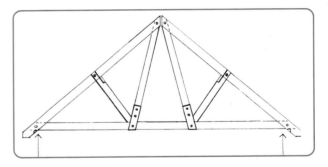

Butterfly roofs

As we saw in Chapter 2, these are a special type of cut timber roof. Commonly found on Georgian and early Victorian town houses, they essentially comprise two separate lean-to half-gable roofs, one either side, with a valley in between. Being rather shallow they're too small to convert. The solution is drastic, essentially involving the construction of an entirely new roof. Such a design will require the party walls on each side to be built up to form new side walls to the loft room. To the front, the existing parapet wall can usually remain in place (or be rebuilt) but the twin half-gable roofs on either side will be dismantled. In their place a very steep mansard front slope is usually constructed, leaving a box gutter running from side to side behind the parapet. To the rear, the existing V-shaped valley wall (between each half-gable) is filled in with brickwork, or lightweight studwork, and built up to form a new rear wall. Finally, a flat or shallow pitched roof is constructed over the top.

There are a number of special issues that are likely to apply:

- These buildings are often three or more storeys high plus a basement. Consequently compliance with fire regulations tends to be more challenging, and extra structural work may be required, such as fitting anchoring systems, with restraint straps at 1.25m intervals between floors and walls throughout the building.
- Period houses are generally more of a challenge structurally for loft conversions, not least because some weren't built very well (apologies to conservationist readers), or they may have subsequently been mucked about with structurally. There is consequently a higher chance of needing expensive foundation work and new support columns.
- Planning permission is always needed, because of the increase in roof height and visibility, plus these properties are often Listed or in Conservation Areas, making the planning process even more rigorous.

TDA bolted truss roof conversions

Many post-war houses were built with a new type of roof structure – the TDA bolted roof truss.

As you might expect, these display similarities both with traditional timber roofs that preceded them and modern trussed rafters that came later. Like cut timber roofs they incorporate large purlin beams that support the rafters, and like modern roofs they utilise trusses that obstruct the loft space and therefore need to be removed. Because the purlins are supported by these trusses, it is necessary to provide an alternative means of support.

Unlike modern roofs however, there are usually no more than three sets of trusses to deal with in an average loft. But these are generally a bit meatier than their modern counterparts, each one commonly comprising a pair of trusses closely bolted together with a small gap in between. The rafters and ceiling joists in TDA roofs are often spaced about every 450mm, as opposed to about 600mm centres for today's trussed rafters. Nonetheless, these loft spaces are considerably more crowded than a traditional roof.

A few roof structures of this age have a different arrangement, better suited for conversion. These incorporate purlin walls, of timber-frame ladder construction, clad with plywood, which can normally remain in place when converting the loft.

Like modern trussed rafter roofs, TDA trusses are designed to span from outer wall to outer wall without any support below. So fundamentally the conversion process is as described below for trussed rafter roofs.

Trussed rafter roofs

Until a few years ago, modern prefabricated trussed rafter roofs were widely regarded as unsuitable for conversion. Contractors tended to avoid such projects and Building Control found it difficult to prove that the job could

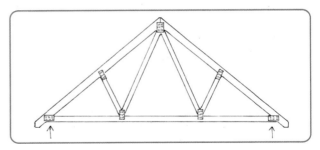

be done safely, especially when it involved cutting into the main outer framework – the all important 'triangulation'. These concerns stemmed from the fact that such roofs are finely-balanced structures that simply aren't designed to be altered in any way. The trusses themselves are manufactured from very thin softwood members (eg 72 x 35mm), and because all the parts are inter-dependent, by cutting one piece you can weaken the entire roof. Even when they're being newly constructed on site, the prefabricated components aren't meant to be cut or modified.

Another obstacle to conversion is that trussed rafter roofs aren't designed to take any extra loadings. They can support their own weight plus that of the roof tiles and any snow loadings. The bottom chords of the triangular trusses form the ceiling joists, which will carry the plasterboard ceiling and insulation. The structure allows for one person walking in the loft together with minimal loadings from water tanks, which must be carefully spread using timber bearers. No other loadings are catered for.

Trussed rafters are designed to span between the main

The strange case of the truss purlin conversion

Dating from the same era as the bolted TDA roof truss (circa 1950s) comes a similarly constructed bolted truss purlin. The problem with these is that you can't cut any of the members. Therefore it's critical to get the staircase in the right place to get the correct headroom height to avoid cutting the trusses.

Studwork complete and floor structure in place.

Truss purlin construction.

New steel beam inserted near base.

Timber stud purlin ladder wall constructed, with original truss untouched.

Insulation fitted to the studwork.

Similar solution to a later 1960s truss purlin.

Converting a trussed rafter roof

A typical conversion might be as follows:

Here we assume the new floor joists have already been installed alongside the old ceiling joists, supported at each end from steel beams, resting in the side walls.

On top of each steel floor beam, a timber stud purlin wall is constructed, to provide new purlin support to the rafters, as close as possible to the existing web struts.

The existing rafters are then doubled up by running larger new rafters (minimum 100 x 50mm) alongside them. This may only be necessary from the ridge down to the new purlin wall (ie not all the way to the eaves). If you plan to fit roof windows between the rafters, note that some skylights require a clear width of 550mm. So to leave enough space, you may need to place the new supporting rafters on the far sides of the existing ones. If you plan to build a large dormer, the engineer may also require a new ridge beam to be installed at or near apex level, or else a pair of high-level purlins near the new ceiling level.

Timber collars (minimum 75 x 50mm) are fixed at high level across the upper 'prongs' of each trussed rafter.

New L-shaped steel restraint ties are fixed horizontally securing the gable walls to the new collars and stud walls, in lieu of those removed earlier.

Now for the scary bit. With the new structure in place all the redundant W-shaped webbing, struts and ties can be cut out and removed. But it's essential that the triangulation of the rafters, purlin walls and floor joists is of sufficient strength.

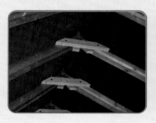 

Job done (in this case the end trussed rafters were left in place).

walls unsupported by any internal walls. However, in some cases they may inadvertently be resting on an internal wall, such as where water tanks are in effect supported from partitions below, or where the internal walls were originally built before all the heavy roof tiles were loaded onto the roof.

As if all this wasn't perilous enough, the trusses themselves are about as stable as a row of dominoes. Of course, all roofs have to occasionally cope with gale force storms. These can impose intense wind pressure to gables at one end, and strong suction at the other. Large masonry gable end walls may look robust, but they don't actually provide support to the roof structure. In fact it's the other way round: the timber roof structure must be strong enough to support the gable end walls. Hence the need for 'lateral bracing' with at least four diagonal strips of timber nailed across the trussed rafters. In Scotland, bracing is provided by timber 'sarking boards' nailed over the top of the rafters.

There are still many original roofs dating from the 1960s and 1970s that weren't built with any lateral bracing or ties to gables, as it wasn't considered necessary at the time. So when you come to convert the loft, this is a good opportunity to strengthen the roof structure.

First impressions can be more than a little off-putting. When you're initially confronted by a complex jungle of W-shaped roof members it can be a trifle difficult visualising how this could ever be transformed into a stunning new loft room. But converting roofs of this type is now considered a fairly routine undertaking, as long as you follow the correct procedures.

Engineers normally specify between two and five new steel beams for trussed rafter conversions. Additional secondary beams may also be required at floor level to trim around openings for stairs or chimney breasts. In a typical 'five steel' roof, the one at the top will act as a ridge beam, two more further down as purlins, and the last two beams at floor level will support the new floor joists. But it's often possible to use only two or three beams, the two at floor level supporting the new floor whilst also acting as purlins via a timber stud wall. The existing rafters are normally doubled up and strengthened, and short timber collars fitted at high level across the upper rafters, acting as ceiling joists. This is structurally important in strengthening the roof by providing bracing across the top of the triangle.

Attic trusses and total replacement

If you're house is less than about 10 years old, there's a fairly good chance that your loft may be constructed from 'room in roof' attic trusses. These are simple to convert, because the trusses are specifically designed with the intention of being fitted out as loft rooms. Such attic trusses are increasingly being installed as standard in new homes, accounting for almost a third of new trussed rafter production.

But what if the opposite is true? What if your roof is the world's worst and is totally unsuited to conversion? Then you may have no other option than to implement the ultimate solution: removing the entire roof and building a completely new one. This needn't be nearly as drastic as it sounds because modern ready-made attic trusses have come to the rescue here as well. Once craned into place you will have the shell of a pre-formed loft room. When budgeting for this type of project, note that crane hire tends to be one of the major costs.

There are different ways you can tackle a roof replacement project. Having stripped the roof tiles, and provided some sheeting for weather protection, the existing trusses can be replaced one at a time. Normally the ceiling can be left intact. This is achieved by cutting the existing ceiling joist (ie the bottom chord) loose from the main truss so it can remain in place, before each truss is removed. Once each new attic truss is installed, the old and new ceiling joists can be tied together. Attic trusses work best when replacing conventional trussed rafters of the same span. Breaking through into the floor below can be done towards the end of the project to keep disturbance to a minimum. However, it's still probably wise to temporarily vacate the premises!

Alternatively, in an empty property it would probably be quicker to totally replace the whole roof and ceiling structure in one, which needless to say is an extremely messy operation. Properly organised, this needn't take more than a couple of, hopefully dry, days.

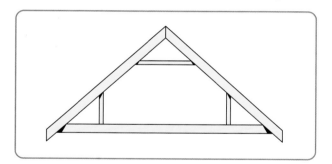

9 DORMERS, ROOF WINDOWS AND WALLS

Photo: David Davies

Photo: Velux

So far, a lot of money and effort has been spent and yet the old loft will still be looking disappointingly dark and dingy. This situation is now about to radically change, as we come to one of the most rewarding parts of the project. As soon as daylight is allowed to flood in, the loft will be transformed into a bright, exciting space. And achieving this magical metamorphosis needn't take a lot, as even the smallest rooflight will dramatically brighten the new accommodation. Once your windows are in place even the doubters will fully appreciate the wisdom of converting your loft.

Let there be light

One of the most fundamental decisions at the design stage is your choice of loft windows. All loft conversions need at the least a skylight or two. These are great for providing light and ventilation, but being flush with the roof slope they obviously won't do much to increase your room height.

Most loft conversions therefore require the construction of large dormer windows, because otherwise they simply couldn't provide enough useable floor area.

Right and below:
A gable wall
window or a pair
of roof windows
may be all that's
needed

Photo: Velux

Roof windows

The development of modern loft windows or skylights has been a major driving force behind the popularity of loft conversions. The Velux brand is synonymous with these products, but there are several other manufacturers with windows available for every type of roof, including 'conservation windows' for traditional buildings. Adding roof windows will not only dramatically brighten your loft room, but can also give it real style, for example by placing a pair together one directly above the other, or even organised in a cluster of four. However, what might look brilliant from the inside can look awkward from outside, defacing a building's architecture, so it's essential to first consider how the windows will impact on the look of your home from the street.

The main point of confusion concerns the terminology. 'Roof windows', 'rooflights' and 'skylights' – what's the difference? Strictly speaking, whereas you can open a roof window, a rooflight is fixed and just serves the purpose of allowing light in. The word 'skylight' is a general term, since skylights can be either of the fixed or 'ventilating' variety, the latter being openable to allow air to pass through.

One of the great advantages of roof windows over bulky dormers is that they normally only require small openings within the roof structure to gain the same amount of light. Often they can slot neatly between a pair of adjoining rafters. This is especially useful in modern trussed rafter roofs, which are notoriously sensitive to any cutting. With their wide 600mm centres between rafters you can fit rooflights in place without any cutting being required to the structure, just trimming with extra timbers around the new opening.

Roof windows are relatively cheap and reasonably straightforward to fit, typically costing around 70 per cent less to install than a comparable dormer. Another advantage is that, being angled towards the sky, they let in considerably more light. Indeed, some advertisements give the impression that all you need do to convert your loft is stick a skylight in your roof. If only.

Selecting skylights

If you thought choosing your roof windows would take ten minutes, think again. There's an incredibly wide range of styles available, and then for each style of window there's a choice of flashings, insulation collars and vapour barriers, along with options for linings, blinds or roller shutters. Then there's the type of glazing to select, such as special obscure

glass for bathrooms. Modern innovations range from rain sensors and programmable ventilation to special controls for humid areas like en-suite showers. Even hard to reach high-level roof windows are no problem with telescopic control rods, or if you prefer an electrically operated opening system.

For flat roofs, there are 'sun tunnels' and flat-roof windows, so you could conceivably incorporate a window on top of your new dormer or on a flat mansard roof.

In order to attract as much light into the loft as possible people are often tempted to order skylights that are larger than necessary. In fact, skylights can allow an incredible eight times as much light to enter a room as a comparable sized wall window, simply because they face skywards. So size shouldn't be an issue. One problem with fitting overly large skylights, is the waste of energy, allowing heat to escape in cold weather, since even the most efficient ones will have inferior insulation compared to the surrounding roof. Larger windows are of course more expensive and require structural alteration work to accommodate them.

Roof windows

Centre-pivot windows
Centre-pivots are the most popular choice of roof window. They're well suited to being positioned higher up, nearer the apex of the roof, above head height. The windows can rotate 180° to allow cleaning of the exterior pane from inside. However, the casement projects down into the room when open, making them less suitable over stairs or for shallow-pitched roofs.

Photo: Velux

Top-hung roof windows
With the hinges located at the top, these windows open outwards from the bottom. This makes them suitable for use at all levels, including lower down near occupants' heads and bodies, in bedrooms. Top-hung skylights offer a wide 45° opening angle, allowing unobstructed views and are suitable for most roofs, including those with a shallow pitch.

Photo: Velux

Roof balcony system
Roof balcony systems form an instant balcony as they open, increasing the amount of daylight and the feeling of space in a loft room.

Photo: Velux

Roof terrace system
The 'walk-out' roof terrace system allows you to walk out to a suitable existing flat roof or balcony. The upper window opens outwards to 45° and the lower window can either be fixed or walk-through.

Photo: Velux

Vertical windows
These are designed for installation to walls below existing roof windows, or to dormers. They are hinged at the bottom for inward opening.

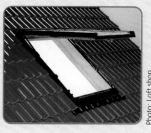

Photo: Velux

Emergency escape/access
These top-hung windows provide emergency escape in the event of fire. Although no longer required for most loft conversions, they may still be worth including as an additional safety feature.

Conservation windows
These traditional style roof windows are available either as centre-pivot or top-hung. There is even a larger emergency escape version. Conservation windows feature a mullion for 'period house' visual appeal. Ideal for traditional steeper pitched plain tiled or slate roofs.

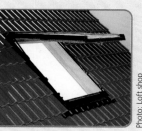

Photo: Loft shop

Photo: Velux

Photo: Velux

Skylight sizes

There is a wide range of sizes and styles on the market. If you want roof windows that are slightly quirky or an odd size, check out some of the smaller manufacturers' products. The standard 550mm width is perfect for most trussed rafter roofs, but for traditional roofs with rafters spaced at 400mm or 450mm, or some peculiar hybrid dimension, it's likely that one rafter will have to be cut.

Common sizes (width x height)

550 x 780mm
550 x 980mm
660 x 1180mm
780 x 980mm
780 x 1180mm
780 x 1400mm
940 x 1600mm
1140 x 1180mm
1340 x 980mm

For traditional roofs, smaller 460 x 610mm conservation rooflights are available.

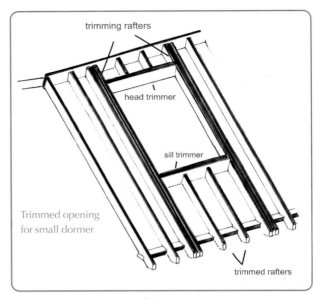

trimming rafters

head trimmer

sill trimmer

Trimmed opening for small dormer

trimmed rafters

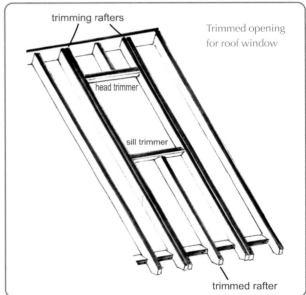

trimming rafters

Trimmed opening for roof window

head trimmer

sill trimmer

trimmed rafter

Trimming around openings

Where rafters need to be cut to create a new opening for a skylight, the remaining rafters that 'frame' the opening will need to be reinforced by trimming. This is basically the same technique as used to strengthen floors around openings for stairs.

Trimming is required to the top, bottom and sides:

■ **Side trimming**
New rafters are fixed alongside the existing rafters either side of the opening, doubling them up to add strength.

■ **Top and bottom trimming**
Where the rafters were cut above and below the new

opening, they need to be trimmed. Their sawn ends are butted against a length of timber at the top (the 'head trimmer') and another at the bottom (the 'sill trimmer'). Below the new window opening, the rafters can be supported on the inside by the new purlin wall.

Dormers

As we saw back at the design stage, choosing the best dormer solution for your roof is one of the most important decisions of the entire project. Sadly, the quality of many existing loft conversions leaves a lot to be desired, as can be seen from the number of ugly dormer boxes built from the cheapest materials, grafted uncomfortably onto incompatible roofs. A badly-done dormer will swiftly become an inaccessible, giant maintenance headache. So it's important to get this right.

It's interesting to consider what type of dormer windows were traditionally fitted in attic rooms. 'Half-dormers' are a feature of many period properties, with the brickwork continued straight up from the main wall below. By comparison, what some regard as the 'true' dormer window would be set back a little, up the roof slope, with its roof finishing well before the ridge. But the decision as to which type is appropriate for your property will have

already been taken, hopefully with the blessing of the local planners. So the task now is to crack on and build it.

Dormer openings

Dormer construction is one of the key stages of a loft conversion project. As we saw in Chapter 6, the first task is to make an opening in the roof, which will initially be used for access purposes. Although this should be a fairly straightforward task, there are some key differences between an opening for a dormer window and one for a rooflight. Because the load from a dormer will be greater, the reinforcement to the rafters surrounding the opening will therefore need to be carefully calculated.

Small dormer windows

Traditional small dormers are usually less than about 1.2m wide, and very often have pitched 'cottage-style' gabled or hipped roofs. Despite their relatively small size, they still normally require one or more rafters to be cut out to form the opening, which then needs to be trimmed.

A head trimmer is fixed across the cut rafters at the top, positioned at an angle to suit the design of the dormer, commonly being installed either vertically, horizontally, or at 45°. In the comparatively rare cases where small dormers have flat roofs, the head trimmer may also need to support the dormer roof joists where they enter the main roof. The sill trimmer at the bottom of the opening should be fixed so that it projects slightly above the rafters

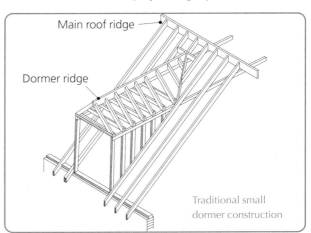

Main roof ridge

Dormer ridge

Traditional small dormer construction

Large box dormers

When it comes to large dormers, there are two basic sizes – big and massive. Otherwise known as 'large box' and 'full-width', both types normally built with flat roofs. The difference between them is that whilst large box dormers leave a small amount of the existing roof in place around them, full-width dormers take out the entire roof slope, so technically they are roof extensions. These don't require any trimming, for the very good reason that there's no roof slope left to trim. Instead, the sides are encased by new brick walls built up from the main side walls or party walls below. However, some full-width dormers are actually set back slightly, retaining some of the original front roof slope, which must be supported from below by new beams.

(which will come in handy later when fitting the flashings).

To minimise the amount of cutting to the structure, on trussed rafter roofs box dormers are often restricted to a width of just under 1200mm, which is equivalent to the width of two 'bays', thereby requiring only one trussed rafter to be cut out.

Although large box dormers don't span the full width of the roof, their substantial size still dictates that a very

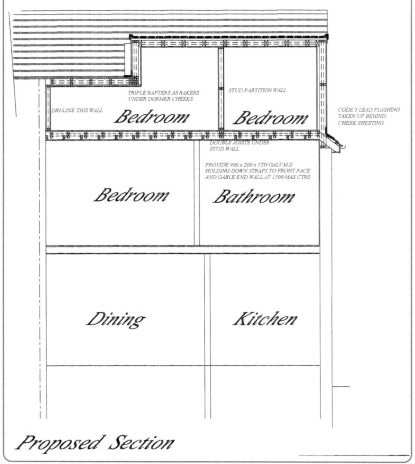

Proposed Section

Drawing: Charles Tidmarsh

Beam positions for large dormers

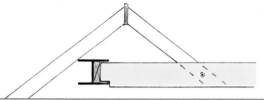

1. Beam to upper rafters, with dormer roof joists set into side of beam and bolted to rafters on dormer side

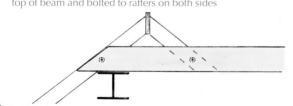

2. Beam to upper rafters with dormer roof joists supported on top of beam and bolted to rafters on both sides

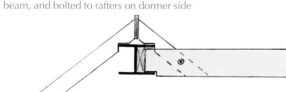

3. Beam under ridge with dormer roof joists set into side of beam, and bolted to rafters on dormer side

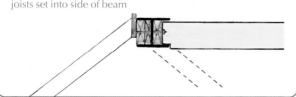

4. Beam at ridge level for maximum room height. Dormer roof joists set into side of beam

large hole needs to be cut to accommodate them. This, together with their significant extra loadings, means that just trimming around the opening would be totally inadequate. Instead, a new steel ridge beam inserted near the apex of the loft comes to the rescue, supporting the dormer's flat roof joists as they enter the main roof at high level. Some trimming is, however, still required:

■ **Side trimming:** Even with very wide box dormers, there should still be at least one original rafter remaining in place on each side. These will now need to be reinforced by being doubled with additional rafters fixed alongside. Support can also be provided by building the dormer's vertical timber sides so that the studs connect to the floor structure below. A third source of support comes from the new studwork purlin wall running along the inside roof slope, below the opening.

■ **Top trimming:** Dormers are often built as high as possible, in order to achieve the greatest amount of headroom inside. Where they're built level with the ridge (the normal maximum permitted height) there'll be no remaining rafters between the ridge and the top of the new dormer. However, where dormers are built a little lower, some sawn-off upper rafters will remain. These can be bolted directly to the new incoming flat roof joists, without the need for a head trimmer timber butting across the ends. This works successfully because the flat roof joists continue past the rafters into the loft, where they're supported on the steel ridge beam (the joists also provide a framework for the new ceiling). Clearly, in order to join with the remaining existing rafters the spacing of the new flat-roof joists will need to match that of the old rafters.

■ **Bottom trimming:** Large dormers are sometimes built right out as far as the main wall, in which case none of the original roof slope will remain at the front. In such cases the front face of the

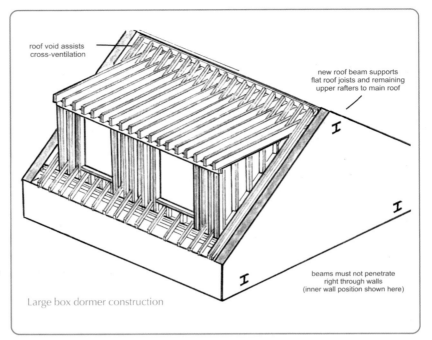

roof void assists
cross-ventilation

new roof beam supports
flat roof joists and remaining
upper rafters to main roof

beams must not penetrate
right through walls
(inner wall position shown here)

Large box dormer construction

dormer is built straight up from the main wall below, either in masonry or timber framework. But in most cases box dormers are actually set back up the roof slope, with a number of short lower rafters running down from the dormer sill to the eaves. These can then either be trimmed with a sill trimmer or bolted directly to the vertical studs in the front framework of the new dormer.

Building a dormer

For a good carpenter, constructing the timber framework of a typical dormer should be a relatively straightforward

task. The dormer's front wall and the side cheeks are built from softwood timber studwork and sheathing. Internally it will be insulated and lined with plasterboard.

Despite their sometimes tank-like appearance and bulky size, the overall additional load imposed on roofs by new dormers is not necessarily that great. Much of the weight on an existing roof is from the tiles, which are of course stripped from this area. Indeed, the total loading may not be significantly increased, due to the dormer's relatively lightweight structure, although some intense localised 'point loadings' need to be supported. But because a large opening has to be cut in the roof, perhaps the most critical part of the job is the strengthening work to the old roof structure, for example with purlins running above and below the new opening.

Building dormers in timber studwork offers several advantages. It's lightweight and yet load-bearing, and of course is fully compatible with the existing roof structure. It's relatively inexpensive and can be built swiftly – always

Because 'centre' measurements are taken from the centre of one stud to the centre of the next, you actually have a net space of 353mm between each stud, assuming you're using 47mm studs. But it's not normally possible to maintain equal spacing across the entire width of the wall, largely because standard window sizes don't co-ordinate with a rigid 400mm grid pattern.

Where studs are bunched together it'll later be necessary to provide extra insulation on the inner face, in order to prevent heat loss from 'cold bridging'.

Headers

In most box dormers, it's the front 'face' wall that takes most of the loadings. The vertical studs to the front wall support a large horizontal timber beam running along the top generally known as the 'header' (also referred to as the 'head beam', 'window header', 'top head' or 'head plate'). Headers are generally formed from a pair of doubled-up joists, but being a key structural component must be approved in advance by Building Control, as per your approved drawings.

Such load-bearing dormer faces are often built up from a floor beam below, upon which they're directly supported. As well as supporting loadings from the dormer's flat roof, headers also provide a ready-made lintel for window openings. One advantage is that they spread the load across the face below, so you don't have to meticulously line up each new flat-roof joist with each vertical stud, thereby saving valuable building time.

Cheeks

The sides of dormers are known as 'cheeks' and are traditionally clad in lead sheet or hung with tiles. In flat roof construction they don't normally take any significant loadings, so their studs can be fixed to the rafters in the roof slopes to either side. It's not unusual to see small dormers on Victorian houses leaning wearily backwards, sometimes at quite dramatic angles, having settled over many years. This is perhaps due to weakness in the rafters on either side, where they weren't strengthened by being doubled-up and trimmed. A more robust alternative is normally to run the side studwork down to the floor below, assuming the floor is strong enough to take the extra loadings.

an important factor when the weather can suddenly turn nasty and you've got a big hole in your roof! If necessary stud walls can even support steel roof beams by incorporating specially designed timber posts (in accordance with engineer's calculations). Also, fitting the insulation boards between the studs should be fairly straightforward.

Soleplates

The first job when building a dormer is normally to construct the base of the timber framework. This is formed with a soleplate, the horizontal strip of timber to which the feet of the vertical studs are then fixed. Soleplates are sometimes also known as 'base plates', 'floor plates', 'sill plates', or 'bottom rails'.

Depending on the precise design of your dormer, the soleplate may be fixed to the new floor or to a timber or steel beam. Where you're building the front wall of the dormer directly up from a main wall below, the soleplate supporting the front timber framework can be fixed to this. Methods of fixing soleplates therefore vary – either shot-firing or bolting them to steel beams, nailing or screwing them to timber joists, or strapping them to masonry walls.

Studs

Dormer studwork is generally constructed from minimum 100 x 47mm (4 x 2in) sawn softwood. Studs are butted together and skew-nailed with at least two nails for each joint, or else joined with metal fixings known as 'framing anchors'.

Where they're load-bearing, the timber may need to be of a minimum strength class of C16. The vertical studs are normally spaced no further apart than 400mm centres.

Noggins

For added strength, it is recommended that load-bearing timber frame walls have a row of staggered noggins fitted at about half-height. As with floors, these are basically lumps of spare wood of the same dimensions as the stud timbers.

Windows and glazing

The dormer framework needs to accommodate an opening for the window, and this requires strengthening with extra studs either side. Some small dormers don't have headers, relying instead on traditional lintels supported by vertical 'cripple studs' on each side of the window. Underneath, the window sits on a timber framework sill.

French windows are sometimes fitted to large dormers. These feature an inward-opening pair of glazed doors and a 'Juliet balcony' balustrade around the outside, and can add a certain style to loft rooms. But there are number of safety issues here. To minimise the risk of falling, guarding should be provided to all opening windows that are 800mm or less above floor level (except escape windows). The balustrade must be a minimum of 1100mm above the finished floor level, and the spacing between the balustrade spindles must be less than 100mm. The guidance for glazing in French windows is more rigorous than normal because the glazing in doors less than 1500mm above floor level must be safety glass. In fact the Building Regulations have quite a lot to say about glazing, both in terms of its overall size and the amount of opening area.

Timber-frame structures are always going to be vulnerable to damp around the window openings, so to stop any damp seeping through and rotting the frame a damp-proof membrane (waterproof plastic sheet) is fixed around the window reveals, overlapping the external plywood sheathing (see below). In exposed areas it's advisable to protect windows by rebating them further back, so the reveals are not less than about 25mm.

Sheathing

Obviously, the sooner you can weatherproof the hole in your roof the better, so once the dormer framework is complete the outside should be clad with timber sheathing. As well as providing protection from the weather and reducing wind penetration, the purpose of sheathing is to stiffen the wall, and to provide a backing for the internal insulation.

Normally external grade plywood sheeting is used, or OSB (oriented strand board) to grade 3 or 4. Boards are typically of either 12mm, 15mm or 18mm thickness, generally the thicker the better.

With plywood or OSB up to 12mm thick, it is best to use 50mm-long corrosion-resistant nails (3mm thick). Boards are nailed to the framework about every 300mm, or 150mm along the edges. Where two boards meet a 3mm expansion gap should be left between them. Because a lot of boards are imported from the US they're sold in standard 8 x 4ft imperial sizes, ie 2440 x 1220mm, and need to be cut to fit a metric framework.

Breather membrane

The next step is for the outer face of the sheathing to be covered with a breather membrane. This layer of roof sheeting material performs the dual purpose of stopping any rain that gets past the outer cladding (*ie* the tiling or lead sheet etc) whilst allowing condensation and water vapour to escape from inside. The breather membrane is tacked to the sheathing or fixed using a staple gun. The sheets should overlap at their sides by at least 100mm and vertically by a minimum of 150mm, with the upper sheet always overlapping the lower one.

Battens

If you've chosen a tile- or slate-hung outer finish, then once the sheathing has been applied treated softwood battens are fixed in place. Each batten should be fixed from at least three supporting points. Where one batten butts against the next, the joints should be staggered and cut at 45°. It's important to note that battens are nailed right through the plywood sheathing into the studs, and not just to the sheathing alone.

In wild and stormy locations there's always a risk that violent gusts of wind-driven rain can penetrate the outer cladding of exposed structures such as dormers, so to provide an additional line of defence an extra layer of vertical 'counter-battens' can be fixed before the normal horizontal battens. This creates a void from which any rainwater can safely drain away, and where air can circulate to help evaporation.

Cladding and walls

The external finish that you've selected for the face and cheeks of your dormers will strongly affect the way the loft conversion appears from the world below. For smaller dormers, best results are usually obtained with traditional

local styles. Tiles and lead sheet are probably the most widely used materials, or you may prefer a smooth render finish, or even glazed cheeks. For large box dormers, timber cladding or UPVC plastic shiplap boarding is popular. Full-width roof extensions have their sides built up from the walls below.

Fire spread between buildings

Ever since the hapless Mr Thomas Farynor of Pudding Lane Bakery, London EC3, caused 13,000 dwellings to burn down, the risk of fire spreading between buildings has been something of a regulatory hot potato. The lessons learnt from this 1666 catastrophe have been distilled down through the centuries into today's 'critical space separation' rule. This means alarm bells start ringing at Building Control where the distance between buildings is 1m or less. For loft converters this might be relevant where, for example, a dormer cheek faces the boundary.

Because materials such as timber cladding or UPVC are highly combustible in a fire, they can't provide the necessary 30 minutes' fire-resistance, and therefore may not be acceptable within 1m of a boundary, unless smaller in area than 1m^2.

But dormers don't just need to be fire-resistant from the outside. Because they're built of timber studwork (except full-width dormers with their brick or block walls), their

cheeks need to be lined with fire-resistant pink-coloured plasterboard. Even where they're clad with slates or tiles (which are naturally fire-resistant), within 1m of a boundary you still need to install a layer of fire-board both internally and externally to protect the studwork structure. This is fixed on top of the sheathing before fitting the breather membrane. If only someone had told poor old Thomas Farynor.

Tile hanging

At the design stage you may have opted to clad the dormer walls in a traditional architectural style that dates back centuries – vertically hung tiles or slates. Tiles are not only a good way of adding some character, they're also extremely practical, since they can help insulate an external wall whilst still allowing it to breathe. Tiling also requires very little maintenance, which may account for its enduring popularity.

A layer of 'underfelt' is first laid below the preservative-treated battens. This should be breather

membrane, *ie* not polythene sheeting. Plain tiles are typically sized 265 x 165mm and each tile is hung on a batten and double nailed in place. Where both the front and the side cheeks of a dormer are tiled, the vertical corners can be clad with special 90° corner tiles for a really neat, waterproof finish.

Leadwork

The premium finish for dormer cheeks in many parts of the country was traditionally lead sheet.

Leadwork is extremely durable and long-lasting. It also looks good, blending in tastefully regardless of whether the dormer roof is tiled, slated, or has a flat roof that's also clad in lead. Today, wall cladding is made using Code 5 thickness rolled lead sheet (to BSEN 12588:1999).

The problem with lead is that it's very prone to expansion, and if wrongly laid it can split. When laying lead sheet the metal must be free to move with temperature changes, so expansion joints are needed even for relatively small areas. Although dormer cheeks don't normally present a very large surface area, the lead is fixed either as overlapping sheets secured with clips or as 'lead welted panels'. Here, individual panels no larger than 450mm wide are separated by a vertical welt, a raised, strengthened seam made from folded-over lead. The fixing clips are concealed in the folded welts. Where clout nails or screws are used, they must be of brass, copper or stainless steel.

In rainy or damp conditions new leadwork can be prone to 'patination' staining, where a layer of white carbonate forms on the surface. This can also cause unsightly white staining on roofs and walls below the leadwork, so to reduce staining, new lead sheeting, flashings and soakers should be treated with a coat of patination oil.

Weatherboarding

Timber weatherboarding is a traditional lightweight wall finish that looks good and works well in combination with timber-frame dormer construction. The downside, of course, is that it's not maintenance-free, so you may need to spend a bit of time up your ladder wielding a brush every few years. Traditional 'barn' cladding is made from rough-sawn feather-edged horizontal planks, typically fixed with a 30mm overlap. Another popular style is rebated shiplap cladding, which uses smooth-planed timber. This is equally weather-resistant, although being laid completely flush means it has less of a 'period house' appearance. If you want to sex up your timber-clad dormers, how about laying your shiplap boards diagonally or vertically?

Timber cladding needs to be fixed to a timber sub-frame of vertical battens, preferably with a sheet of roofing membrane underneath for better weather protection. It's good practice to apply at least one coat of stain or paint before fixing, so that there are no bare strips peeping out at you between courses when the timber inevitably shrinks. Rough-sawn timber can drink large amounts of wood stain and needs a reapplication about every seven years.

The amount of time required for keeping up appearances can be reduced by using special low-maintenance wood stain or microporous paint. To protect against rot, all wood should be pre-treated with preservative, ideally arriving on site already pressure impregnated. Otherwise it will need liberal coats of preservative brushed well in, especially to the grain at cut ends.

If you prefer a maintenance-free lifestyle, some of the more expensive 'fit and forget' timbers, such as cedar or heat-treated redwood, may be worth investigating. Other cheaper options are cladding made from fibre-cement board or UPVC, which is available in a range of different colours. Whether UPVC cladding will look right will depend on the age and type of your property. It may be just the thing for large dormers to some 1960s or 1970s houses, but for traditional architecture you can't beat real wood for style and quality. Something both UPVC and timber cladding have in common, however, is that their use is restricted within 1m of a boundary (see above).

Render

A smooth, honey-coloured traditional render finish can look superb on dormer cheeks. But cement render is normally applied to walls built from blockwork, and here we're dealing with a timber framework. The solution is to apply it to a special base of metal lathing that has a layer of building paper incorporated, which helps contain the render within the mesh. Battens are fixed through the sheathing and breather membrane into the studwork to create a cavity between the back face of the render and the sheathing. The cavity allows any water that penetrates the render to drain out, and allows ventilation to disperse any damp from condensation.

Alternatively, smooth render or textured cement finishes can be applied to fibre-cement cladding boards or cement-bonded particleboard fixed to battens.

Selecting the right colour sand for your render is important if you don't intend to paint the surface. To avoid ending up with a gloomy looking grey cement colour you could lighten the mix by adding a dash of lime. Special colour enhancers can also be applied, or you can buy ready-made coloured render mixes.

Render is normally applied in two coats. For a smooth finish the final coat is rubbed down with a float or trowel. As with most cement-based materials, care should be taken to avoid applying render in frosty conditions, otherwise cracking can occur.

Plain render is often painted, and is therefore not maintenance-free since it requires decoration every five years or so (although some paints claim up to 15 years before needing recoating). Masonry paint comprises special water-based emulsion with anti-bacterial properties, incorporating reinforcement for strength. But before painting newly cement-rendered walls the underlying surface must first be allowed to fully dry out, which, depending on the weather, can take several weeks. Once dry, the render can be sealed with a stabilising solution before painting, to bind the surface and make it less absorbent.

full-width dormer, or where a new gable end wall is constructed to replace a side-hipped roof. Matching the existing brickwork or stonework requires some skill so that the new walls don't obviously stand out and ruin the look of your home (see below).

Although more expensive to build than timber studwork, masonry walls offer several advantages for loft conversions. They have excellent resistance to fire, are largely maintenance-free, and can provide relatively good sound-insulation qualities. Where it's not possible to safely build on top of existing old walls, for example where their condition is questionable, lightweight studwork construction with a tile-hung or rendered finish may be a better option.

To build the side walls for a new full-width dormer, normally just the rear part of the existing side gable wall (or party wall) will need to be built up. Most dormers are located on rear roof slopes, so adding a new triangular-shaped wall here is essentially an infill job. To build on top of an existing party wall, it's obviously going to be a lot easier on properties where the party walls were originally built up 'through the roof' in the form of a parapet wall (as

Masonry walls

As a rule bricklayers don't get rich working on loft conversions. The only time when there's much bricklaying is when the existing walls are built up to form the sides of a

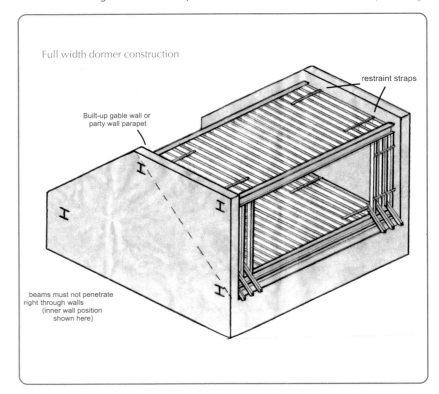

Full width dormer construction

restraint straps

Built-up gable wall or party wall parapet

beams must not penetrate right through walls (inner wall position shown here)

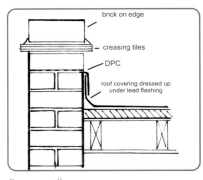

brick on edge

creasing tiles

DPC

roof covering dressed up under lead flashing

Parapet walls

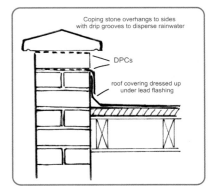

Coping stone overhangs to sides with drip grooves to disperse rainwater

DPCs

roof covering dressed up under lead flashing

found on Victorian terraces in London). Once built, the new side walls will need to be secured with steel restraint straps to the dormer's floor structure, roof joists and face studwork.

The new side walls are actually built higher than the level of the dormer's flat roof. They need to be built as parapet walls extending either side by a minimum of 225mm above the highest part, which is normally where it joins the main roof. Because flat roofs usually slope down slightly towards the front to allow rainwater to disperse, the outermost end will typically be about one course of brickwork (75mm) lower, on a typical 3m-deep flat roof.

The reason that the walls need to be this height above roof level is that, to be fully watertight, the flat roof covering needs to lap up the walls either side by a minimum of 150mm, leaving room for another couple of courses of brickwork above. It's very important that these new parapet walls are finished with a suitable capping on top, such as with traditional coping stones, or leadwork dressed over boards, or a line of bricks laid on their sides over projecting 'creasing tiles'. The precise choice will depend on the architectural style and age of the building. But whatever type you choose, it's important that they're laid over a DPC and project sufficiently either side of the wall to protect the brickwork below.

Hip to gable conversions

As noted earlier, for houses with hipped roofs, in order to achieve a decent amount of head-room in the loft it's often necessary to replace the original side roof slope by building up the existing side gable wall.

Apart from the lack of headroom, another problem with hipped roofs is that there's nowhere you can easily support new steel loft beams at high level, because instead of a wall there's a roof slope on the side. So a hip conversion will also make it possible to install the new beams that may be required to support the dormer's flat roof.

New gable walls can equally be constructed above existing traditional solid masonry walls or modern cavity walls. One side-effect of enlarging the gable wall is that it substantially increases loadings on the building, especially if built in masonry (as opposed to timber studwork). The additional area of new tiled roofing to the front and rear, however, shouldn't be vastly greater than the amount removed from the side.

The first task in a hip conversion is for the tiles on the side roof slope to be stripped, and then the rafters and battens removed. As far as possible the front and rear roof slopes are left undisturbed, unless you need to cut an opening for a new dormer to the rear. Once the new gable wall has been built, the main roof can be extended across to meet it by fitting new front and rear rafters to a new ridge board. The previously stripped tiles can then be re-used to clad the extended front roof slope, thereby achieving a nice, neat match with the existing roof coverings.

The job of extending gable walls probably qualifies as

potentially the most hazardous part of a loft conversion. While they're being built, large freestanding walls are highly vulnerable to gusts of wind, and are at risk of collapse, so temporary timber supports should be used to prop them up.

Once built, gable walls need to be tied to the new roof structure with steel restraint straps. A strap is provided near the highest point of the roof, and additional straps fixed every 2m (or closer) down the roof slopes. In most cases walls are also strapped to the floor structure.

Matching bricks

In order to get new brickwork to blend in satisfyingly it may be necessary to track down suitable reclaimed bricks that harmonise with the old walls. Although these can cost more than three times the price of ordinary common bricks, the numbers required are fairly small. But getting as perfect a match as possible isn't the only important consideration. Brickwork at high level is obviously going to be very exposed, especially on parapet walls that stick out above roof level. The problem is, with old reclaimed bricks it's not possible to select ones with high frost-resistance or low salt content (to reduce the risk of sulphate attack), as you would for new bricks. Also, their 'crushing strength' will be an unknown quantity, which could be an issue where new walls have to support any beams.

One solution may be to investigate the world of new 'retro' bricks. There are over 1,200 different types of bricks currently available in the UK, some of which are designed to provide a very realistic match with traditional bricks, without the technical risks. The standard modern metric brick size (dating from 1974) is 215 x 102.5 x 65mm, but sizes compatible with old imperial stocks are also available. These come in a range of traditional heights such as 80mm, 67mm and 50mm, although they're usually the same length and width as modern metric bricks. To achieve an original-looking gable there's also another essential ingredient – the style and colour of the mortar pointing. For an authentic look this may mean using traditional lime mortar on older buildings.

If matching old bricks proves troublesome, or if your walls are rendered, an easy solution is to build in 440 x 215mm lightweight blockwork for a rendered finish.

Hip conversions

CONVERSION 1: Traditional hip to gable conversion with gable wall built up in lightweight block and matching brickwork. Double height roof window to front slope.

CONVERSION 2: Hip extended with large 'part gable, part dormer' to side, extending to rear with flat roof. A small portion of the original hipped roof is still visible. Tile clad to timber framework and blockwork inner leaf. No roof windows.

Although conventional blocks are 100mm thick, aerated concrete blocks are now available in thicknesses including 'full-width' 200mm, 215mm, 255mm, 265mm, 275mm and 300mm – which covers pretty much any wall you're likely to encounter at this level. Building onto a cavity wall using fat blocks that can span the full wall width in one go makes them ideal for work at upper gable level, as they're very light and quick to lay. Their compressive strength, however, can be relatively low, requiring a weaker mortar mix. The mortar joints should be recessed to provide a key for the later render surface coat.

If the idea of a rendered gable doesn't sound appealing, you could choose from a selection of tiles, slates or timber cladding fixed to battens. Many Edwardian properties featured tile-hung upper gables above brick side walls, so this may be an appropriate choice for properties of this era.

Pitched dormer roofs

Small dormers normally have cute cottage-style pitched roofs designed to match the tiled or slated main roof. Although flat roofs are easier to build, they rarely look good, and so are normally reserved for large box dormers and full-width roof extensions. The most popular pitched roof style on smaller dormers is the classic A-shaped gable. In many cases hipped roofs may also be architecturally appropriate but are more complicated to construct.

Because of their small size such roofs rarely require any extra support internally from purlins or collars.

The rafters on a small gable roof are typically spaced at 400mm centres, and are nailed to the ridge board at the top. A small V-shaped cut is made in the rafters to ensure the rafter feet mate securely to the timber wall plates with a 'birdsmouth joint'. The ceiling joists span the short distance from side to side, fixed onto the timber wall plates on top of the side cheeks.

If you live in a house with a hipped roof you may want to construct new dormer windows with small matching hipped roofs of their own, to blend in with the original architecture. But hipped roofs are relatively complicated to build. The difficulty is that the carpenter needs to make a lot of tricky angled cuts where the three (front, rear and side) roof slopes meet. These 'corners' of a hipped roof are made from special hip rafters, usually clad with round 'hip tiles' (similar to ridge tiles) or with upturned 'bonnet tiles'. Due to their weight, hip tiles normally need a protruding metal strip called a 'hip iron' at their base, to discourage any loose ones from slipping off and hitting innocent passers-by.

Matching the slates or tiles on new dormers with those on the existing main roof can usually be achieved by recycling the ones that were stripped off earlier when making the opening. Otherwise reclaimed materials from reclamation yards may be worth investigating. In any case, suitable new ridge tiles will need to be found, as well as hip and valley tiles for some designs.

Roof felting and battening

The same breather membrane material that was fixed earlier to the studwork walls can now also be used to underfelt the dormer roof. Rather like high-tech mountaineering clothing, sheets of breather membrane cleverly prevent rainwater from getting in, and yet allow any water vapour to escape from inside the loft.

This should be installed as soon as the basic roof structure is complete, starting near the bottom at the eaves and working upwards. Rough-sawn softwood roofing battens treated with preservative are fixed horizontally to secure the underlay to the rafters (see also 'counter battens' below). An overlap of at least 100mm must be allowed where one sheet joins another. To preserve their strength, the joints between lengths of battens should be staggered, and the smallest battens should span across at least three rafters. Batten sizes are typically 32 x 19mm where the rafters are spaced

apart at no further than 450mm centres. The precise spacing between the rows of battens will depend on the size and lap of the tiles and the pitch of the roof. Tile manufacturers can normally carry out the necessary calculations.

In Scotland the rules are different. Rafters must first be covered with rigid 'sarking boards', a traditional form of timber cladding. Over this base a breather membrane underfelt is laid, held in place by counter-battens running up the rafters, before conventional battens are fixed across them. This leaves a ventilated air space under the tiles.

Because your dormer roofs are newly built, achieving the required insulation standards should be a lot easier than for the old main roof which has to be upgraded from inside. As we shall see in the next chapter, the need for thick insulation boards and generous ventilation spaces at rafter level in loft conversions can consume a lot of valuable space, so it often makes sense for the roof slopes to be built up slightly to increase the available space for insulation. This can be done by first raising the height of the rafters by applying counter-battens down them, before the 'real' battening is done. But because you're effectively extending the height of the roof this must be agreed at the design stage.

Soakers, secret gutters, flashings and valleys

Most roof failures occur at junctions, so the joints between dormer walls and existing roof slopes are best formed in hardwearing, traditional lead. The attraction of lead is that it enjoys a healthy lifespan in excess of 80 years, and can easily accommodate small amounts of movement.

Where dormer cheeks meet the existing roof slopes the junction can normally be weatherproofed using lead 'soakers' hidden under the tiles. These are strips of lead sheet (usually

in Code 3 lead) fixed underneath the tiles or slates on the main roof and turned up at the dormer cheeks, behind the battens but on top of the breather membrane underlay, to form discreet 'secret gutters' – a neat solution.

To the front face of a dormer there should be a special lead 'apron' flashing dressed down over the tiles below by about 100mm, to make the joint watertight. These horizontal lead strips are turned up at their tops and fixed under the windowsills or behind the battens. Lead aprons should be formed from thicker Code 4 or 5 lead, and secured with clips to prevent wind uplift.

Perhaps the trickiest joint of all is the one at the back where the new dormer roof meets the existing main roof slope. At this junction the old roof tiles in the immediate area will have been stripped to expose the structure, and so that new valleys can be formed at the join. This is done by placing timber valley boards ('layer boards') diagonally onto the existing rafters.

Because valleys channel rainwater from the surrounding main roof slopes they're a common weak point, requiring good-quality weatherproofing. For traditional tiled roofs the best solution is often to fit purpose-made valley tiles that match the style of the existing plain tiles. Alternatively a lead-lined 'open valley' or a 'mitred valley' with strips of sheet lead underneath can be made. Today GRP fibreglass linings are widely used, which are cheaper but unlikely to last as long as lead.

Large mansard roof extensions with their sloping front 'walls' don't normally join directly to the main roof slopes, other than perhaps with a new valley gutter to the front. Instead they abut newly-built walls on either side, where the joints are waterproofed using traditional flashings made of Code 4 or 5 lead. This is also the case for full-width dormers, although a lead apron may be required to the front where they're set back slightly up the roof.

Flat dormer roofs

Large dormers normally have flat roofs because these achieve the maximum possible space inside a loft room.

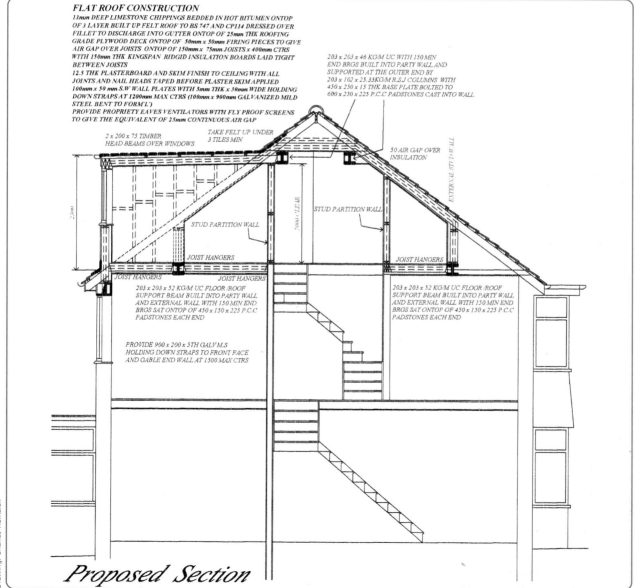

FLAT ROOF CONSTRUCTION
13mm DEEP LIMESTONE CHIPPINGS BEDDED IN HOT BITUMEN ONTOP OF 3 LAYER BUILT UP FELT ROOF TO BS 747 AND CP114 DRESSED OVER FILLET TO DISCHARGE INTO GUTTER ONTOP OF 25mm THK ROOFING GRADE PLYWOOD DECK ONTOP OF 50mm x 50mm FIRING PIECES TO GIVE AIR GAP OVER JOISTS ONTOP OF 150mm x 75mm JOISTS x 400mm CTRS WITH 150mm THK KINGSPAN RIDGID INSULATION BOARDS LAID TIGHT BETWEEN JOISTS
12.5 THK PLASTERBOARD AND SKIM FINISH TO CEILING WITH ALL JOINTS AND NAIL HEADS TAPED BEFORE PLASTER SKIM APPLIED 100mm x 50 mm S.W WALL PLATES WITH 5mm THK x 30mm WIDE HOLDING DOWN STRAPS AT 1200mm MAX CTRS (100mm x 900mm GALVANIZED MILD STEEL BENT TO FORM 'L')
PROVIDE PROPRIETY EAVES VENTILATORS WITH FLY PROOF SCREENS TO GIVE THE EQUIVALENT OF 25mm CONTINUOUS AIR GAP

2 x 200 x 75 TIMBER HEAD BEAMS OVER WINDOWS

TAKE FELT UP UNDER 3 TILES MIN

203 x 203 x 46 KG/M UC WITH 150 MIN END BRGS BUILT INTO PARTY WALL AND SUPPORTED AT THE OUTER END BY 203 x 102 x 25.33KG/M R.S.J COLUMNS WITH 450 x 250 x 15 THK BASE PLATE BOLTED TO 600 x 250 x 225 P.C.C PADSTONES CAST INTO WALL

50 AIR GAP OVER INSULATION

STUD PARTITION WALL

STUD PARTITION WALL

JOIST HANGERS

JOIST HANGERS

JOIST HANGERS

JOIST HANGERS

203 x 203 x 52 KG/M UC FLOOR /ROOF SUPPORT BEAM BUILT INTO PARTY WALL AND EXTERNAL WALL WITH 150 MIN END BRGS SAT ONTOP OF 450 x 150 x 225 P.C.C PADSTONES EACH END

203 x 203 x 52 KG/M UC FLOOR /ROOF SUPPORT BEAM BUILT INTO PARTY WALL AND EXTERNAL WALL WITH 150 MIN END BRGS SAT ONTOP OF 450 x 150 x 225 P.C.C PADSTONES EACH END

PROVIDE 900 x 200 x 5TH GALV M.S HOLDING DOWN STRAPS TO FRONT FACE AND GABLE END WALL AT 1500 MAX CTRS

Proposed Section

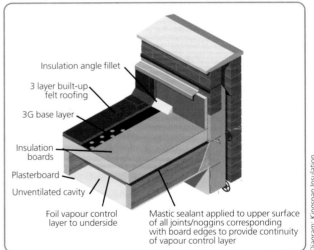

Typical box dormer structural support

Timber header

New beam supports flat dormer roof and main roof

Original purlin (retained where possible)

Purlin wall

Purlin wall

New beam supports floor and roof loadings

New beam supports floor, roof and dormer loadings

New loft floor may need additional support from existing internal wall

Of course, flat roofs aren't actually flat. By definition anything up to a 10° pitch counts as flat, the slope or 'fall' being necessary so that rainwater can swiftly disperse. The Building Regulations encourage a minimum fall of 1:40, but that hasn't stopped some roofers actually building them totally flat. If built correctly rainwater should discharge efficiently into the gutters without puddles forming on the surface.

Flat roofs are the simplest of all roof types to construct, being built in a similar way to floors. Once the dormer's timber stud walls are complete, and the large header beam positioned above the front window, the roof joists can be installed. To the front, the joists are strapped to the header. At the other end, support is normally provided from a new steel ridge beam inside the loft.

Before ordering roof joists you first need to know the required size, length and stress grade, which will be specified in the drawings. As with floor structures, the sizes and spacings are calculated by the length they need to span and the load imposed on them. In this case the loadings simply comprise the insulated roof deck plus an allowance for potentially violent gusts of storm force wind and accumulated snow. Common joist sizes are 50 x 200mm or 50 x 175mm, and they're normally spaced at either 400mm or 600mm centres. A typical span would be about 3m. (See span tables on website).

The joists are actually fitted perfectly level, so that the ceiling below will be level. The required outward fall is achieved by nailing thin tapered timber strips called 'firring pieces' along the tops of the joists. Timber merchants can supply firrings cut to the required fall.

As well as being fixed to the front header beam and to the ridge beam inside, the joists can be bolted to any remaining rafters of the main roof that they overlap. The structure is then strengthened with strutting fitted between the joists, in a similar way to floors. To complete the roof structure, a deck of 18mm or 25mm-thick marine-grade plywood is laid over the joists and secured with galvanised nails. Ordinary chipboard is not recommended, as it can disintegrate when damp.

Before applying the outer roof covering, in order to comply with the Building Regulations flat roofs must contain an adequate amount of thermal insulation. A plastic-sheet vapour barrier is laid on the deck, prior to placing thick polyurethane foam insulation boards on top. This is known as a 'warm roof' with the insulation carried above the roof joists (see Chapter 12). Because of the thick insulation boards sitting above the deck, there's no cold surface underneath for any warm, moist air escaping from the room below to condense against, therefore

Insulation angle fillet

3 layer built-up felt roofing

3G base layer

Insulation boards

Plasterboard

Unventilated cavity

Foil vapour control layer to underside

Mastic sealant applied to upper surface of all joints/noggins corresponding with board edges to provide continuity of vapour control layer

Diagram: Kingspan Insulation

Flat lead roof with rolls

Photo: Velux

there's no need to provide a ventilation space above the ceiling. This also means that recessed lighting can be fitted to ceilings.

Finally, the roof covering can be laid over the insulation boards. There is, however, a potentially useful short cut. Instead of going to the trouble of installing separate layers of deck, insulation and roof covering, you could use ready-made 'composite' decking which combines a triple sandwich of plywood, insulation and felt covering all bonded into one.

Flat roof coverings

Flat roofs have something of a dubious reputation. Quite simply, they don't last very long. Or at least, mineral-felted roofs often have an embarrassingly short lifespan. Having to re-cover a felt roof on a garage or single storey extension may be an inconvenience, but attempting the same thing to an inaccessible third- or fourth-storey dormer can be a major headache. So it's not normally a good idea to fit a cheap mineral felt roof that may only last around a decade.

The premium choice of flat roof covering is lead on account of its high durability. Flat roofs need relatively thick Code 5 or 6 lead. As noted earlier, the problem with lead is that it's notoriously prone to expansion in hot weather. This is going to be much more of an issue for flat roofs than for cheeks because the areas covered are normally far greater. Any large areas without expansion joints will eventually cause splits and buckling. Sheets should therefore not exceed 2.5m in length (for Code 6 thickness lead). Expansion cracking can be prevented by building in suitable 'rolls' parallel to the slope direction. At joints with walls the sheets should be turned up and lapped over by a separate lead flashing.

If your budget won't stretch to lead sheeting, a good-quality mineral felt correctly laid may be acceptable. Felt is the most common covering material for domestic flat roofs and is traditionally laid in triple layers bonded to the insulation boards on the deck with hot bitumen. But be sure to keep your distance when scolding bitumen is being dispensed at high level.

To keep rainwater from spilling over the edges, the sides of the roof surface are built up slightly using triangular pieces of timber called 'tilt fillets' nailed to the edges of the decking (except, of course, where full-width dormers have new parapet walls to the sides).

One major reason for the short lifespan of felt roofs is the effect of the sun on their relatively dark surfaces. South-facing roofs are more likely to fail early because of damage caused by continual expansion and contraction. So felt roofs need protection, such as from a solar-reflective finishing layer of white mineral chippings. But unless securely bedded in hot bitumen the chippings tend to get blown away over time, ending up in the guttering. One alternative is to paint the surface with bright silver solar-reflective paint that protects it from ultraviolet radiation. Today this can be avoided by fitting three or four layers of high-performance glass-reinforced polyester, which doesn't need to be covered with chippings or solar-reflective paint.

The biggest weak point on flat roofs is normally at the joint where they meet a wall. Full-width dormers have walls on either side and, as noted earlier, the felt should be dressed up the wall by at least 150mm (known as the 'upstand') and fixed into a mortar joint and bedded in mortar. The sharp bend where the felt is folded up the wall is a common weak-point, because it can easily split and leak. The solution is to reduce the sharpness of the angle by placing a small strip of timber called an 'angle fillet' under the felt. The job is then completed with a lead flashing (cut into a joint in the wall above) dressed down over the felt, finishing no closer than 75mm above the roof surface. Any pipes or ducts passing through the roof are another point to watch, and the joints around such things as soil pipes, flues or roof lights poking up through the surface must be carefully waterproofed.

Eaves, fascias, soffits and bargeboards

One of the key design details that make dormers look right is the detailing at the edge of the roof. The best approach is normally to copy the detailing on the main house.

On pitched roofs, the projecting rafter feet at the top of

the main walls are commonly 'boxed in' by the eaves, which comprise a front fascia board and a soffit infill underneath. This is the classic 'box eaves' arrangement where the soffits normally have vents to allow air to flow through up the roof structure. Alternatively, where the rafter feet don't project, fascias are sometimes fixed directly to the wall. Although fascia boards can provide a handy place to secure the gutter clips, they are a little out of vogue at the moment. The current fashion is to leave the rafter feet exposed, a traditional style that suits small cottage dormers. On flat roofs fascias are still necessary to cover the ends of the roof joists, the choice typically being between timber and UPVC. When ordering timber for external use it should always be preservative-treated.

Bargeboards are the strips of timber found under the roof edges of a gable wall. Small gabled dormers often sport such timber bargeboards under the verges. But this isn't the only option. You may prefer the look of naked masonry, which can be equally appealing, perhaps featuring some traditional 'dog-tooth' brickwork along the top.

Rainwater fittings – gutters and downpipes

When the roof is complete, installing the rainwater fittings should be a relatively simple task – assuming you have safe access. So this is best done whilst the scaffolding is still in place. But first the timber fascia boards, or rafter feet to which the gutter clips are to be fixed, should be painted.

At the design stage the route of the rainwater escaping from new dormer roofs should have been planned. Often it can discharge discreetly down onto the main roof, perhaps via a short length of new downpipe near the front of the dormer. Or there already may be a convenient existing downpipe nearby to which it can be connected.

The need for new downpipes can be more of a headache when there are several small traditional half-dormers built directly up from the main walls. The problem is, if you want to run a single length of guttering straight across the front, it may obstruct the windows, or at least look rather clumsy. So several short lengths of gutter are often required between each dormer, each one needing its own downpipe connected down to surface water drains at ground level.

The variety of guttering on the market is extensive, but you'll probably want to select the style that matches that of the main house. Good old black PVC is the most popular choice, since it's relatively cheap and is adequate for most purposes.

And finally...

When all the roofing, rainwater fittings, eaves and bargeboards are complete, the scaffolding may no longer be required. But don't be too hasty. The 'snagging' process may yet reveal defects at roof level, such as leaking skylights, loose flashings, or leaking gutter joints. Also, decorating timber windows and external joinery will be a lot easier whilst direct access is still possible. Fortunately the extra cost of leaving the scaffolding in place for another week or two rarely seems to worry scaffold-hire firms unduly, so hang on to it while you can.

STEP BY STEP

Installing a roof window

There's some debate about whether it's better to install roof windows from inside the loft or from outside. Whilst the job can sometimes largely be done from inside, the preliminary stage of removing slates or tiles is normally better carried out externally. This is because it's very difficult to loosen and remove traditional slates or plain tiles from inside without causing some to cascade dangerously down to the ground. However, where roofs are clad with large interlocking tiles (such as the modern concrete side-interlocking type) removing them from inside should be a lot easier, but you'll still need to cordon off the danger area down below as a precaution. Being only single lapped, rather than double lapped for plain tiles and slates makes them easier to lift. Natural slate coverings are probably the most difficult since slates are nailed in place.

To work successfully from inside the loft, you'll need a stable platform, such as a good pair of step ladders, that

Tools required
- Screwdriver
- Hand saw
- Craft knife
- Spirit level
- 90° set square
- Silicone gun and sealant
- Adjustable spanner
- Angle grinder/tile cutter
- Wooden dressing tool for leadwork ('lead dresser')
- Safety goggles and gloves

Materials
- Roof window
- Lead sheeting kit for head and sill (typically Code 3 lead approx 300mm wide), normally supplied with window
- Code 4 lead for side flashings: two rolls 150mm wide x 3m long (or flashing kit supplied with some windows)
- Step ladders
- Scaffold tower and roof ladders
- Timber battens and fillets
- Tiles: special 'one-and-a-half' size edge tiles, and shorter eaves tiles (or equivalent slates or tiles cut to size); for a plain tiled roof you need about 10 to 14 of each for a 600mm high window.

allows you to stand up comfortably through the opening in the roof, to about elbow height (much higher and there can be a risk of falling).

The job of fitting roof windows tends to be undertaken either by roofers or carpenters. Quite naturally, the former tend to favour the outdoor approach, shown in the example below. If external access is good, with scaffolding or a decent scaffold tower to work from, and for most bungalow loft conversions, the outdoor option should achieve swifter results. Either way, the tasks undertaken are essentially the same.

One of the first and most important decisions to make is, of course, whether any rafters should be cut. If possible this should be avoided as it weakens the roof structure. There are many standard roof windows (eg 550mm wide) that will fit easily between modern rafters, spaced at 600mm centres. With older houses where the rafters are more closely spaced (eg at 400mm centres), special conservation windows designed for period properties with limited space may be suitable. Fitting two smaller windows side by side (or one above the other) is often preferable to one larger window, as it can avoid the need for structural cutting to rafters. Also, a combination of smaller windows tends to look better architecturally from outside than one clunking great rooflight.

Where cutting rafters is inevitable, the timber framework around the window – ie the rafters either side and the top and bottom trimmers – must be doubled-up.

The higher up the roof you fit the windows, the more light should flood in. At the design stage you need to picture the finished room and consider your desired view. From a practical perspective you normally wouldn't fit windows any higher than about six courses of plain tiles or slates below the ridge. Any higher and the works can cause the ridge tiles to become loose and need re-bedding.

It's not unknown for builders to wrongly install roof windows. Inept weatherproofing at the flashings can sometimes cause leaks, and in some cases windows have even been fitted upside down! Different manufacturers' windows have varying installation requirements, explained in the instructions with each product, but the following should be a useful general guide. The roof window featured here is an externally fitted Replica 1 model from The Rooflight Company, with a structural width and length of 550 x 700mm. Finally, before cutting large holes in your roof don't forget to schedule some decent weather!

Personal safety
For any work carried out at height, please refer to the Working at Height Regulations and wear a safety harness. Note that if you need to cut tiles or slates using a tile cutting disc or angle grinder, always wear goggles and gloves.

1 First, temporarily remove the opening part of the window, the glazed casement, from its 'base-plate' or sub-frame by unscrewing the hinge bolts or pins. Take care not to scratch the protective coating to the paintwork, and set the casement safely aside. Measure the dimensions of the base-plate. Mark the approximate position of the window on the rafters.

2 Working from the outside, carefully lift and remove some tiles or slates. Expose an area roughly equivalent of the base-plate plus an additional two or three rows and courses beyond, around the frame. Unlike traditional slates, most tiles aren't nailed in place and can simply be lifted off, making them easier to work with. To remove interlocking tiles from inside the loft, first cut and remove an area of underfelt exposing the battens and the underside of the tiles. Then gently lift the nibs of each tile and carefully slide them back between the battens.

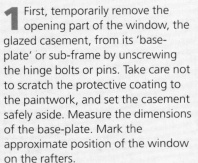

3 In this example, the window base-plate is designed to sit across a pair of rafters once the battens have been cut and removed. Having marked the outline of the base-plate on the battens, they can be carefully sawn and the opening for the base-plate made. In this example the battens are cut to almost meet the sides of the base plate, but with a 5mm expansion gap. Where any batten ends are left unsupported, timber packing strips can be nailed along the sides of the rafters below. Note that different manufacturers' roof windows vary in this respect. Some are designed to sit on top of battens around the opening secured with external brackets.

4 Working from the outside, the underfelt (or in some roofs, timber sarking boards) can now be cut away to approximately the size of the window base. If working internally this will have been done at stage 2.

5 To complete the timber framework which will support the window, timber trimmers must be fitted to the top and bottom of the opening, between the rafters either side. Normally 100 x 50mm sawn treated timber can be used, or a similar size to match the rafters. First, mark the base-plate's top and bottom position on the rafters, using a 90° set square. Then skew-nail or screw the trimmers securely in place.

6 Cut a strip of 300mm wide lead sheet. This will be used to form an apron below the window at the sill, extending 150mm either side of the base-plate. (Step 8).

7 To smooth the path of the lead sheet, a small triangular 'tilting fillet' (sawn treated timber) should be placed along the top of the first row of tiles, below the opening. Then lay a thick line of silicone roof sealant along the surface of the lead apron. This will ensure water-tightness to the joint when the base-plate is fitted.

8 Dress the lead sheet down so that it laps generously over the tiles below. At its top, the lead sheet should cover the bottom trimmer of the frame.

9 Carefully position the base-plate so that it sits in the prepared framework. Check that it's level and square. Small adjustments can be made by adding thin strips of timber 'shims' as necessary.

10 The base-plate has a pair of fixing brackets either side which are securely bolted into the rafters with coach bolts, once any small gaps have been filled with timber packing.

11 The sides of the window are made watertight with lead soakers tucked under each course of tiles. These are small oblong strips of lead cut from the 150mm-wide roll of lead flashing. The size depends on the size of tiles or slates (being roughly three-quarters the length of the tile). For the traditional 265 x 165mm plain tiles shown, strips about 200mm long should be adequate.

12 Starting at the bottom of each side, fold each oblong strip of lead so that it tucks down into the side of the base-plate. Then hang a tile onto the batten and nail it in place (using non-corrosive roofing nails). Bend the lead over the top of the tile and dress it at least halfway across the tile. This is then covered and secured by the next tile to the course above. Continue until each course of tiles covers a lead soaker.

13 To achieve an even edge to the tiles on each side of the window, extra-wide 'one-and-a-half' tiles are used on every alternate course (the same type used at roof verges). By spacing out all the tiles in a row slightly wider than normal, any gaps can be accommodated.

14 To make the top of the base-plate watertight, a head flashing is fitted. This is formed similarly to the lead apron at the sill by cutting a strip of 300mm-wide lead, extending 150mm either side of the base-plate. The lead sheet is dressed over the battens above, and tucked under the roofing felt below the topmost batten. The lower edge of the lead sheet is lapped over the top of the base-plate, and dressed down into it. As shown earlier, a small triangular timber tilting fillet is first placed along the outer edge of the base-plate to help smooth the path of the lead sheet.

15 The top of the window is finished by replacing rows of tiles nailed to the battens. The lowest course of tiles should be shorter eaves tiles. These cover the head flashing.

16 The glazed window casement can now be reattached to the base-plate by connecting it through the hinge posts using the original bolts and washers.

17 To the inside, the window reveals are lined with strips of insulation. Because the bracket for the window handle or winder will need to be firmly screwed in place, a strip of timber must be fixed to the centre of the lower reveal before insulating.

Other makes and models

Like cars, roof windows come in all kinds of different qualities and styles. The roof window shown here is an all-steel type that's designed to sit discreetly, relatively low within the roof slopes. Some other roof windows have a timber frame instead of a base-plate, which is fixed to the rafters with metal brackets so they sit on top of the battens. Special flashing kits suitable for different types of tile or slate roofs are sometimes supplied. Before fitting, always refer to manufacturers' instructions for the specific type of roof window.

Photo: Velux

Photo: Velux

Photo: Velux

18 Finally, plasterboard strips can be cut to cover the window reveals to the sides, top and bottom. These should slot neatly into the ready-made groove in the window frame.

Photo: Velux

Photo: Velux

Loft Conversion Manual

10 STAIRS AND INTERNAL WALLS

We are now fast approaching the stage when the new loft accommodation will finally assume its rightful place – as part of your home. Until now, the loft has existed in a kind of parallel universe, physically divorced from reality like an island floating in space, accessed only via scaffolding or a precarious ladder. But that's all about to change.

The full onslaught will begin when the new stair opening is cut through the old ceiling, inviting a tsunami of dust, mess, noise and then even more dust to rain down. It's for this reason that you may choose to delay fitting the stairs until as late as possible – perhaps when all the partition walling, joinery, plumbing and plasterboarding is safely out of the way. Alternatively, putting the new stairs in now should make access considerably easier for all the internal finishing works.

Back at the design stage the precise position of the loft stairs was, of course, one of the key considerations. The need to achieve sufficient headroom at the top of the stairs may even have dictated the overall layout, perhaps necessitating the construction of a large dormer, or gable conversion.

If you're lucky, installing the new stairs may simply be a matter of running a new flight above the existing staircase.

As we saw in Chapter 3, this is the most common arrangement in Victorian terraced houses thanks to their frequently generous headroom and landing space, although you might still need to sacrifice a cupboard or two.

In more modern houses, finding sufficient room for the new stairs and landing may mean losing part of an existing bedroom or demolishing an airing cupboard. Many post-war properties are well endowed with cupboard space separating the front and rear main bedrooms, an ideal location for the new stairs. Here they can run sideways off the main landing, rising upwards in the direction of the party wall, although this arrangement might mean having to take out a central chimney breast to free up extra stair space. If the amount of elbow room in your loft was in short supply from the outset, your drawings may instead show a spiral

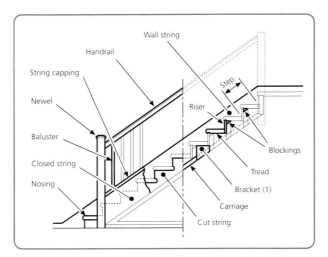

Wall string
Handrail
String capping
Newel
Step
Baluster
Riser
Closed string
Nosing
Blockings
Tread
Bracket (1)
Carriage
Cut string

staircase or special space-saving loft stairs.

So now comes the moment of truth. We're about to discover whether all those calculations and assumptions made earlier by the designer will actually cut the mustard when translated into 3D reality. No matter how many times you checked and double-checked the measurement from the floor below to the surface of the new loft floor above, it always comes as a mighty relief when the new stairs slot into place as planned (after a spot of planing and adjustment!).

The language of stairs
- **Balusters:** The thin vertical spindles below the bannister handrail. Alternatives include boarding or horizontal 1970s ranch-style strips.
- **Bannister:** The outer handrail fixed between newel posts.
- **Goings:** The main part of a tread that excludes the nosing.
- **Newel posts:** The big upright posts at the top, bottom and landings. Handrails are run between the newel posts.
- **Nosings:** The small overhanging front part of the treads – the bevelled front protruding lip.
- **Risers:** The vertical part of each step, an infill panel between treads, sometimes left open.
- **Strings:** The long strips of timber that form the stair sides, running from top to bottom, with the steps sandwiched in between.
- **Treads:** The steps that you put your feet on.
- **Winders:** Tapered triangular shaped steps where the stairs turn a corner through 90 or 180 degrees.

Stairs

Stairs are a prime location for accidents in the home, and hence are one of the most rigorously enforced parts of the Building Regulations. Indeed the term *flight* of stairs is strangely appropriate, given that a dramatic headlong stair plunge is a staple feature of so many period crime thrillers.

It's therefore all the more surprising that the regulations for loft stairs are relatively relaxed. The reason for this uncharacteristically

laid-back attitude from the authorities is easily explained. If conventional stair rules applied, a large number of loft conversions would simply not be possible.

Concessions for loft stairs

Headroom
For your main stairs the regulations require a clear headroom of 2m, but as noted in Chapter 3, for loft stairs you need only achieve a reduced minimum headroom of 1.9m above the centreline of the stairs. This means that if the ceiling slopes at right angles to the stairs, the headroom on the lowest side can be just 1.8m – it only needs to be 2m on the highest side.

In some older properties where the main stairs were built with relatively low headroom (such as some 1930s semis and period cottages) Building Control may accept the argument that the loft staircase should be 'no worse than' the existing stairs.

Stair width
Normally 800mm is the minimum acceptable stair width, but for loft stairs serving one habitable room 600mm would constitute a reasonable minimum width, although 800mm is preferred. Where you have tapered corner treads ('winders'), they must have 50mm minimum tread width at the narrow inner end, and the centre of each 'going' must be to the same depth as those on the straight.

Space-saver stairs
In some houses it simply isn't possible to find space for a conventional flight of stairs to serve the new loft room. Fortunately, you should be permitted to fit special space-saver stairs where you can prove that it would be impossible to accommodate a conventional staircase. But these can only be used to serve one habitable room (which includes a new loft bedroom with an en suite bathroom).

Conventional stairs – the rules
- **Pitch** – No steeper than 42°.
- **Headroom** – Measured vertically above each step, you need a minimum clearance of 2m (across the full width).
- **Goings** – No smaller than 220mm deep.
- **Risers** – No higher than 220mm.
- **Winders** – Must be 50mm deep at their narrowest inner end, and no less than 220mm at the centre.
- **Handrails** – Only essential on one side, but to a minimum height of 900mm (measured from the pitch line up the stairs). At landings, handrails must also be minimum 900mm high.
- **Balusters** – The gap between spindles must not exceed 90mm.

Space-saver stairs must have handrails on both sides and can only be used as straight flights, *ie* without bends. There are two main types – alternating tread stairs (ATS) such as paddle stairs, and fixed ladders (FL). Note, however, that retractable loft ladders are *not* acceptable. The advantage of space-saver stairs is, of course, their compact size. Their main disadvantage is that they may not be safe for young children or oldies – plus any clinically obese or less agile citizens in the household may struggle to negotiate the steep incline.

Landings
There's something about the terminology of stairs that hints of danger, such as with the word *landing*. And where

Going up - paddle stairs

Compact stairs

Landing at base of loft stairs (within lobby with fire doors)

New landing and lobby at top of loft stairs

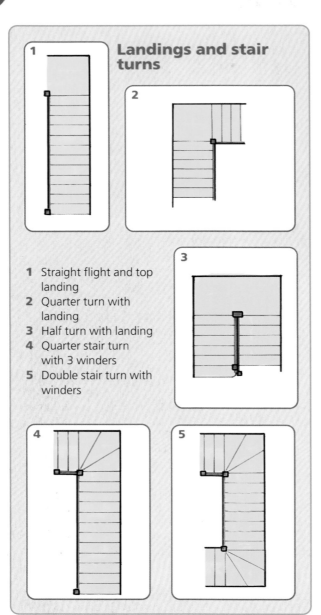

Landings and stair turns

1 Straight flight and top landing
2 Quarter turn with landing
3 Half turn with landing
4 Quarter stair turn with 3 winders
5 Double stair turn with winders

Mezzanine landing

Photo: Wooden Hill

Where stairs change direction, you have two choices. First, you can opt for either conventional flat landings, or stair turns with winders. Second, they can be positioned at the top or the bottom of a flight of stairs, or both. To be really different you could have a landing halfway up. But as a general rule, changes of direction are best made at the bottom of the stairs – simply because there are fewer accidents that way. Sometimes the word 'dogleg' is used to describe turns in stairs. This simply means 'a sharp bend or angle' such as a 90° turn.

Stair crazy

Although you can buy ready-made stairs 'off the peg', these are best suited to newbuild projects which are designed and built to standard sizes. Loft conversions, in contrast, are custom-built projects, often with curious dimensions, so it's unlikely you'll be able to just pop a flight of pre-manufactured stairs straight in. Although the stairs are one of the more complex pieces of joinery in the house, it should be fairly easy for a good joiner to build them in situ – in which case you might want to include some design features that match the age of the house, such as Art Deco motifs for 1930s houses, or for 1970s properties how about 'open risers' that you can see straight through? Or perhaps something super-modern in brushed steel and glass? Specialist manufacturers can custom-build stairs to your dimensions although it's preferable for such firms to take their own measurements – so that you can't be blamed if they turn

there's any risk of danger, the Building Regulations a re there to soften the potential blow. Stair landings therefore need to comply with some good common-sense safety rules.

For obvious reasons, you can't have doors that recklessly swing open directly onto a landing. However, a door is allowed to swing across those at the bottom of a flight of stairs if it leaves a clear space of at least 400mm when open.

You also can't have a doorway that joins straight onto a flight of stairs without a landing – a surprisingly common design error when building side extensions. In terms of size, landings must be at least as wide as the stairs. So if the stairs are 800mm wide, the space at the top and bottom should be a minimum of 800 x 800mm.

New spiral stairs in Victorian house above main staircase

Types of loft stairs

Spiral stairs – not exclusive to lofts, but spiral stairs can add a sense of style and permit access centrally in a room.

Alternating tread 'paddle stairs'

Loft ladder stairs

out not to be 100 per cent accurate! But for anything custom built, always check that scheduled delivery dates aren't so far in the future that global warming will by then have consumed the planet.

Fitting the stairs

Fitting the stairs is potentially one of the most problematic aspects of a loft conversion. If it turns out that the stairs don't quite fit you can, of course, shave a tiny bit off here and there, but because all the risers must be of equal height, including the top and bottom ones, we're only talking in terms of a couple of millimetres. The safest approach is to fit all the new floor joists and trimmers to the loft before finalising that crucial measurement from the floor surface below to the new floor surface in the loft room. However, even at this stage the new floorboards may not have been laid and it's essential to allow for them (typically 22mm thick) when measuring, plus any subsequent laminate flooring etc.

When fitting a typical straight flight, the inner side will be fixed against a wall. The outer side ('string') terminates

at newel posts to the top and bottom. These posts are in turn fixed to the floor joists, or to the trimmer timbers that butt across the ends of the cut floor joists. The inside string is screwed or bolted into the wall, and at the top is fixed to the trimmer timber at the new loft floor landing. Normally the stairs are designed to enter the new loft room parallel to the joists, so as to minimise the amount of cutting and trimming of floor joists.

Obviously, headroom is a major factor with loft stairs, and one thing that sometimes gets overlooked – especially in period properties – is the presence of projecting, head-banging ceiling beams. Another limiting factor that can sometimes cause last-minute surprises is the extent that the headroom is reduced due to the thickness of insulation and plasterboard that has to be applied under the rafters, although this should be shown on the plans. One possible solution, if stair headroom is very tight, is for a small skylight to be placed at a key point in the roof. This can provide valuable extra clearance of around 50mm, which could make all the difference. But even here there are potential dangers. To prevent any risk of decapitation, best opt for the outer-opening top-hung variety, rather that central-pivot 'swing-down' roof windows.

Partition walls

Once the loft is weatherproof and all the structural work is complete, you can at last begin to focus on how you want the finished space to look. Partition walls are likely to be required where the new accommodation is going to be subdivided to provide more than one room, for example a bedroom with an en suite shower/WC. Also, in many cases partitions are needed to separate the loft room from the new upper landing lobby at the top of the stairs, or as firewalls encasing the loft stairs. Either way, before the electrician and plumber can do their stuff the walls will need to be erected. These are normally framed in 100 x 50mm timber studwork which is then clad in plasterboard once the first fix electrics and plumbing have been installed.

Fire precautions

The easiest way for a fire to spread from one floor to another is always via the path of least resistance – in other words, up the stairs. So to prolong precious escape time in an emergency, loft stairs need to be protected from fire and smoke. If you're simply adding a flight of new stairs above the existing ones, then they should already lie within the 'protected stairway' zone, safeguarded by fire doors to the rooms off the landing and hall. But in some cases new loft stairs may need to be directly enclosed by constructing fire-resistant walls either side, forming a protective compartment around the stairs. To provide the necessary 30 minutes' fire resistance these walls are normally built from timber studwork with a layer of special pink-coloured 12.5mm fire-board (or a double layer of ordinary 12.5mm plasterboard), which is then given a skim plaster finish. In such cases a fire door with minimum 20 minutes' fire-

Front roof window provides natural light to lower stairs. Rear box dormer provides headroom and natural light to landing

resistance needs to be installed either at the bottom, as you approach the stairs, or to a new landing at the top.

Similarly, if there's an open-plan living room on the ground floor of your house, without a separate entrance hall, then a new fire-resistant partition wall will most likely be required to form the necessary protected escape corridor leading out to the final exit door, as described in Chapter 4. Although this will inevitably shrink the size of the living room it's an essential part of the loft conversion process, unless, of course, Building Control have accepted a suitable alternative, such as a sprinkler system. At this point it's not unknown for less scrupulous builders to advise clients to 'pull a fast one', and the new partition walls mysteriously disappear directly the Building Control Officer has stepped out of the building! But there's a massive assumption being made with this dodge. Further spot visits are always a possibility. Even a drive-by inspection can give the game away, and there's no way that the all-important completion certificate will be forthcoming without such mandatory safety measures in place. Also, one fine day when you come to sell the house the surveyor or solicitor should point out the potential seriousness of this non-compliance to their client, something guaranteed to frighten off all but the most flame-proof of buyers. But above all, removal of a firewall means gambling with the dreadful prospect of loved ones suffering horrific burns or a gruesome death by asphyxiation or incineration trapped in a raging house-fire.

New enclosed loft staircase with fire door at bottom. Discreet raised roof window creates extra headroom

Stud partitions

The position of any loft-room partition walls will have been considered in some detail at the design stage. The engineer may have concluded that to support such extra loadings, the new floor joists underneath the walls should be strengthened by being doubled up.

Keeping the weight down is an important factor in many loft conversions, which is why the internal walls are built exclusively in lightweight timber studwork rather than concrete blockwork. However, a modern alternative favoured by mainstream housing developers is the use of metal frame partitions. Once clad with plasterboard it's hard to tell the difference, except that the metal variety are usually thinner (and magnets stick to them!).

If you have an eye for interior design, at this stage you might want to 'sex up' your internal walls with a little glamour, perhaps in the form of a few glass blocks. These are best encased in a surrounding timber framework within the wall. Just one or two strategically placed blocks can do wonders to brighten an otherwise plain bathroom or bedroom.

Once the framework for the stud walls is complete, the door linings can then be fixed in place – see below. The wall is then left to await any cables and pipework before being plasterboarded and skimmed. (See Chapter 13).

One drawback with stud walls is the potential problem of sound transmission, which may be an issue with bathroom walls. Fortunately it's a simple task to fill the

hollow cavities between the studs with thick sound-deadening quilt to boost their insulation qualities. If noise is a serious concern, special acoustic boarding can be fitted in place of ordinary plasterboard.

Purlin walls and eaves storage

As we saw earlier, studwork purlin walls look rather like a ladder resting on its side propping up the rafters (hence their alternative name of ladder walls). In most cases purlin walls form a key part of the new roof structure, taking roof loadings down to new beams at floor level. But in some cases they may not be load-bearing, for example where the engineers specified independent new beams at purlin level.

If they haven't been built already, these short 'knee walls' around the edge of the room are needed to create the eaves storage cupboards. This is space that would

otherwise be wasted. Dark recesses with ultra-low sloping ceilings are of very little use except for storage. As noted in the next chapter, they're also very useful for channelling air for roof ventilation, so the walls must be fully insulated. These spaces will be in great demand as a home for all the stuff that used to clutter up the loft! Indeed, you may have already reserved some of the space to relocate water tanks and pipework.

Some key points to consider when finishing the purlin walls include fitting the insulation, deciding on the number of access doors, and remembering to board the floors.

Door linings

Openings left in internal walls for doors will need door liners to be fitted. These are simple planks of wood, rather than the purpose-made doorframes used for external doors. The linings consist of two side jambs and a head, and are normally installed before the walls are plasterboarded. Linings have traditionally comprised handy leftover floorboards, but today ready-assembled kits are available in differing sizes to fit walls of varying widths. Door liners are deliberately wider than the studwork in the walls in order to accommodate the depth of plasterboard and plaster. They're typically made from 130 x 30mm planed softwood for installation against 100mm-thick internal walls, but where the walls are thinner, say 75mm, 105 x 30mm liners may be used. Timber liners are easy to fit to stud partition walls since they're screwed or nailed directly to the timber subframe. The screws should be fitted in pairs to prevent frames from twisting as doors are opened and closed.

NB: Fire doors may need a special frame – see 'Fire doors' in Chapters 4 and 13.

Building a timber stud wall

Stud partition walls are normally built from 100 x 50mm (4 x 2in) softwood sawn timber.

1 First you need to mark out the wall's position by drawing lines on the ceiling and floor. Horizontal timbers can then be fixed along the lines to form the header plate and base plate respectively (a.k.a. the top plate and soleplate). Nail through the floorboards into the joists. Fixing to concrete floors is done with screws and plugs.

2 Fixing should be fairly straightforward if your new wall runs at right angles to the floor joists. If it runs the same way as the joists, then unless it's directly above a joist you'll need to provide extra support for the base plate in the form of strips of timber noggins (minimum of 50 x 38mm) between the joists. The same applies at the top, at ceiling level.

3 Next the vertical timber studs are fixed in place, normally at 400mm, 450mm or 600mm centres. The

precise spacing should match the size of plasterboard used. Standard plasterboard sheets are imported from North America and have imperial dimensions (8 x 4ft or 6 x 3ft), so the studs should be placed to allow the boards to join over a timber stud.

4 For added strength you need to fit at least one row of horizontal noggins, between the main vertical studs at about half height, which also provides an essential fixing point for the plasterboard sheets. When constructing the frame, skew-nailing – *ie* with the nails hammered in at an angle – is the quickest method of joining the various pieces. For the less experienced, it often helps to drill a pilot hole first.

5 If you know you'll later need to hang stuff off this wall, such as radiators, towel rails or toilet cisterns, or you need to fix sockets or pictures, now's the time to fit extra rows of noggins at the appropriate height so that you'll have something meaty to drill into. Alternatively, clad the walls with a plywood sheet before plasterboarding.

Fitting doorstops to the liners is normally left until the doors are hung, nearer completion. Remember that door linings are decorative surfaces that will be visible in the finished room, so they need protection from damage, especially if they're to be varnished or stained.

The next step

Right now you're probably standing on some temporary plywood sheeting laid over the bare floor joists. Hopefully, this decking will be securely fixed in place and perfectly steady.

There are two good reasons why you might decide to leave installing the proper floorboards until the final stages. First, because any necessary pipework for bathrooms or radiators, and any cables for power and lighting, first need to be run. And second, if your loft room is going to boast a splendid and expensive varnished wood flooring it'll look a whole lot better if it doesn't get sprayed with paint and plaster or scarred by power tools.

On the other hand, it may well be possible to run all the pipes and cables through the eaves cupboards, and the lighting cables through the new mini-loft. In which case it may suit you to crack on with the flooring now, making very sure that the surface of the new floorboards is well protected with temporary sheeting.

Instant protected stairway

Existing stairs open to living room, and face towards the front-door entrance lobby.

New door opening formed in entrance lobby stud wall.

New studwork wall encloses stairs and creates new hallway.

View from entrance lobby, showing new doorway.

Looking down.

FIRST FIX: ELECTRICS AND PLUMBING

Photo: Velux

Photo: Boundary bathrooms

The time is now right for 'first fix'. This means routing all the electrical cables for power and lighting through the loft room's timber skeleton while it's is still exposed. If your new accommodation includes a bathroom, the pipes supplying hot and cold water will also need to be tucked away behind wall and floor surfaces, along with the waste pipes and those for radiators.

Don't be too alarmed if at the end of first fix the job appears incomplete, with lots of cables and pipe tails poking forlornly out of the walls. As the name implies, a 'second fix' will later take place once all the new pipe and cable runs are safely concealed behind sheets of plasterboard.

In the meantime there may come an unwelcome surprise from elsewhere in the house. It's not unusual at this point to discover that your existing electrics and heating systems are, frankly, getting a bit past it. At best, they'd struggle to cope with the extra demand imposed by the additional loft accommodation. Such unanticipated upgrading of old systems is always fertile ground for builders seeking profitable 'extras'.

Loft conversions normally lend themselves to first fixing without too much anguish, thanks to easily accessible spaces behind eaves cupboards and new mini ceilings. It's important to note that although pipes and cables can be run next to stud walls and through floor joists, the roof rafters must not normally be cut or drilled.

Electrics

Unless you've already provided a set of drawings showing exactly where you want your new switches, sockets and light fittings, the electrician will most likely do it the easiest way.

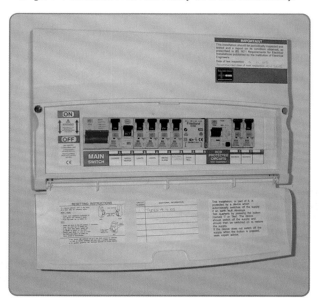

Photo: EGLO

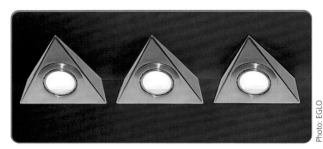

Photo: EGLO

Although a lot of electrical work isn't particularly difficult, this is not really an area for the DIY enthusiast, unless you know exactly what you're doing. Anything with a risk of death attached isn't normally worth saving a few quid over. Although much DIY electrical work is now restricted under Part P of the Building Regulations, a non-qualified person can still carry out electrical work as long as Building Control are informed and it's officially tested upon completion.

The usual advice is 'if in any doubt, always consult a qualified electrician'. But how do you go about choosing one? First, it's essential that they're registered with an appropriate organisation, such as the ECA (Electrical Contractors Association) or NICEIC (National Inspection Council for Electrical Installation Contracting). If you're employing subcontractors directly, always get more than one quote, and make it clear that payment for the job will be subject to first receiving a test certificate upon completion.

The electrician's first job will be to route all the cables around the timber frame structure and then fix the boxes in place. He'll return later to do the second fix work, installing covers to the switches, sockets and ceiling roses once the boarding and plastering of the walls and ceilings is out of the way. The loft rooms may simply be run as a continuation of the existing ring and light circuits to the floor below, or the electrician my want to run new circuits from your consumer unit, which could involve some disruption to supplies and minor damage to décor.

If you need to add some extra power point sockets or light fittings, now is the time. Don't wait until everything is all beautifully plastered. Any special requirements must be clearly communicated, although there are limits to what you can request. Remember that the Building Regulations require that power sockets must be positioned no lower than 450mm above the floor, and light switches no higher than 1200mm from the floor, and that no sockets are allowed in bathrooms.

Lighting style

Adding some creative lighting to your loft room can be the icing on the cake, and it needn't add much to the cost. Seductive features such as discreet LEDs embedded in floors, recessed ceiling lights, wall-mounted fittings and uplighters can all make loft-living feel super-stylish. And why pick boring white switches when there's a choice of brushed aluminium, brass or chrome?

At this point you won't be surprised to discover that your new lighting not only needs to look good, it also has to be green. So in addition to conventional fixed lighting, Part L1B of the Building Regulations now requires a minimum number of energy-efficient light fittings to be installed. At least 25 per cent of all fixed lights must be of an energy efficient type – *ie* compact fluorescent lights

Photo: EGLO

(CFL rather than old GLS or tungsten halogen ones). The minimum requirement is for at least one fitting per 25m^2 of floor area in your loft. Most lofts are smaller than this,

Photo: EGLO

Photo: EGLO

but if your floor happens to be just a tiny bit larger than 25m^2 then you'll be required to fit two eco-lights. This target will inevitably increase in the next few years, so you may as well go the whole hog and fit as much green lighting as possible.

Provision of energy-efficient lighting
In relation to floor area

Floor area of loft extension (m²)	Minimum number of energy-efficient light fittings required
0–25	1
25–50	2
50–75	3
75–100	4

Provision of energy-efficient lighting
In relation to number of conventional fixed light fittings

Conventional fixed light fittings in loft extension	Minimum number of energy-efficient light fittings required
4–7	1
8–11	2
12–15	3

Photo: EGLO

How many sockets?

One of the most common complaints amongst house buyers is the discovery that there are insufficient power points for all the various PlayStations, foot spas and smoothie-makers that modern life demands. You can never have too many power points, so be generous with the DSSOs (double-switched socket outlets) in your new rooms, since the cost of adding a couple of extra ones here or there at this stage is peanuts. A typical loft room will

require at least four DSSOs plus one for landings. In bathrooms only shaver sockets are allowed, and these are run from the lighting circuit.

Running cables

Having gone to so much trouble at the design stage to carefully calculate that your loft room will be structurally safe, you don't want the floor joists to now be seriously weakened by having huge chunks hacked out of them to accommodate pipe and cable runs. Although a lot of the cabling in loft rooms can be run through eaves cupboards, you may also need to run some through floors, which means drilling holes in timber joists and feeding them through. The critical points structurally in joists are at their centres and ends, so there are strict rules about how to do this without weakening the joists:

- Holes should be drilled about halfway down the joist, at its centre.
- Don't drill near the joist ends – not within the first quarter of the joist's span from the wall.
- The size of holes should be no bigger than ⅛th of the depth of the joist.
- Don't drill holes too close together (no closer than three times the hole's diameter).

When it comes to gable walls or party walls in lofts, these are commonly plasterboarded to a timber stud framework infilled with insulation. Here, cables can be run through the timber framework, and where necessary protected behind flat steel shields or plastic conduit tubes and trunking. In walls, cables are normally fixed vertically from the outlets they supply, so that the following trades know where not to drill holes. But electric cables run within thermal insulation can be at risk of becoming overheated, and any contact with polystyrene insulation can react with and soften the PVC sleeving. If there's no other option, run them immediately next to the plasterboard rather than being totally encased within thick layers of insulation. It's also a good idea to use a higher capacity cable than necessary in the immediate area.

Smoke alarms

The biggest killer in most house fires is not incineration by flames, but being overcome by smoke. Silent, deadly smoke and fumes can engulf the average home in a few minutes, snuffing out lives in an instant. So the Building Regulations insist that this threat is taken very seriously at the design stage both in terms of early warning and safe escape.

A smoke alarm waking you up before it's too late can literally be a lifesaver. Smoke alarms must be wired to the mains (normally the lighting circuit) so that flat batteries don't render them impotent at the critical moment. The minimum requirement is for one smoke detector fitted on each storey, and the detectors interlinked (so that a solo detection in one triggers them all). In some homes, smoke alarms are found in the most bizarre locations, but correct positioning is important to prevent false alarms. To prevent sensors being obstructed they need to be more than 300mm away from light fittings, and also about 300mm away from walls, because smoke tends to avoid the corners of rooms. They should be no further than 7.5m away from the doors of habitable rooms such as bedrooms. Locate them well away from cooking areas, heaters and bathrooms, since steam and fumes can set them off.

Ventilation for occupants

In most modern houses the air that you breathe indoors is actually more polluted than the air outside the house, even in cities. Air quality is a serious health issue, especially when you consider that people may spend as much as 90 per cent of their time indoors. So your new loft room will need to be well ventilated, with musty, unhealthy atmospheres banished forever.

In the next chapter we stress the importance of fitting

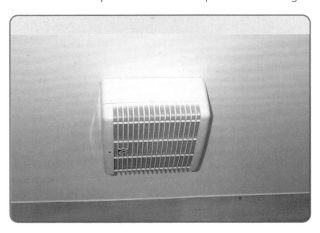

vapour barriers so that any moist air from rooms is prevented from penetrating into the timber roof and dormer wall structures where it can cause damage. But all that water vapour has to go somewhere. So instead of being trapped within the room (or forming condensation within plasterboard linings) it needs to be ventilated away, or expelled via extractor fans. By getting rid of all those litres of humid air swirling invisibly around the atmosphere of modern homes, it should be possible to prevent problems from condensation such as ugly black mould staining. There are three types of room ventilation: rapid purge, background, and extract:

■ Rapid purge ventilation might sound like something unpleasant involving the US military, but it simply means having openable windows, so that any malodorous stuffy fug can be swiftly purged from your loft. Openable windows are therefore required in all habitable rooms, such as bedrooms and living rooms. The regulations stipulate that the size of the opening part of a window (ie the casement or sash) must be at least as big as 5 per cent of the room's floor area. In some loft rooms you may have pivoted or hinged windows with their opening restricted to 30° or less, in which case the area of the opening part needs to be at

least 10 per cent of the room's floor area.
■ Background ventilation means continuous low-rate ventilation, and this is typically provided by small trickle vents in window frames, or wall ventilators. So that the room doesn't feel draughty, these need to be located at least 1.7m above floor level.

■ Extract ventilation, as the name suggests, is typically provided via extractor fans. This is required in rooms where there are high levels of water vapour or foul odours.

Wet room ventilation

Nowhere is ventilation needed more than in bathrooms. This is where steamy air from showering can do the most damage, condensing against cold surfaces such as loo cisterns and window frames, before dripping into puddles and soaking into the walls and ceilings.

Bathrooms must have minimum ventilation equivalent to 2500mm², which is easily achieved with an opening window. But then it's not always practical to provide windows for loft bathrooms where, for example, they're

Photo: Velux

designed with exclusively internal walls. So the Building Regulations require the provision of extractor fans. Bathroom fans must to be capable of shifting 15 litres of air per second, and for cloakroom/WCs the rate is 6 litres per second. If there's no opening window, fans should have an overrun of 15 minutes, which seems like a lifetime as they continue to whine irritatingly, long after you've departed.

If there's an opening window (with trickle vents), mechanical extraction is still required, but without the fan overrun.

Another drawback with fans is that they're commonly wired into the lighting circuit, so no matter how steamy it is in the daytime, such fans don't work unless you put the light on – which is fine if you bathe exclusively after dark, but not very green otherwise. Thankfully there are now 'intelligent' extractor fans with humidistats. These relatively quiet, automatic humidity-sensing fans only come on when needed, regardless of whether the light is on or not.

Electric fans mustn't be located anywhere they could be touched by someone using the bath, and they should be positioned safely away from the risk of shower spray. If the bathroom's so small that this isn't possible, consider fitting special low-voltage bathroom units.

Fans may be built into walls, with the moist air directly expelled to the outside, or they may be fitted to ceilings and linked to outdoors via a length of round, flexible concertina ducting that runs up through the eaves cupboards or loft space to a roof vent.

Plumbing

There are three main areas where plumbing supply work may be required in loft conversions: the hot and cold water to new bathroom fittings, pipework for additional radiators, and the relocation of the old water tanks. If your new loft room is going to include a new bathroom or (less commonly) a kitchen, then the existing water supplies will need to be extended. But before the first monkey wrench is removed from the tool bag it's always a good idea to discuss the desired layout of new pipes and fittings with your plumber. There will, of course, be some physical limitations as to where pipework can be run, but with a little thought you can normally agree simple solutions, perhaps saving a lot of unnecessary expense.

Photo: Quadrant hero

Unlike work to the electrics or gas appliances, the only restriction on DIY plumbing is competency. If you feel confident, there's no reason why you shouldn't carry out some of the work yourself. Installing new bathroom fittings shouldn't be too difficult. The fact that the pipework and fittings are brand new makes things a lot easier. But obviously the new system to the loft accommodation will at some point need to be joined to the existing hot and cold supplies and waste pipes. Water

Photo: Velux

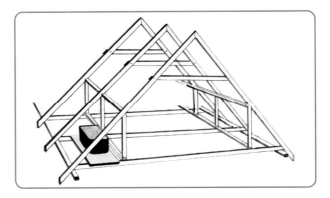

pipes run through cold spaces such as eaves cupboards should be lagged with purpose-made foam insulation wraps, which, incidentally, also help deaden the sound of rushing water.

Cutting joists

Water pipes may be surface-mounted along walls, or concealed in the new timber floor. It's worth keeping a record of the location of any hidden pipe runs in case access is required in future.

The rules for cutting notches into joists without inviting disaster are similar to those for electric cables. As noted earlier, the critical points structurally in joists are the centre and the ends and it's a good idea to fit small steel shields over the top of cut notches to protect pipes from subsequent puncturing should anyone carelessly hammer nails into floorboards.

■ Don't cut too near the joist ends – not within the first quarter of the joist's span out from the wall.
■ Don't cut notches closer than 100mm to holes drilled for cables.
■ Cut no deeper into a joist than an eighth of its total depth, *ie* about 25mm in a 200mm-deep joist.
■ Joists should always be notched from the top.

Water tanks

Back in Chapter 6 the old water tanks in the loft were moved out of the way to clear space for the new loft rooms. Since then, a temporary arrangement may have

sufficed. Now, unless you've decided to dispense with water tanks altogether and have a new Combi boiler or pressurised system installed, they'll need to be properly repositioned.

This may be a good opportunity to replace old tanks with durable plastic ones of 225 litre (50 gallon) or even a generous 330 litres capacity, especially if the old ones are more than about 30 years old and made of steel, asbestos or fibreglass.

The preferred place in which to relocate water tanks is the

new eaves cupboards around the edges of loft rooms. Bear in mind, however, that access will be needed for maintenance, so they can't simply be walled up and forgotten about. This means fitting insulated cupboard doors and at least 1m² of access boarding around each tank. Other favourite places are in cupboards above the loft stairs, or high up in the new mini-loft, if space permits. These remaining loft areas suit water tanks because the ventilation helps prevent condensation forming and causing damp.

The most critical issue of all is how to support the loadings. A full water tank can weigh about 230kg, the same as three fully-grown adults, and clearly the loft floor must be designed to handle this load. The deck should be of exterior grade plywood (rather than chipboard, which can disintegrate when damp) and needs to be placed over four thick timber bearers, which in turn should rest on at least three joists.

Any internal load-bearing walls can be used to help support loadings from tanks.

It's important to remember that the water pressure at your taps depends on the water tank being placed as high as possible above the bathroom in order to provide enough 'head'. If this isn't possible, fitting a pump can overcome such difficulties. Finally, make sure the tanks are tucked up warmly in a thick insulation jacket and have a fitted lid to keep dirt and small creatures out of your water supply.

Waste pipes

Modern plastic waste pipes should be trouble-free if properly installed. This means fitting sufficient support-clips and allowing sufficient falls – DIY plumbers sometimes forget that water runs downhill. To achieve enough height to provide a decent 'fall' on a longer run, mounting basins or shower trays a little higher can sometimes do the trick.

Internal waste pipes and fittings are of the white, plastic, push-fit variety, usually 32mm for basins or 40mm for baths, showers and sinks. External pipes are normally run in UV-resistant grey plastic.

The position of your new bathroom will have been planned very early in the design process, so that it's located as near as possible to the existing one downstairs. The reason for this is to ensure the waste pipes have a reasonably short run to join up with the existing SVP (soil and vent pipe).

The main limitation when installing loft bathrooms is the fairly short distance that you can run new waste pipes before there's a risk of siphonage. This peculiar phenomenon occurs when the 'seal' of water sitting in the U-bends of traps under basins and baths etc is literally sucked out by a deluge of outgoing waste water, creating a build-up of pressure in its slipstream. The resulting

ingress of foul odours is frequently accompanied by a cacophony of rude gurgling noises. To avoid such horrors, there's a maximum permitted length to which pipes of each diameter can be run before siphonage becomes a risk. Hence there's a maximum distance that you can safely locate your new basin, loo and bath away from the waste stack. These distances are typically 3m for baths or showers, and less than 2m for most basins. For WCs you normally have 6m to play with.

If this restriction cripples your otherwise excellent bathroom layout, it may be possible to work around the problem by fitting special 'anti-siphonage' traps or bigger-bore pipes. Or you can cheat by using non-return valves that don't need a water-sealed trap at all, such as HepVO valves.

There's another potential snag that's sometimes overlooked with loft conversions – namely, what to do about your existing SVP stench pipe. Let us explain. The stench pipe (a.k.a.

Can you smell drains? Old SVP terminates directly under new loft window

Maximum pipe lengths

	Max length	Pipe diameter	Fall
Basins	1.7m	32mm	18–90mm per metre run
Baths and showers	3m	40mm	18–90mm per metre run
Toilets	6m	110mm	10–30mm per metre run

soil stack, or soil and vent pipe) is the large vertical pipe that vents the foul drainage system. In pre-war houses they normally run up the side or back wall, terminating at roof level. In most post-war houses they're run internally and boxed in, extending up through the edge of the loft before ultimately poking out through the roof. The rule is that these stacks should extend at least 900mm above any opening window that's less than 3m away. This is so they can dissipate the 'stench' as anonymously as possible. Any lower down and the unfortunate occupants could be treated to the sweet aroma of sewer gas.

So when new windows suddenly appear at roof level within range of a malodorous vent pipe, something clearly needs to be done. The obvious solution is to raise the existing SVP higher up, well above any new windows or rooflights safely out of harm's way. But unless designed with care, this can look awkward and clumsy. Another problem is that ancient cast iron or asbestos-cement SVPs don't take kindly to being extended at their time of life, plus they're more difficult to connect into than modern plastic pipes. The worst-case scenario may mean having to fork out to replace your old SVP with a new plastic one.

Where a standard-sized 110mm SVP is obstructed, for example by new beams or dormers getting in the way, then it should be permissible for the upper part of the SVP diameter to be reduced to 50mm to help negotiate the restricted areas.

If it's not possible to connect to the existing stack, an air admittance valve (or 'Durgo valve') may be acceptable internally, but this needs to first be approved by Building Control. Unlike SVPs these aren't permanently open. Instead, they're capped with a rubber diaphragm that opens automatically to relieve pressure, admitting air into the system before sealing closed again, thereby relieving excess pressure without emitting odours. Because no unpleasant smells are emitted, they don't need to terminate way up above roof level, and instead can be neatly boxed in within the eaves cupboards.

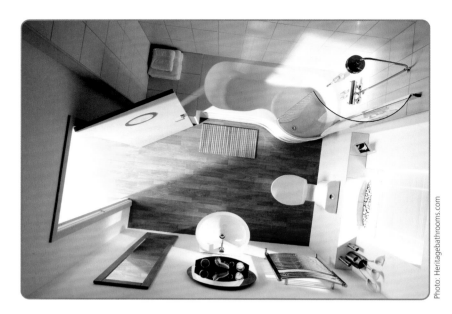

Photo: Heritagebathrooms.com

WCs

For those who crave a new loo located on the far side of the house, well away from the existing waste

plumbing, there's an alternative solution that can offer complete toilet freedom. With this handy device, the frustration of trying to fit within the limitations of the existing waste pipes can be safely ignored – by using a 'macerator'. These devices apply technology to toilets by mashing up the waste into a liquid so that it can be pumped out through narrow-bore 32mm or 40mm pipes rather than requiring the normal cumbersome short-range 110mm WC pipes. When you flush a macerator WC, you may notice a curious and slightly off-putting whirring sound. This is because macerators rely on electric power to do the crucial pumping. The snag is, in the event of a power cut they're totally unserviceable, which means you're not allowed to rely on them exclusively. A home must have at least one conventional loo. The regulations also require that for every new WC you must also fit a nearby washbasin with a supply of hot and cold water.

Photo: Quad Sphere

Photo: Manhatten Quad

Showers

Photo: Bow Tribeca

Showers are widely installed in en suite loft bathrooms in lieu of baths. But before acquiring the world's cheapest possible shower cubicle on eBay, it's worth bearing in mind that surveyors widely regard shower trays with the utmost suspicion. This is because, over the years, there's a very good chance that water will get down the seals at the edges of the tray, or else will infiltrate the wall tiling. Which is why it's advisable to tile onto a marine plywood or 'aquaboard' base rather than ordinary plasterboard. The worst offending trays are thin acrylic ones, which can be prone to flexing and distortion, especially when new timber floor joists start to shrink. Ceramic or stonecast trays are preferable. Or, best of all, take no chances and fit a modern all-in-one moulded cubicle. But whichever type you choose, it's important to build in an access point underneath so that the trap can be cleared.

Alternatively, you could dispense with the tray altogether and build an exotic 'wet room' with a drain fitted inside the floor void (which must be able to cope with a flow of 30 litres per minute). Here, the floor needs to be waterproof, and slope inward towards the drain at a fall of about 1:40 for a distance of 1m around it. What this means in reality is that timber floors need to be built up in

order to provide a 25mm central depression. It has to be said however that putting a wet room at the top of your house may not be a great idea. Unless very carefully fitted and maintained, wet rooms are generally best confined to the ground floor.

Unlike other sanitary fittings, showers need to be thermostatically controlled. The water temperature is adjusted automatically, preventing unwitting shower-users suddenly getting scalded with super-hot water because someone else has just run a nearby cold tap and unintentionally upset the mix.

Showers also need a consistently powerful water supply, for which modern mains pressure hot-water systems are ideally suited. Otherwise the flow rate of existing water supplies may need to be beefed up by fitting powerful pumps. It's also often necessary to install a separate cold supply direct to the shower from the cold-water tank.

Heating and hot water

Boilers

It's estimated that as many as a third of all loft conversions result in boilers being replaced, because adding extra radiators to a creaky old heating system can be the straw that breaks the camel's back.

As a rough guide, depending on how they're maintained, boilers may last no more than around 20 years, considerably less for some combination boilers. So renewal may be overdue anyway.

Boilers are rated according to the power they produce, measured in BTUs

Photo: MHS classico

(British Thermal Units). As a rule of thumb, a 40,000 BTU boiler should be capable of heating at least seven radiators, as well as producing hot water. But you need to carry out a heat calculation for the whole house to determine how much boiler power is needed.

Even when the existing boiler is retained, the controls should be upgraded to comply with minimum standards. A system with modern controls can be up to 30 per cent cheaper to run, thanks largely to programmable thermostats that raise or lower temperatures at pre-set times. Replacing old valves with modern thermostatic radiator valves (TRVs) can make a big difference, and is a reasonably straightforward DIY job.

By law, all new boilers must be of a high-efficiency condensing type. Only CORGI-registered engineers are permitted to install gas boilers, or OFTEC-registered for oil-fired systems. If you're having a new boiler installed you may want to consider fitting a combination type. Combis currently account for half of all UK boiler sales. The great thing about them is that they're very efficient at providing endless hot water instantly, as well as taking care of your space heating requirements. They're bulkier than ordinary boilers since they contain a built-in hot-water vessel, but the need for separate water tanks and cylinders is dispensed with, as well as all the costly associated plumbing. So although dearer to buy, they're cheaper and easier to install. Their limitations have traditionally been their low flow rates, so look for ones than can achieve more than 1.5 litres per minute.

Boilers are awarded energy efficiency ratings, from A (90–94 per cent efficient) to G (50–70 per cent efficient). But as well as running costs, reliability is probably the single most important factor. The choice of available brands and models should be discussed with the contractor early on in the project, otherwise you may get lumbered with some obscure make for which spare parts are scarce.

Central heating
By now you've probably already mulled over at some length where all the furniture is going to be positioned

once the new loft space is finally habitable. But such well-laid plans could be ruined when you discover that someone's stuck a bulky radiator in just the wrong place. The moral is, unless you provide the plumber with a clear set of drawings showing exactly where you want your radiators positioned, they'll probably get bunched back-to-back on internal walls, to save on pipework.

Conventional central heating (CH) systems work by pumping hot water from the boiler to radiators in each room, via pipework which comprises separate parallel 'flow and return' circuits, usually in 15mm or 8mm copper or plastic pipes. The 'flow' circuit feeds the hot water to each radiator and the 'return' circuit takes the cooler used water back to the boiler. The pipework can either be surface-run along the walls and boxed in, or else concealed within the floor space. Pipework should be supported with a clip at least every 1.4m and at each change of direction, because poorly supported pipes can make irritating noises as well as being prone to damage.

Before installing radiators you need to calculate what size is required to provide sufficient heat in each room. As with boilers, radiator output is measured in BTUs, calculated according to the size of each room and its level of insulation. For optimum room warmth, the best position for radiators is normally under windows, since this is often the point where the room is coldest. For bathrooms, a radiator towel rail is a useful addition.

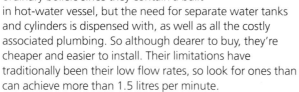

Photo: Boundary bathrooms

The majority of new homes built today have pressurised sealed CH systems such as Megaflo or Vantage. Because there are no loft tanks for emergency expansion they're referred to as 'unvented' systems, and any expansion is instead taken by a vessel connected to the hot water cylinder, which is capable of storing hot water at mains pressure.

In areas without a gas supply electric heating is quite common, typically comprising fixed storage heaters. These take down cheaper off-peak electricity at night, store it in special bricks and release the heat the next day. But electric heating is not only the most expensive system to run, it is also the least controllable and the biggest CO_2 emitter. However, despite the higher running costs, given the relative ease of installation it can often make sense to fit it in smaller, highly insulated rooms – such as loft accommodation.

Designer rads

Adding new radiators to your loft space could present an exciting opportunity to splash out on some seriously cool design. Modern designer radiators can provide a focal point to an otherwise neutral room if you're willing to invest a little more money than for a bog standard white panel rad. For the style conscious, the sky's the limit, with

Photo: Boundary bathrooms

all kinds of fun shapes to choose from, such as 'gnarled tree stump' sculptural steel radiators, or perhaps a stunning multi-column vertical tube design.

But expensive 'arty' rads are less efficient than the conventional panel variety with fins that vastly increase the surface area for giving off heat, and they therefore need to be larger, which may not be ideal if space is limited in your loft room.

If, instead, you hanker after a charming period piece, salvaged radiators are an option, but they may not be easily compatible with modern pipework. Reclaimed school radiators are popular, costing from a couple of hundred pounds, but they tend to be bulky and extraordinarily heavy, so make sure your floorboards can take the weight.

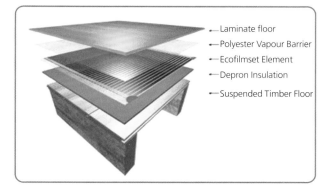

- Laminate floor
- Polyester Vapour Barrier
- Ecofilmset Element
- Depron Insulation
- Suspended Timber Floor

Underfloor heating

Although underfloor heating (UFH) is currently very popular, it's generally better suited to ground floors, where it can provide consistent background heat. There are two types: wet systems, which use warm water pumped at low pressure through concealed pipework within the floor; and dry systems, which use electric heating elements such as ultra-thin flexible mats, which can be laid directly under new floor coverings.

For a typical loft conversion, electric mats might be suitable to take the chill off cold stone or tile floors in en suite bathrooms. But a possible problem with UFH in loft rooms is its slow response time – a wooden floor can take well over 30 minutes to warm up or cool down. Wet systems tend to be relatively expensive to install over small floor areas, plus, of course, timber acts as a heat insulator. So to boost the upward transfer of heat through the floorboards into the room, special aluminium diffusion plates need to be fitted underneath, significantly adding to the cost.

Photo: Loft shop

Photo: EGLO

12 ENERGY CONSERVATION

Photo: H+H Celcon Ltd

Photo: Charles Grosvenor

The second most common complaint about new loft rooms is that they're uncomfortably hot (the main gripe being low ceiling heights). This isn't entirely surprising because warm air from inside the house will tend to rise up, accumulating in the top floor. And in the summer months, attic rooms can easily overheat as a result of direct solar gain passing through the roof structure. With large expanses of roof tiles baking in the sun on either side, you're effectively sandwiched within a potential hothouse. Adding glazing may only serve to increase the greenhouse effect further.

Like conservatories, loft rooms can suffer from cold in winter and stifling heat in summer. But unlike conservatories, such problems in lofts can be designed out, by making sure your loft is energy-efficient and well-insulated. Adding insulation is essential to combating such problems.

Fitting the latest energy-saving materials should not only keep your room temperatures comfortable, but will also boost the 'miles per gallon' factor of your home, shrinking fuel bills by achieving minimal heat loss. This has been demonstrated in Scandinavia, where super-highly insulated houses have been shown to require minimal heating, despite the sub-zero weather outside. So if you

want a loft that's warm in winter and pleasantly cool in summer, read on.

In actual practice, you have no choice but to make your new loft energy-efficient, since preventing heat loss is now a major concern of the Building Regulations. By the time your new loft room is finished it may very well end up being the most highly insulated part of the entire house, benefiting the rest of your home by stemming leakage of heat through the roof. Even historic Listed Buildings and properties in Conservation Areas are only exempt from energy efficiency requirements where compliance would 'unacceptably alter the building's character or appearance' – which is unlikely to be a problem when you're insulating the inside of a loft space. So when Building Control throw the energy conservation book at you, take a look at the title as it whizzes past. It's called Approved Document L1B.

Keeping warm

Creating a nice new room in your loft is all very well, but unless done properly it could leak large amounts of heat through the roof and cause some nasty

Photo: South London Lofts

Where are you leaking heat?

The main offenders when it comes to heat leakage through the different elements of a typical home's 'thermal envelope' are:

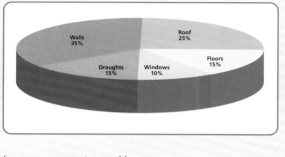

Walls 35%
Roof 25%
Floors 15%
Draughts 15%
Windows 10%

(source www.cat.org.uk)

condensation problems into the bargain. Before the loft was converted, a layer of insulation quilt laid above the bedroom ceilings would have separated you from the cold loft space above. Now however, this first line of defence will need to be moved upwards, so it's literally packed right up to the rafters.

To ram home the importance of energy conservation, homes now require an energy performance certificate when they're sold or rented. This means your home will be officially labelled as anything from an excellent Energy Rating 'A' down to an embarrassingly chilly 'G'. So when, one day in the future, you come to sell your beautifully converted home, the highly insulated new loft may drag the old house into a higher performance bracket – something likely to please potential purchasers.

The Building Regulations are very hot on the subject of insulation. This is explained in terms of 'U-values', which show how much heat is allowed to escape from different parts of the property. The larger the number, the more heat can be lost. So if, for example, the walls have a stated U-value of 0.30 W/m2K it means 0.30 Watts is the maximum amount of heat permitted to pass through each square metre of wall (technically, that's for every degree Kelvin of temperature difference between the inner and outer surfaces of the wall). Conversely, the lower the U-value, the better insulated the structure is. For example, a wall with a U-value of only 0.5 will leak heat half as fast as a wall with a higher U-value of 1.0.

Just to make things more confusing, when you pop out to buy the individual materials to construct, for example, a wall or roof, they're often labelled in terms of their thermal resistance, known as 'R'. The more they resist the passage of heat the better, so materials with higher R-numbers are better insulators. If you add together all the R-numbers of the various components, such as tiles, blocks and plasterboard, it will give the total resistance of that wall or roof. Cavities or air gaps within the structure will help increase the total R-number further, since they boost the overall resistance. Finally, to translate this into the all-important U-value for the whole element, you take the number 1 and divide it by your total R-number. So the larger your total R-number, the smaller the U-value will be.

Thermal elements

The Building Regulations describe buildings in terms of their 'thermal envelope'. This basically means all the major elements that can leak heat, such as the main walls, windows, roof and ground floor. Each of these thermal elements is given a target for the maximum amount of heat they're allowed to lose.

So when you replace a thermal element, such as the roof or the windows, by law it must be carried out to meet the performance standards, specified in U-values, shown in Document L1B.

Should you find it impossible to meet one of the target values, fear not. You may be able to trade-off a reduced level of insulation in one element, such as the roof, in return for a higher level elsewhere, for instance by fitting high-performance glazing. Or you may be allowed to fit less insulation in exchange for fitting a more efficient boiler. This is normally acceptable as long as you can still meet a relatively undemanding low minimum threshold U-value in each element.

Obviously it's going to be a lot easier achieving super-high insulation standards if you're building a new house from scratch, rather than renovating an ancient dwelling. Which is why there are a number of exemptions to the rules when refurbishing property – for example, where the cost of insulating wouldn't pay back financially within 15 years, or where sticking lots of bulky insulation on the walls would decrease a room's floor area by more than 5 per cent.

Different standards
There are different standards you need to meet depending on whether you're building something completely new, or retaining an original part of the house.

If your loft conversion is fairly straightforward, where the original roof remains intact apart from, say, a couple of discreet roof windows, then it would come under the 'retained' standard. Except, of course, for the windows, which are new.

But there's one little sting in the tail of Document L1B. Where more than 25 per cent of the surface area of an element, such as a roof, is being renovated, then you'll have to upgrade the whole of that element to meet 'retained' U-value standards. But then, you were planning to insulate the whole roof anyway, so in most cases it shouldn't make too much difference.

Picking your energy targets

Newbuild
Not surprisingly, new construction will demand the highest thermal standards. In a typical loft conversion this would apply to new dormers, or where you've converted the old hip with a new upper gable wall. Specifically, the new thermal elements in a dormer would include:

New dormer walls	U-value 0.30
New dormer roof	U-value 0.20
New windows	U-value 0.35
New French windows	U-value 2.20
	(a 'controlled fitting')

Retained/renovated
In most loft rooms the existing gable end walls and roof slopes will become part of your home's thermal envelope. Fortunately, the Regulations recognise that there are difficulties improving existing buildings, so upgrading only needs to be carried out if it's technically and economically feasible. Typical retained elements in a loft conversion would include:

Existing roof slope	U-value 0.20
Existing side wall	U-value 0.35

Replacement
This is unlikely to apply to most loft conversions. This is where an existing component is replaced with a new one that's the same, like-for-like; for instance, where you completely remove an original roof slope and replace it with an identical new element in the same position.

Insulation materials

	Conductivity
PIR (poly-iso-cyanurate) – foil-faced	0.017
PF (phenolic foam) – foil-faced	0.020
PIR (poly-iso-cyanurate)	0.021
PU (polyurethane) with pentane – foil-faced	0.021
PF (phenolic foam)	0.025
PU (polyurethane) with pentane	0.027
Extruded polystyrene (XPS) with CO2	0.033
PU (polyurethane) with CO2	0.035

Types of insulation

The world of thermal insulation has advanced light years since large itchy rolls of glass fibre or mineral wool represented the peak of sophistication. Today highly-efficient rigid foam insulation boards are routinely installed, with specific types designed for use in walls, roofs and floors. The key objective of insulation manufacturers is to supply products that can achieve maximum performance standards whilst keeping the thickness of the insulation to a minimum. And of course, nowhere is this more essential than in cramped loft spaces.

The three most common types of rigid insulation boards are polyurethane (PUR), phenolic foam (PF) and poly-iso-cyanurate (PIR).

These materials are all widely used to insulate attic rooms, and can be applied both to the roof slopes at the rafters, and to flat roofs. Traditional white expanded polystyrene (EPS) boards are only half as efficient as these modern alternatives, which means you would need at least twice the thickness for the same result. Consequently they're considered too bulky for rafter insulation, but are sometimes still used on flat roofs where there's more space.

Manufacturers often quote performance standards in terms of 'heat conductivity values'. The lower the conductivity figure, the better it is, and the less thickness you need. Boards that are foil-faced on both sides are the most efficient. Manufacturers can normally advise on the required thickness for specific locations to meet target U-values.

Perhaps the best-known UK insulation manufacturers are Celotex and Kingspan. Their boards are available in a range of thicknesses, typically from 20 to 70mm. Thicker 'all in one' composite sheets of insulated plasterboard are also available incorporating 12.5mm plasterboard and a vapour barrier. Rigid sheet board sizes are commonly supplied as 2400 x 1200mm.

Multifoils

There is another, more controversial, type of insulation on the market – 'multifoil'. These are shiny 'radiant heat barrier' sheets, supplied in large rolls looking like a thin hi-tech sandwich of Bacofoil and Kleenex. At only 30mm thickness (when not compressed) they can provide the equivalent of 210mm traditional loft quilt insulation. The best known brand is the Tri-Iso Super range made by the French company Actis.

Despite being relatively expensive, multifoils were becoming widely used for new roof construction until the NHBC and some Local Authority Building Control Departments recently declined their use due to doubts

about performance on-site matching the standards claimed by the manufacturers. However, at the time of writing some Building Control bodies still accept them.

The reason this is of interest to loft-converters is that multifoils are also suitable for refurbishment projects, their space-saving qualities making them potentially very attractive. They can be fitted to the underside of rafters to existing roofs, while in newly constructed areas such as dormer roofs they're normally laid above the rafters. A 30mm layer is claimed to increase thermal efficiency to an amazingly low U-value of 0.19. But in reality it's only likely to be accepted in tandem with foam boards, a mixed solution for which there's a strong technical argument. But because of the current regulatory uncertainty it's essential to get this approved at the design stage.

Multifoils work by reflecting the heat of rooms back inside whilst also reflecting away incoming solar radiation from outside, thereby significantly reducing summer overheating and winter heat-loss. They can achieve excellent air tightness, which is important in attic roofs, but to work efficiently they need an air space either side, to a minimum of 20mm, which in effect can limit their space-saving potential. For installation, see the section on 'Pitched roofs' below.

Condensation

Apart from stopping heat leaking out, there's one other major challenge your new loft accommodation will need to address. Creating a room in the roof means there'll now potentially be lots of moist air from the new living space that's free to escape into the roof structure, where it can condense into harmful damp. So to protect your roof timbers a dual strategy is required: vapour check, and ventilation. On the inside, a vapour control layer will limit the passage of any water vapour entering the roof from the new loft room. So once your insulation is in place, a polythene sheet can be fixed to the room-side surface of the insulation (the 'warm side') before plasterboarding. Alternatively, foil-lined plasterboard or special foil-faced insulation boards can be used, as the reflective silver foil serves the same purpose.

But in case any moist air does get through, either from inside or outside, your roof design must incorporate ventilation to swiftly disperse it.

Ventilation

With so much insulation material being installed, it's easy to forget that lofts were originally designed to be draughty and well ventilated, so that any damp from rain or condensation could easily evaporate away. Such cold roof spaces are traditionally sealed from bedrooms down below with thick layers of loft insulation laid above the ceilings. This arrangement describes a typical empty loft, and is known as a 'cold roof'. But as soon as you build a room in your loft, the insulation barrier needs to be moved upwards to roof level, along with the new ceiling and must include an air space for ventilation. Failure to provide adequate ventilation can lead to dampness becoming trapped in the timbers, causing outbreaks of rot.

So, before fitting any insulation, a 50mm air space must be left directly below the underfelted roof tiles (or, in older roofs without any underfelt, directly below the tiles and battens). This ventilation path will allow any moisture-laden air to safely ventilate away before it can condense and cause dampness. To separate you from the cold, thick insulation boards are then wedged between the rafters, so that the outer face is the 'cold side'. But what's to stop these insulation boards, which are simply friction fitted between the rafters, from later slipping down and blocking the airflow? The solution is to first nail thin battens along all the rafter sides, at about half their width, so as to leave a minimum 50mm clear outer space. Or a thin panel of plywood can instead be fixed in place to separate the outer air space from the insulation boards.

However, there's no point going to all this trouble if a healthy flow of air can't enter from outside and do the ventilation job. So to encourage a good airflow, small openings need to be provided down at the eaves and sometimes also at the ridge. At the eaves this must be equivalent to a 25mm continuous gap on both the opposing sides. Such eaves-to-eaves roof ventilation relies on wind power to push the air in from one side and out

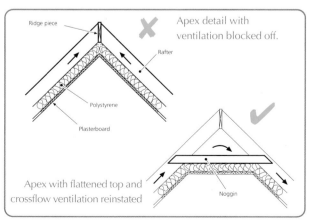

Apex detail with ventilation blocked off.

Ridge piece

Rafter

Polystyrene

Plasterboard

Apex with flattened top and crossflow ventilation reinstated

Noggin

Cutting circular holes in eaves soffit for air vents

through the other. However, the additional use of ridge vents (equivalent to a 5mm continuous gap) is recommended for roofs steeper than 35°. This means wind passing at high level over the ridge will help suck fresh air up from the eaves, improving the thermal upflow, thereby avoiding the risk of stagnant air pockets forming on calm days.

This, of course, is all very well when building a new roof where it's an easy job to incorporate special plastic dry ridge vents when fitting the ridge tiles. But having to alter perfectly sound ridge tiles to an existing roof can mean a lot of unnecessary expense and hassle, and on period properties you certainly wouldn't want to damage historic crested terracotta features. Fortunately, in older houses where the existing roof doesn't have any underfelt, roof vents aren't required as the airflow will filter through the existing tiles or slates. Otherwise it's worth checking with Building Control, as you may not need to go to the trouble of providing ridge ventilation if the air can flow satisfactorily up from one side and down the other.

Loft rooms are usually built with three roof voids – the two eaves cupboards, one either side at low level, and the small triangular mini-loft above the room. This allows ventilation to swirl up from the eaves on one side, over the

top and out through the eaves on the other side.

If you don't already have vents, or a continuous air gap at the eaves (normally to the soffit under box eaves), fitting new ones should be fairly straightforward. Small plastic air vents with an insect-resistant 4mm mesh can be installed. But take care if the soffit board under the eaves is made of asbestos cement – this must not be drilled, as dangerous fibres might be inhaled. In such cases a specialist contractor must be employed.

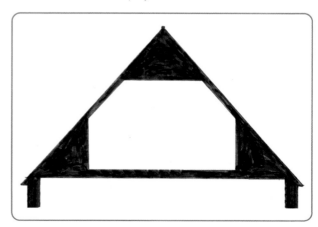

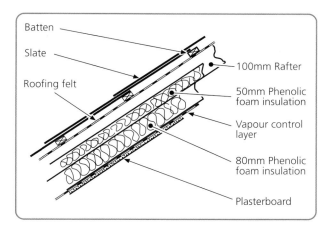

Batten
Slate
Roofing felt
100mm Rafter
50mm Phenolic foam insulation
Vapour control layer
80mm Phenolic foam insulation
Plasterboard

In some houses the fascia boards are fixed directly against the upper walls, without any soffits for eaves ventilation. Unless vents can be fitted to the fascias (without obstruction from gutters) it may not be possible to easily accommodate new soffit or fascia vents.

The solution here is to fit special vents directly to the tiles or slates (fitted right through the roofing felt below so that the air gets through). There is a risk that these may only introduce air into the gap between one pair of rafters at a time. Fortunately, most loft rooms have eaves cupboards that act as a sort of communal air space providing cross ventilation at the base of all the rafters, which saves having to fit one vent specially for each individual rafter void.

So far so good. But you also need to consider any obstacles to the air path that could allow 'dead air zones' of damp, stale air. Imagine air flowing into an eaves vent and happily travelling up between a pair of rafters until it encounters a trimmer timber blocking the air path where a roof window has been installed. In order for air to flow freely where roof windows are fitted, you need to drill 10mm diameter holes centrally through the rafters on either side, both above and below the window (check any proposed drilling of rafters with your structural engineer first). A similar lack of cross-ventilation can occur between the short 'jack rafters' at the corners of roof hips, which again may require small air vents to be drilled.

But what if you've just built an enormous full-width dormer on one side of the roof – how do you provide cross-ventilation? As we shall see, flat dormer 'warm roofs' don't require ventilation, so the remaining roof slope on the other side can be vented from the eaves up to the ridge.

Most loft conversions have highly insulated timber stud walls which form the new eaves cupboards. The space within the eaves cupboards will remain draughty and well ventilated, just like the old unconverted loft. In these fringe areas there may still be some thick loft roll sitting above the edges of the bedroom ceilings to stop heat escaping. This commonly poses a problem at the eaves, namely how to keep the air ventilation paths clear without them getting blocked by loft insulation, when at the same time

you want to prevent any 'cold bridging' to the ceilings below from poorly insulated gaps, which can cause black mould staining. This apparent conflict can be reconciled by fitting special plastic ducts above the soffit vents leading into the loft, allowing the eaves to at once be ventilated and insulated to exactly the right extent.

There remains, however, one intriguing question. Why does the air gap need to be such a generous 50mm, given that gale force draughts seem to be able to blow through the tiniest gaps elsewhere in the house. One reason might be that most roofs have traditional underlay made from heavy black bituminised Hessian, which was designed to sag slightly between rafters, therefore the air gap needs to accommodate this. But where you have a roof with modern breather underlay a reduced 25mm space is acceptable. The ventilation rules can actually be waived altogether for some very small roofs, notably those to 'cottage' dormers and small porches.

In fact, new technology means that ventilation may in some cases not be required for new pitched roof construction. Modern breather membranes are now used instead of traditional underlay and these allow water vapour to escape. Also, many new roofs are now built with the insulation boards placed above the rafters, creating 'warm roofs' that don't need ventilating (see below).

Fitting insulation

Before you had the crazy idea of converting your loft, the roof may have been responsible for losing about a quarter

of all the heat escaping from your home. Even if your old loft space was fairly well insulated, you now have a good opportunity to substantially boost your property's overall thermal efficiency, and save money on future fuel bills. So now we come to the tough part – actually doing the job, and meeting all those demanding heat-loss targets.

Pitched roofs
Target U-value: 0.20 W/m2K or lower

Because most loft conversions involve upgrading original roofs from the inside, you might reasonably expect the heat-loss target to be a little less ambitious than for totally new roofs. Bad news – the standard for insulating new or existing roof slopes is exactly the same.

The reason the rules aren't relaxed about this is because roofs are such a major offender when it comes to leaking heat. Indeed, the Building Regulations actually require a lower U-value for the roof structure than for just about any other element of a house.

When building a new roof, the simplest and most effective method is to lay the insulation boards over the

top of the new rafters, rather than between them or under them. This is known as a 'warm roof', because the whole structure is encapsulated within a thick layer of insulation. This is standard construction on flat roofs, but is a fairly recent innovation on pitched roofs. With this method, ventilation isn't required because the underside of the insulation is relatively warm, so any humid air that gets into the roof won't condense into moisture against a cold surface.

When re-roofing an existing property, warm roofs should be acceptable, provided that the resulting small increase in roof height doesn't cause problems with adjoining roofs, and that the planners are happy. But this is only likely to be cost-effective where the old roof coverings have reached the end of their life and need to be replaced. However, when building new dormer pitched roofs this is often the best method to adopt.

Most loft conversions involve upgrading the existing roof from inside with a choice of fitting insulation between the rafters, under the rafters or a combination of both. The decision must take into account the following factors:

- Where insulation is placed between the rafters, a minimum 50mm air gap must be left above it, on the cold side, to allow a cross-flow of ventilation under the tiles.
- Unless insulated on their room-side, rafters act as a thermal bridge that lets heat escape at a faster rate than through the surrounding insulation.
- Insulation placed under rafters projects into the room, reducing valuable headroom.
- A vapour-check barrier is required on the inside to prevent moist warm air from the room getting into the roof structure, causing damp from 'interstitial' condensation.

In a traditional pitched roof the rafters are commonly sized about 100 x 50mm (4 x 2in). Although modern trussed rafters may only be 72mm deep, in practice the engineers would normally want to see these doubled up with conventional 100 x 50mm rafters alongside to strengthen them. Then, by adding 20mm-deep battens along the inside of standard '4 x 2' rafters you can increase their depth to 120mm. After deducting the necessary 50mm outer air space there should be enough space left for 70mm insulation between the rafters. This means you only need an inner layer of approximately 50mm-thick insulation plus 12.5mm plasterboard (or 62.5mm composite board).

If you can't achieve a minimum 120mm rafter depth you're going to need some bloody long dry-wall screws to hold the 70 to 80mm thick inner lining of insulation plus plasterboard in place. Screws need to achieve a 'bite' into the timber of at least 25mm. The loss of headroom due to fitting thick insulation boards to the inside of the rafters could prove critical in some smaller lofts, and in special cases it may be possible to argue for reduction. Alternatively, as noted earlier, it's sometimes permissible to reduce the ventilation gap. If you can fit 75mm insulation between 100mm-deep rafters and still leave an acceptable air gap, then a depth of only 50mm or less laid on the room side may be sufficient. When constructing new pitched dormer roofs, using thicker 150mm rafters will accommodate a healthy 100mm depth of 'between rafter' insulation.

When fixing thick insulation boards in place, care must be taken to ensure that the ventilation isn't blocked at the apex. This is easily achieved by leaving a new mini-loft area above the ceiling, which is a natural part of the design where high-level collars are installed. But this may be harder to achieve where a large rear box dormer is extended out from ridge level (see the section on 'Ventilation').

Note that any recessed lights in the new ceiling should have a sealed air space around them so that they're not covered in insulation that could cause overheating.

A thinner air gap may be acceptable to old roofs without underfelt

What thickness of insulation do you need?

This is a question that can cause considerable debate, even down at Building Control HQ. Typically a combined thickness of about 120mm insulation (*ie* the total insulation between and below the rafters) plus 12.5mm plasterboard is likely to be required. The Building Control Officer will expect to see the full thickness of insulation specified on the plans to be provided on site.

Assuming you have typical 100mm-deep rafters, the insulation mix could be as follows:

Option 1
Modern breathable felt
25mm air gap
75mm insulation between rafters
50mm insulation across the inside face of the rafters.

Option 2
Traditional non-breathable felt
50mm air gap
50mm insulation between rafters
75mm insulation across the face of the rafters

(alternatively where rafters are extended with 20mm internal battening, fit 70mm insulation between rafters and 50mm to inner face plus 12.5mm plasterboard – see main text).

Option 3
Traditional non-breathable felt
50mm air gap
50mm insulation between rafters
30mm multifoil insulation quilt across inner rafters..

In most cases the type and amount of insulation is ultimately down to the discretion of the Building Control Officer. Usually an acceptable compromise can be reached.

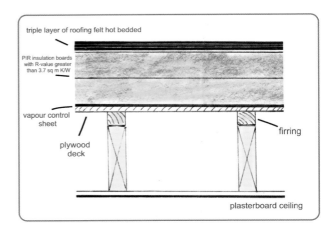

triple layer of roofing felt hot bedded

PIR insulation boards with R-value greater than 3.7 sq m K/W

vapour control sheet

plywood deck

firring

plasterboard ceiling

Mixing and matching – insulating under the rafters the multifoil way

Once the rafters have at least 50mm depth of foam insulation fitted between them, the next step is to insulate on the room side of the rafters. But instead of using thick wedges of insulation boards, sheets of multifoil could provide a slimmer, hi-tech alternative. However, this method must be checked with Building Control in advance.

The main attraction of multifoil is the potential saving in room space. The multifoil itself is about 30mm thick (less when compressed) but the battens can add at least a further 25mm. It may therefore not be significantly thinner than the equivalent foam boarding, and can be more expensive.

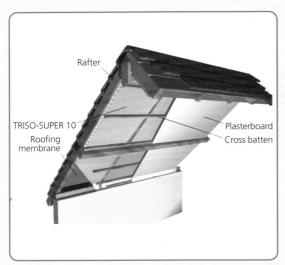

Rafter

TRISO-SUPER 10
Roofing membrane

Plasterboard
Cross batten

- Unroll the insulation, starting along the top of the roof.
- Fix the foil to the underside of the rafters, stretching it tightly and taping at joints. Staple the joints every 50mm with galvanised 14mm staples. Overlap the joints by at least 50mm and cover them with metallic tape.
- At the bottom of the roof pitch, staple the insulation directly onto the timber wall plate. Remember to pay attention to edges – continuous insulation is just as important as the thickness.
- To provide the necessary air gap around the multifoil, 25mm battens are then fixed (25 x 35mm minimum) along the inner face using appropriate nails. Then proceed as described above with a vapour control sheet before plasterboarding. Ensure that there's a minimum air gap of 20mm between the insulation and the plasterboard lining.

Flat roofs

Target U-value: 0.25 W/m2K or lower

The regulations are less demanding for flat roofs than pitched roofs, with a target value of only 0.25 W/m2K. Here, foam insulation boards are normally laid on top of the deck or the roof joists to create a 'warm roof'. It's fairly common to use 120mm insulation boards, but if height is an issue, for example where a large flat roof dormer mustn't be any higher than the existing roof ridge, it may be possible to use thinner insulation on top, combined with additional insulation boards fixed between the roof joists. The total depth of a flat roof, comprising the joists, firrings (thin tapered timber strips), deck and felt, can sometimes exceed 220mm at the highest point on a large box dormer spanning about 3m. Special purpose-made boards are used on flat roofs, as their surfaces may need to resist the application of scalding bitumen, used to bed roofing felt.

Masonry walls

Target U-value: 0.30 W/m2K or lower

It's not unknown for some less scrupulous 'loft specialists' to forget to insulate any existing masonry walls either side of your new loft room. This may sound picky, but it needs to be done to comply with Building Regulations. The external walls are obviously a major thermal element, although the actual wall areas found in loft rooms are relatively small. Even if you happen to live in a mid-terrace house without any external walls to the loft, or in a detached property with hipped roof

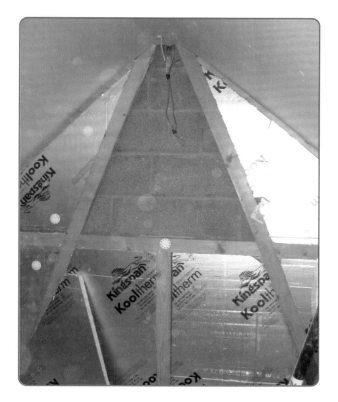

Existing masonry walls – how warm are they?	U-value W/m2K
Modern cavity wall Brick outer leaf, 115mm cavity with 65mm insulation, insulated blockwork inner leaf	0.35
1990s cavity wall Brick outer leaf, 100mm cavity with 50mm insulation, insulated blockwork inner leaf	0.45
1980s cavity wall Brick outer leaf, 75mm cavity with no insulation, insulated blockwork inner leaf	1.00
1930s–1970s cavity wall Brick outer leaf, 50mm cavity with no insulation, brick or blockwork inner leaf	1.60
Pre-1930s, Victorian etc Solid 229mm brick wall	2.10

slopes on all sides, there may still be dormer walls that need insulating. In most lofts there'll be at least one gable wall or internal party walls to insulate.

Where a typical side gable wall needs upgrading to a loft room, the first question to ask is how does it currently score in insulation terms? This will largely depend on the age of the property. Surprisingly, the requirement to insulate new houses was only introduced as recently as 1985. This encouraged the use of lightweight thermal blocks on inner leafs as a replacement for conventional dense concrete blocks. So in all but the most modern houses, unless you've had cavity wall insulation injected, there will very likely be some serious catching up to do.

It's well known that timber-frame houses score relatively highly for insulation. Here the inner leaf of the cavity walls is built from timber, and the outer walls are of conventional brick, stone or rendered blockwork.

The worst energy performance of all is from traditional solid masonry walls, common on pre-1930s properties. These are poor insulators, so where one is incorporated within the conversion's thermal envelope it must be upgraded to achieve an improved U-value.

Although solid brick walls are not acceptable for new construction, building up an existing solid wall using similar brick or blockwork should normally be permitted. Aerated concrete blocks have good insulation properties, but these alone won't hit the insulation target. So you'll need to dry-line the wall internally. If you're building up an existing cavity wall, any cavity insulation will need topping up to bring it up to the apex.

Upgrading existing masonry loft walls normally means dry-lining with 50mm insulation board plus plasterboard (or 62.5mm composite).

Composite boards can be fixed direct to the wall using plaster dabs, or you may want to first build a timber stud framework to the wall, which can be infilled with insulation boards before covering with a vapour control sheet and plasterboard. Note that any electric cables should have an air space around them to prevent over-heating.

Timber stud walls
Target U-value: 0.30 W/m2K or lower

In loft conversions there are two main areas where timber studwork will require insulating: dormer walls and purlin 'ladder' walls. To achieve a U-value of 0.30 dormer studwork normally needs 100mm foam insulation boards to be friction-fitted between the 100mm timber stud framework. An additional layer of insulation can be provided internally where

necessary. Adding external cladding or render is, of course, a useful way of boosting insulating without sacrificing room space indoors.

Correct insulation to the timber stud purlin walls that form the eaves cupboards is crucial, but is sometimes skimped. Although they're internal walls, they form a key part of the thermal envelope around the new loft room, as well as normally playing a major structural role. Insulation needs to be continued from the roof slopes down to the purlin walls, to resist the cold ventilation air swirling up through the eaves cupboards.

Achieving a good thick layer of insulation here should be very easy to achieve, since losing a few inches of space at this level makes no real difference to the room. Plus you've already got a full 100mm depth of studwork to play with, and there's bags of space behind the wall within the eaves cupboard itself that could be utilised. So this might be a good place to over-achieve on U-values if you want to negotiate a trade-off for a reduced level elsewhere. A typical arrangement might use 80mm insulation between the studwork plus an extra lining to the room-side of the wall of 37.5mm composite board (*ie* 25mm insulation plus 12.5mm plasterboard). But there is still one glaring weak point in your defences that often gets overlooked. Remember to fit super-snug insulated cupboard doors to your eaves cupboards (without vents in them), otherwise all the warmth in the room will swiftly drain away. (See final chapter.)

Windows
Target U-value: 1.8 W/m2K or lower

Windows and doors are relatively poor insulators, so to limit the amount of heat lost through them the maximum total size of all new openings is restricted to the equivalent of 25 per cent of the floor area of the new accommodation (plus an extra amount equivalent to any original windows or doors that were sealed up as a result of the work). This should be more than enough for even the brightest loft rooms.

Just to briefly revisit the issue of lofts overheating in summer, it's worth noting that windows positioned higher up the roof slope are much better at controlling the build-up of room heat. Windows at lower levels are less effective in dispersing warm air because it rises, accumulating around the ceiling apex level.

The target U-vale for new windows is 1.8 W/m2K. This includes windows fitted to new openings in existing houses, such as roof windows and dormers. However, where you're simply replacing old windows with like-for-like new ones in the same place, they need only achieve a U-value of 2.0. Incredible though it may sound, through clever design and the use of special low-energy glass some advanced windows can actually achieve a net thermal gain rather than losses. But this is very much something for the future, as most windows available today still represent an energy loss low point.

Thermal bridging

Moist warm air will always seek out the coldest spots in a house on which to condense, which in time causes ugly damp black mould staining. Cold spots are commonly found in places where the insulation was omitted, or where it hasn't been possible to break the 'cold path' from outside to inside, typically across window reveals or through rafters. This is why it's recommended that internal insulation is continued across the reveals of roof windows. Document L1B has increased the emphasis on minimising thermal bridging and air leakage at all gaps, joints and edges.

But even if you exceed all the thermal efficiency targets in the book, it's sobering to think that modern insulation technology still has something to learn from William the Conqueror's time. When existing buildings are upgraded with insulation fixed to internal surfaces, they tend to warm up relatively rapidly, and when the heating is turned off they can likewise cool fairly swiftly. This is because insulation materials have a low thermal mass, unlike old super-thick masonry castle walls.

STEP BY STEP Fitting the insulation

Tools required
- Fine tooth handsaw
- Hand padsaw
- Small rasp (a'surf')
- Craft knife
- Cordless screwdriver
- Safety goggles, mask and gloves

Materials
- Insulation boards as specified
- Foil-backed 12.5mm plasterboard
- 75mm and 100mm dry-wall screws
- A can of polyurethane expanding foam

When it comes to insulating your new loft accommodation, the general idea is to turn the living space into an insulated 'box'. This means you'll probably need to insulate at least three different types of surface. The exact type and depth of insulation required to meet the target U-values in each case will already have been specified on your approved Building Control drawings. The products shown are Kingspan phenolic insulation boards. Photos courtesy PBdrylining.co.uk and Kingspan Insulation.

Rafters

The main roof slopes are insulated in two stages. First an outer layer of insulation is wedged between the rafters, and then an inner layer is fixed across the rafters, facing the room. The following works should easily achieve the target U-value of 0.20 W/m2K.

1 Before insulating, it's essential to leave a 50mm-deep ventilated air space under the existing roofing felt (or in older unfelted roofs, directly under the battens). This means the insulation can't just be stuffed all the way in otherwise it would block the airflow between the rafters. Because there's also a potential risk that the slabs of insulation could later slip and block this ventilation path, the first job is to fit timber battens along the rafter sides. These act as 'guide rails' for the slabs to rest on, and are nailed in place 50mm in from the outer face of the rafters (using sawn treated 25 x 38mm battens).

2 If necessary, the existing rafters can be made deeper in order to accommodate a thicker layer of insulation. Here we have traditional 100mm deep '4 by 2' rafters that are being extended by nailing 20mm thick battens along their inner faces, to achieve a total depth of 120mm.

3 Before installing the first layer of insulation between the rafters, an extra row or two of horizontal battens (say 50 x 50mm) may need to be fixed between rafters, flush with their inner face. This will later provide extra support for the inner layer of insulation in stage 8.

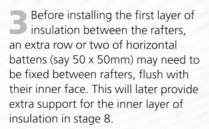

4 Next, slabs of insulation are measured, marked and cut into suitably sized chunks to fit between the rafters, using a fine tooth handsaw. To achieve a tight friction fit, the board can be cut slightly oversized on one side, or at a slight angle. The insulation shown is of 70mm thickness.

5 Push the chunks between the rafters. They should be fitted flush with the inner surface of the rafters. A small amount of adjustment and trimming can be done in situ using a handsaw. If required, screws can be used to hold boards in place.

6 Next, the inner face of the rafters will need to be clad. First mark the boards and cut to size with a handsaw. To achieve a snug fit, the sides of the boards can be planed with a small rasp.

7 All edges of boards must be supported on rafters or battens. In this example, 62.5mm-thick insulated plasterboard sheets are used (50mm insulation combined with 12.5mm plasterboard).

8 Secure the boards in place with dry-lining wall screws.

9 Where the loft room has a new mini-ceiling, this first layer of insulation to the rafters needn't continue any higher than the ceiling joists. If there is no ceiling, the rafters should be insulated up to the ridge, taking care not to block the air path. For optimum performance the insulation on adjoining boards should meet.

this is the final surface. Otherwise, a final layer of plasterboard will later be needed (foil-backed or with a separate vapour barrier). The plasterboard will be secured with screws through the insulation into the rafters, which also helps hold the insulation in place (see next chapter).

10 Where insulation boards meet the ceiling, they need to be cut at an angle, to neatly butt against the ceiling surface. If you're fitting insulated plasterboard, a neat joint here is especially important as

11 At its base, the insulation needs only to extend down as far as the top of the purlin walls. If there are no purlin walls, then it should continue right down to the wall plate, taking care not to block the eaves air vents.

Window reveals

1 To achieve a neat, well-insulated joint around roof windows, board right across the room, as described above, including the windows (temporarily). Before this is done, the dimensions and approximate positions of each window opening are first marked in pencil on the board.

2 Using a padsaw, a rough hole is cut allowing some light in, leaving at least 25mm extra board protruding inward around the window opening.

3 The reveals around the window are filled with pieces of insulation cut to fit, typically about 50mm thick.

4 The opening is then neatly formed by cutting off the surplus board using a padsaw leaving it flush with the surface of the insulated reveals.

5 Strips of plasterboard are inserted over the insulated reveals and pushed firmly into a purpose-made slot in the window frame. The inner edges are trimmed to achieve a neat finish, prior to taping or skimming.

Ceilings and stud walls

Loft ceilings follow a similar procedure to rafters, although there's normally no need for extra battens because the area being covered is generally very small and the inner layer of insulation is held in place by gravity. Cables for lights will, however, need to be accommodated. On trussed rafter roofs there may be some awkward shapes to fill, where the old prongs were cut. Gaps should be sealed with expanding polyurethane foam. Here we're fitting 100mm insulation between the joists and 37.5mm insulated plasterboard along the underside to achieve a minimum 0.2 U-value.

The procedure for insulating studwork walls is also similar to that described for rafters. In some cases extra battens may be required, or a plywood backing, so that the boards can't slip out. Cables and boxes for electric socket outlets and switches will need to be accommodated. Small gaps can be sealed with expanding foam. Here we're fitting 80mm insulation between the studs and 37.5mm insulated plasterboard along the inside surface. This should comfortably exceed the 0.3 target U-value (compensating for any heat loss through cupboards etc).

At junctions between purlin walls and the rafters above, the surface layer of insulated plasterboard will need to be cut at an angle for a neat joint.

If required dormer studwork can normally accept 100mm rigid insulation boards friction-fitted between timber stud framework, to achieve the target 0.3 U-value or better.

Gable walls, floors and flat roofs

Gable

Masonry walls can be lined with 50mm insulation board before plasterboarding (or you can use the combined 62.5mm composite variety). Insulation can be fixed direct to the wall using plaster dabs or held in place with circular plastic and steel fixing discs hammered into the wall. Alternatively, boards can be fixed to a timber stud framework. In this example, the remaining trussed rafters at each end were infilled with 50mm insulation and extra battens, and lined with 37.5mm insulated plasterboard along the inside surface to achieve a U-value of 0.30.

Floor

If your loft floor is above a cold space such as a garage, a 100mm depth of floor insulation can be wedged between the new floor joists, with plenty of room to spare. It can be fitted either from above or below. Obstacles such as pipes, cables and herringbone bracing straps will need to be accommodated with a small amount of trimming. This should achieve the target 0.23 U-value.

Flat roof

To achieve the target 0.25 U-value 120mm-thick insulation boards are placed on top of the roof deck to create a 'warm roof' (see chapter 9).

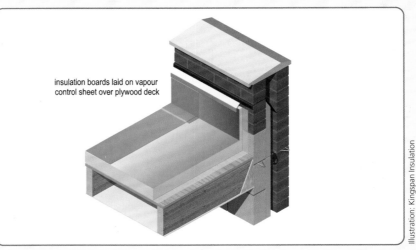

insulation boards laid on vapour control sheet over plywood deck

13 COMPLETION

Photo: South London Lofts

Photo: designer-radiators.com

Photo: Charles Grosvenor

Photo: South London Lofts

It may seem a little optimistic to start talking about completion right now. With a profusion of wires and pipes poking through lots of shiny insulation boards, your loft will probably be looking more like the inside of the TARDIS than a penthouse suite. But that's all about to change. As soon as the walls and ceilings are tacked out with plasterboard, and the second fix electrics and plumbing are sorted, you'll be within spitting distance of that luxurious loft-living lifestyle. But that doesn't mean you can take your eye off the ball. A large percentage of snagging issues that arise after completion relate to poor finishing, notably shrinkage cracking and plastering defects. So vigilance is everything.

Of course, it may be that you've already completed much of the dry-lining process by fitting 'all in one' insulated plasterboard sheets at the insulation stage as shown in the previous chapter, in which case the decision will now need to be made whether to opt for a skim plaster finish or perhaps to decorate direct. See page 205.

Dry-lining with plasterboard

The next step is to fit large sheets of plasterboard in place to form the ceiling and wall surfaces. These are installed using special dry-wall screws fixed to the timber studwork, wall battens or rafters, thereby helping to securely contain the insulation so it's sandwiched permanently in place.

But first there's a more immediate problem – how to physically transport giant sheets of plasterboard up into the loft. This is where having a large opening in the form of a box dormer can come in very handy, especially if the window frame can be temporarily removed. Of course, this will still require considerable amounts of wrestling with the boards as they reluctantly ascend the scaffolding. Hiring a small winch at this stage

Photo: Celotex.co.uk

Photo: Celotex.co.uk

could be money well spent. Alternatively, if your loft stairs are already in place the boards can be carted up one or two at a time – unless, of course, the designer specified spiral stairs or the steep compact variety!

In reality, however, it's often more practical to order smaller-sized boards which are easier to manoeuvre into place.

Plasterboard is sold in thicknesses of 9.5mm and 12.5mm and comes in two main sheet sizes – giant economy size 2400 x 1200mm, and the not quite so back-breaking 1800 x 900mm size.

Your choice of plasterboard sizes will normally depend on how the joists are spaced. The thicker 12.5mm type is needed where ceiling joists are at 600mm centres. The thinner 9.5mm variety can only realistically cope with spans of up to 400mm between joists without bowing. If you've spaced your studs any differently, the boards will have to be specially cut to fit.

This is a job that should be within

Left: Exposed undersides of stairs may need extra fire protection.

Below: Suspended ceiling to bedroom below hides new loft WC waste pipe

the capabilities of most seasoned DIYers, although you normally need to work in pairs to manhandle larger boards into place. The job is made more challenging by the cables and pipes sprouting out of the walls. Neat and accurate

fixing is crucial to the finished appearance of ceilings and walls, especially if you plan to decorate direct to the board surfaces instead of plaster skimming.

Plasterboard sheets can be fixed to masonry walls, such as gable ends, by means of a timber framework of battens infilled with insulation boards. Where it's possible to meet the required U-values, the boards can instead be squashed into place on a brick or block wall with blobs of plaster known as dabs.

When fixing boards, they should not all be neatly lined up next to each other. The joints should instead be staggered, so as to reduce the risk of cracking. It's also good practice to leave a tiny gap of about 2mm between adjoining sides of boards. Cordless power-screwdrivers take a lot of the sweat out of screwing boards in place.

Most plasterboard comes with a grey surface suitable for either skimming or decorating. However, for direct decoration it's best to use boards with a tapered edge, which allow a seamless surface that hides any visible shrinkage and hairline cracking – see opposite.

The other big decision when ordering plasterboard is whether to plump for the more expensive foil-backed variety. The purpose of the foil is to act as a vapour barrier, preventing moist air from the house penetrating into the roof and condensing into damp. The alternative is to first install 500-gauge (150 micron) polythene sheeting prior to boarding. This is generally considered to offer a better solution, since it covers any small gaps between boards.

In some cases you might want to specify special types of board, such as pink fire-resistant plasterboard for protected escape routes, or moisture-resistant board for steamy bathrooms. For beefed-up sound insulation try gypsum fibre boards, which are highly durable and strong enough to accept wall fixings directly.

Whether you're fitting thick insulated boards or bog standard 12.5mm wall board, one of the trickiest areas to get right is around rooflight windows. As shown in the last chapter, the way professionals sometimes approach this is to tack a large sheet right across the rafters as if there were no windows there, having first pencil-marked the oblong window shape on the boards. Using a hand-held pad-saw a rough opening can be cut out leaving about 25mm extra all round the window reveals. Pieces of insulation are then cut to size to fill the reveals. The rough

window openings in the large sheet can then be cut accurately, before the reveals around the window jambs are finished with strips of plasterboard.

Skimming

Despite the fact that mainstream house-builders sometimes decorate directly to plasterboard, a thin coat of smooth plaster skim is generally considered to provide a superior finish. Once the taped and filled joints are dry, a surface coat is applied direct to the plasterboard to a depth of about 2mm. This can be trowelled off to produce a smooth 'polished' surface where walls are to be emulsioned. The thin plaster typically sets within about

Decorating direct onto plasterboard

◼ If you want to decorate direct to the surface without plastering it is best to use 'tapered edge' boards rather than square edged. These have thinner sides so when they're butted together a shallow recess is formed either side of a joint.
◼ The recess can be filled with jointing compound and then covered with joint tape.
◼ When dry, 2 more coats of jointing compound are applied, each one sanded down when dry. Each coat has a setting time of roughly 90 minutes.
◼ Going over the edges with a damp sponge helps disguise the joint, leaving a smooth surface.
◼ Finally the surface can be sealed before receiving 2 coats of emulsion.

Photos: Lafarge Plasterboard Ltd

one-and-a-half hours, and can normally be decorated within 48 hours. Any exposed pipes and cables are best protected with Clingfilm or tape, since plastering by its nature can be a messy business.

To achieve a neat finish at the corners of walls, door openings and window reveals, angle beads or special joint tape (paper containing a strip of galvanised metal or plastic) can first be fixed in place over corners before being skimmed over. Beading must be carefully aligned using a spirit level and can be set in dabs of plaster or anchored with galvanised masonry nails prior to plastering.

Fireboard

In the space of only 30 minutes, untreated softwood can burn through to a depth of at least 25mm, enough to weaken a timber structure sufficiently to bring about collapse. Fortunately, plasterboard is naturally fire-resistant and can normally protect the timber behind it. But despite being reassuringly non-combustible and inert, to be fully fireproof the regulations require a coat of skim plaster, so that the paper lining

205

doesn't get burnt and peel off. In locations especially at risk from fire-spread, such as to garage ceilings with rooms above, the plasterboard needs to be laid to a double thickness as well as being skimmed.

Tough though they undoubtedly are, steel beams react badly when confronted by fire, being prone to alarming degrees of buckling and twisting. This plainly isn't desirable when your floors and roof are dependent on them for support. In short, any exposed beams will need protecting. In most conversions the beams will already be hidden away within floors or purlin walls, so this shouldn't be an issue.

The beams that are most likely to be exposed and in need of treatment are the ones up near the apex of the roof (if not already concealed behind a new mini-ceiling). Where the loft floor has been strengthened from below any exposed beams at ceiling level within existing bedrooms will also need protection.

Protection can be provided in the usual manner – *ie* a single layer of special pink-coloured 12.5mm fireboard with a skim plaster finish (or a double layer of ordinary 12.5mm plasterboard with a skim finish). However, if your design is meant to feature exposed steel beams for that cool Manhattan loft apartment look, then coating them with special intumescent paint should do the trick, although Building Control will insist on it being professionally applied and certified by the installer.

Photo: EGLO

must be of an energy-efficient type for each 25m² of floor area in your loft.

Bathroom light fittings must be concealed, such as sealed downlighters, to prevent any risk of direct contact with water.

Otherwise the second fix electrics should be a straightforward process, assuming there are no last minute changes of plan. The various switches and socket covers are normally fitted before decoration, although any tiled wall surfaces should, if possible, be completed beforehand. The decorators will nevertheless later need to go round loosening the covers so as not to ruin their appearance by camouflaging them with artistic daubings (they will then regard it as someone else's job to screw them all back again). Any unfinished safety earth-bonding must be completed before appliances are connected. The consumer unit to the main house electrics may also need to be upgraded, so it's best to time this when the family aren't all glued to their favourite TV soaps or YouTube. Finally, upon completion of the job, the electrician should hand over a signed BS 7671 electrical safety certificate.

Second fix electrics

This is the stage when your new living space really starts to feel like home. All the socket covers and switches can now be connected up to the loose cables and boxes that have lain dormant since first fix. But it's the sudden appearance of the lighting that really lends the loft a homely aspect.

As noted earlier, smoke detectors must be wired in, and to comply with Part L1B of the Building Regulations at least one light

Photo: EGLO

Second fix plumbing

Second fix for heating and plumbing may prove a little more arduous than for the electrics. The pipework tails now need to be connected to the sanitary fittings. But even if you opted for an all-in package loft conversion, selecting (and paying for) the sanitary fittings is normally something

Photo: EGLO

words 'loft room' and 'Victorian cast iron bath' are ones you'd prefer not to find in the same sentence. If you really insist, then you're going to need the assistance of Mr Iron-Man and his mates to wrestle a back-breakingly heavy original bathtub up the stairs. The alternative of craning it up the scaffolding and thence through a large dormer roof opening is only a marginally more appealing prospect. If your lifestyle truly demands such design statements, then fitting a relatively lightweight replica plastic roll-top bath instead has to be a better option. The biggest problem with cast-iron originals is their miniscule claw feet, which transfer incredibly high loadings to the floor surface – as much in terms of pounds per square foot as a Challenger tank. A bit of chipboard floor panelling under the bath just isn't going to be up to the job. So if you don't want a moving experience when sitting in the bath be sure to first strengthen the floor.

Photo: Boundary Bathrooms

Regardless of the style of fittings, once the job's done it's important to pay careful attention to the detailing at the edges of baths and shower trays. Probably the most common cause of leaks in bathrooms comes from the joints to walls, particularly if fitting acrylic or plastic units that typically suffer from a degree of 'flexing'. Never rely on grout, but use purpose-made sealing trim strips instead, or a suitable silicone mastic sealant. Many homes bear testament to such defects in the form of ugly brown stains on downstairs ceilings, with the associated risk of hidden timber decay.

that's left up to the customer. You supply the bathroom suite and your contractor does the fitting. So like it or not, the client often tends to get lumbered with the responsibility for ordering and co-ordinating delivery at the right time. And of course it's sod's law that the suite you really want will have an estimated delivery date three months in the future, and therefore needs to be ordered as early as possible. This state of affairs has come about because contractors know from bitter experience that some homeowners can be prone to peculiar memory lapses and changes of mind when they see their new bathroom in the flesh on site. Somehow it doesn't look the same as it did in the brochure. If the contractor does supply them, his price should be pretty close to the sum you'd pay to buy them yourself. Although he'll want to add a profit margin for the trouble of ordering them, trade discounts mean this should pretty much even out.

In an ideal world, new plumbing systems would be leak-free from the word go. But in reality a loose connection here or an unsoldered joint there isn't unusual. Small leaks usually manifest themselves within the first couple of days. It's therefore a wise precaution to fit a stopcock that can turn off the loft water supply independently from the main house, and also to ensure that the plumber hasn't disappeared without trace at the crucial moment. When all the plumbing is complete and all the radiators, basins, baths, WCs and showers are fully connected up, Building Control may want to carry out checks, such as ensuring non-return valves are in place to the various water supply pipes. They'll want to be sure that waste water discharges fluently, and that all the above-ground waste plumbing has been tested as fully watertight, which means the system being capable of holding water or air under pressure for at least three minutes.

En suites

Most loft bedrooms are today designed to include a small en suite shower or bathroom. But there are limits on the type of fittings that may be appropriate. As a rule, the

Second fix joinery

The job isn't over until your internal joinery is neatly finished. As well as the floorboards, doors, architraves and skirtings, there's usually a mixed bag of other jobs that might also include fitting staircase balustrades, boxing in pipes, and even fixing picture rails. You need to be clear what style of skirting and architraves you want, whether traditional Victorian ogee, or 1930s 'Ovolo', or plain modern chamfered. Choose from softwood, hardwood or MDF, to be either painted, stained or varnished. But whichever type you pick, it needs to be consistent throughout, if possible matching the joinery in the main house.

The quality of finish is very important as it's one of the things that most people really notice. A lot of snagging items are concerned with getting the detail right. You can usually judge a good quality loft job by the skill of and attention to the joinery – small details like securely fixed skirting boards and neatly mitred joints.

Floor coverings

In some loft conversions the timber flooring is laid as soon as the joists are installed. The advantage of doing it early is that you then have a decent platform to work from, but it's often wise to wait a little, until the plasterboarding and plastering is safely out of the way. This is because expensive timber flooring can lose its appeal when defaced with unsightly blobs of plaster and paint, or deep gouges from rogue power tools. So once fitted, take good care to keep it protected.

Floor coverings play an important secondary role, adding strength to the floor structure. However, when it comes to nailing down the new boards over freshly run pipes and cables it's not unknown for disaster to strike – although the consequent leaks and short circuits may not

occur until later, when the water and electricity supplies are connected.

Traditional floorboards versus chipboard panels
You have two main choices when it comes to selecting your timber flooring: softwood floorboards or chipboard panels. For a traditional timber floor that you can leave exposed with an attractive varnish or stain finish, pine floorboards are ideal. Although chipboard panels are cheaper and quicker to lay, they will need to be covered, perhaps with laminate or carpets, which obviously adds to the cost. But it also means they can be fitted directly the floor structure is in place since they can withstand a fair amount of wear 'n tear in the meantime. Hardwood flooring is a possible third option if you're willing to pay considerably more. But whichever type of floor coverings you choose, a 10mm expansion gap should be left at the edges by the walls. These will later be concealed under the skirting.

Floorboards
Softwood floorboards are commonly available in 18 x 121mm or 22 x 125mm sizes, sold in varying lengths. Such traditional timber floorboards can be prone to shrinkage, which results in unsightly gaps between boards and creaky floors, so it's best to allow the new boards to acclimatise for as long as possible by placing them loose and flat for a while

in the loft room before being finally fixed. This should cut the moisture content down from around 18 per cent, thereby reducing the risk of shrinkage once fitted. Either PTG (planed tongued and grooved) or plain-edged boards may be used, but plain-edged boards may need to be overlaid with hardboard to meet fire standards. If you want the beauty of a nicely sanded and sealed surface, PTG boards are fine, but they'll allow noise transmission, which can be reduced by insulating between the floor joists. To reduce sound further you could lay a thin finish surface of wood flooring or laminate, but then you may as well fit cheaper chipboard as a base.

Floorboards are traditionally fixed across the joists using special large flat nails called brads, since the heads are easily embedded in the boards without the need for

punching-in afterwards. Boards should be laid in a staggered pattern. For added strength, the tongues can be glued into the grooves.

Chipboard

Flooring grade chipboard panels with tongued and grooved edges are probably the most widely used loft flooring, mainly because they're relatively cheap and fairly easy to lay. Chipboard sheets are also highly resistant to rot and beetle. Typical board sizes are 2440 x 600mm or 2400 x 600mm. The 22mm-thick panels can span 600mm between joists, but thinner 18mm panels can only manage 450mm. Although chipboard is unlikely to shrink it has been known to disintegrate when wet, so the moisture-resistant 'green' type must be used (V313 grade or BS 7331:1990 standard). However, unless it's fitted with scrupulous care chipboard is extremely prone to developing creaks over the years, as a result of panels springing away from the joists. Also, should access be required for future maintenance to pipes or cables it's very difficult to replace undamaged once lifted.

The boards should be laid across the joists, rather than along them, and staggered at joists for increased rigidity. To reduce the risk of creaking it's recommend that boards are secured using purpose-made screws rather than nails, and that PVA adhesive is applied at the joints (as long as you're never going to need access in future). Where their edges are unsupported at walls, timber noggins (50 x 75mm) are required to prevent the boards from sagging.

Chipboard is notorious for blunting tools because it's so dense, so it's worth drilling pilot holes first. The tongued and grooved edges of the panels can become easily damaged, so never hammer directly onto the edges without first protecting them under a spare offcut. Also, beware of sharp particles which can fly out when sawing, which makes wearing eye protection essential.

If noise transmission is an issue, special sound-resistant 'acoustic sandwich' panels are available, but these need to be specially sealed around the edges of the room.

Internal doors

As we saw in Chapter 4, complying with the fire regulations can be one of the most challenging tasks of the entire project. Properties with open-plan ground floors may require a separate hallway to be specially constructed or a costly sprinkler system installed.

Fortunately, in the majority of homes the existing walls to the landing and entrance hall effectively split the house into compartments that can delay the spread of fire. The problem is, they're compartments with door openings in them, and old ill-fitting doors with paper-thin panels will be about as effective at resisting fire as a pair of crimolene trousers. Therefore fire doors that can resist flames for at least 20 minutes must be fitted to the rooms along the escape route, including the door to the loft room itself.

Bathrooms and cloakrooms are the notable exception to this rule (unless they happen to contain a boiler).

But doorways aren't the only weak-point along the escape route. Fire can swiftly vanquish any glazed areas, such as glass panels set within doors or frames. Ordinary glass will crack when exposed to heat and is liable to disintegrate and fall out very early in a fire. But wired 'Georgian' glass of 6mm thickness can withstand exposure to fire for an incredible hour or more before it finally reaches a temperature high enough to soften it.

From a design perspective, fire doors were traditionally plain and boring. A choice of featureless flush finishes was about as exciting as it got. Today, a selection of varieties and designs is available if you're prepared to pay a little more. These should look perfectly fine in many homes, but architecturally they're no substitute for many of the high-quality original doors that grace a lot of period properties (1930s and earlier). Which is why you can be pretty sure

that up at 'Posh Mansions' their hand-carved original mahogany doors aren't about to be chucked into a skip, simply to comply with the fire regulations.

In many cases it would be criminal to trash original antique doors that add so much character to older properties. Indeed it is quite literally a criminal offence to do so without consent if you live in a listed building. The quality of pre-war timber was often far superior to much of today's cheap mass-produced product. But how do you retain these valuable original features and at the same time comply with Part B of the Building Regulations? There are two possibilities – the illegal one and the ingenious one.

It's not unknown for loft contractors to make a suggestion along the following lines to grief-stricken homeowners: 'We'll put in some cheap new fire doors, then once you've got your Building Regs certificate, the old doors can go back in.' The problem with this approach is that when you sell, the buyer's surveyor may spot the dodge (unless, of course, you swap them round for a second or third time!); plus, if there's a house-fire, it won't look too clever on your death certificate.

A better option would be to upgrade your existing doors so that they comply with fire-resistance standards. This can be done for little more than the cost of fitting new fire doors, but the system you choose must be agreed with Building Control well in advance. Of course, you can't

Antique and irregular sized doors can be upgraded rather than replaced

Before paint

After paint

Door photos: Envirograf.com

make a fire-proof silk purse out of a pig's ear, so the existing doors must be of reasonable quality to start with.

There are a number of products on the market that claim to allow you to upgrade old doors to achieve the necessary fire resistance. Upgrading may involve fitting a layer of special fire-retardant paper over the inner surface, or it might be possible to achieve satisfactory fire resistance by applying a coating of special intumescent paint to the door. Such coatings must be applied by a 'competent person' and Building Control will ultimately require a certificate from the contractor confirming adherence to the manufacturer's instructions. See website.

Loft doors

The entrance door to your loft accommodation must be to a minimum FD20 standard. However, where you have doors between adjacent loft rooms they don't need special fire-resistant qualities. Internal doors should only be hung once the timber door liners have been fitted and the plastering completed. Never cut doors to size until the finished floor level is established, including any floor tiling or laminate. Obviously decisions need to be made in advance as to whether doors should open inwards or outwards, and which side of the frame the hinges should

hang from.

From a design viewpoint, part-glazed doors are a useful way to boost the amount of light in a room. You may want to create a sweeping entrance to a room with a pair of glazed double doors, but any lower panels that are glazed will need to be fitted with safety glass.

When it comes to selecting standard internal doors, as opposed to fire doors, you essentially have two choices – hollow or solid. The majority of factory-made internal doors are of the hollow, lightweight variety. These comprise a simple timber frame with a honeycomb cardboard core, clad on both sides with moulded panelled surface covers. But before hanging hollow doors be aware that the inner timber frame running up the side to be hinged is often manufactured slightly thicker to accommodate the screws, and should be marked 'hinge side'. You also need to locate the solid wood block part of the frame that will house the door latch (the metal tube that's embedded inside the door).

Solid doors, in contrast, are commonly made of pine or similar softwood and have a more expensive feel, giving a more pleasing chunky sound when they shut. Timber internal doors are either stainable or paint-only grade. Paint-only ones are often remarkably good value, being made from cheaper timber containing knots. Stainable solid softwood doors can be twice as expensive, but don't cost anything like as much as solid hardwood oak or meranti doors. Hardwood veneer might be a less expensive compromise.

Standard internal door sizes are 1981mm high by either 762 or 686mm wide (ie 78in high x 30in or 27in wide), and are normally 35mm thick.

Fitting latches and locks in solid doors should be fairly straightforward. However, it's worth noting that doorknobs need to be set further in from the edge than is necessary for handles, so that you don't scrape your knuckles on the frame every time you open the door. The hole in the latch determines how close the handle will be to the edge of the door, so you need to use a longer 75mm latch rather than the standard 63mm size.

Most internal doors can be supported by a pair of butt hinges – brass ones are preferable, especially in

bathrooms, since they won't rust in the most air. Upper hinges are positioned about 150mm from the top and lower ones 200–225mm from the bottom. Fire doors, being considerably heavier, require a third hinge.

Doorstops and architraves

Once the new door is swinging smoothly on its hinges and

the catch clicks satisfyingly into place, the frame can be completed by fixing the doorstops in position. These are the long strips of 30 x 12mm softwood that are fitted along the middle of the liners, literally stopping the door from swinging through the frame. Each doorstop can be nailed into place on the liner using small 'lost-head' oval nails, their heads punched and buried below the surface ready for filling. Fire doors may need special treatment as described earlier. Which just leaves one problem – what to do about the ugly joint between the door liner framework and the plaster.

Architraves are the time-honoured solution. These long strips of decorative moulded timber are fixed around the sides of the doorframe, neatly covering rough gaps. You can fix them in place using lost-head nails driven into the liner at an angle, or, if you believe the claims made by glue manufacturers, nails may not be required at all. The architraves are normally set back about 6mm from the inner edge of the door liner. At their top corners they're mitred and pinned together, and at their feet they may project out slightly, being traditionally a little thicker than the adjoining skirting boards. The architraves can then be skew-nailed into the skirting boards.

Eaves cupboards

Given all the hullabaloo made about insulation and thermal efficiency, it's rather surprising that when you mention the subject of doors to eaves cupboards no one seems particularly bothered. These provide access to

storage space at the edge of the room which may also be the new home of your water tanks. But eaves cupboards are cold and breezy places, just like your old loft which is why the stud walls that incorporate the new cupboard doors will be stuffed to the gunnels with insulation.

A typical loft can have four or more eaves cupboard doors, and if they're uninsulated this will clearly be a major chink in your loft's thermal armour, with alarming scope for heat-loss. It is possible to track down specially-made insulated doors, but these can be expensive, and only available in a very limited range of styles and sizes.

A cheaper solution is to acquire suitably-sized kitchen wall- or base-unit cupboard doors, and fit some of the leftover insulation board (of which there'll be plenty!) to the inside. Because these cupboard doors are likely to be used only infrequently, they can be fitted as 'pull-off/push-on' doors with magnetic catches to a prepared frame recessed about 10mm into the wall surface. Otherwise they can be conventionally hinged. A draught excluder can be used to good effect around the lip of the frame to seal the edges, and finally some suitably stylish handles fitted.

Loft hatches

One thing that loft firms sometimes forget to include in their quotes is making good to the old redundant loft hatch to the remaining ceiling below. The old opening

The old loft hatch is now redundant

should be sealed with plasterboard, and plastered to match the surrounding surface as closely as possible.

If there's a new mini-ceiling above your new loft room, you may need a new loft hatch installed for access, particularly since storage space will now be at a premium. Most new loft hatch openings are about 600mm square, but must be no smaller than 520mm square and not located directly over the stairs. Hatches are rebated within timber linings similar to those for doorframes and must be fully insulated.

Medium density fibreboard

Good old MDF. It pretty much made the career of 'Handy Andy' and other television DIY celebrities. There's not much in the way of internal joinery that you can't buy in MDF – picture rails, dado rails, architraves, skirting. Unlike real wood, it doesn't warp, split or shrink, nor does it suffer from the inconvenience of knots that need priming. But unlike timber its raw appearance isn't attractive and it needs to be painted, which is why it comes pre-undercoated, ready for the topcoat, saving time and money. Once painted it's virtually impossible to tell apart from the real thing. Unfortunately, however, there's a potential health issue when cutting and drilling the stuff: ultra-fine dust particles emitted when cutting with electric saws can cause irritation to skin, eyes, and lungs, so it's essential to wear a suitable dust mask.

Skirting and matchboarding

The purpose of the humble skirting board is traditionally to disguise unseemly gaps where the plastering on the walls comes face-to-face with the floor. Skirting is by no means essential, and is sometimes absent in properties where the detailing is neat enough to be left exposed. But it's an extremely handy device for covering the expansion gaps that must be left at the edges of various types of floor coverings, such as laminates. Skirting may be screwed, glued or nailed to the walls. The accuracy of mitring and fitting is more important when the wood is left exposed and varnished or stained, whereas a small amount of filler is permissible when it's to be painted.

An alternative design treatment to the lower walls is Victorian-style pine matchboarding fixed vertically between skirtings and dado rails. This can add some authentic period charm, especially to flights of stairs, and is useful for hiding pipes and cable runs.

Window boards

Until now, the new window frames for insertion into gable walls or large dormers may have been left fairly loose so that they could be temporarily removed, facilitating access for occasional bulky deliveries of materials. These can now be finally secured, and the inside sills finished by fixing the window boards in place.

In many cases this will have been done earlier in the build, but fitting the interior window boards is best left as late as possible to avoid damage. With wooden window frames the boards should rebate neatly into special horizontal grooves along the inside of the base of the frame. The boards are fitted level and flat, with the curved 'nosing' edge projecting into the room. They usually extend roughly 50mm wider than the window itself, beyond the plastered wall reveals.

Decoration

Victory is now so close that you can almost grasp the completion certificate shimmering tantalisingly on the horizon. But it's not over until the decorators have done their job. This is the stage when you may notice a number of outstanding 'no man's land' tasks – work left incomplete because each trade believes it's another's responsibility. For example, exposed bathroom waste pipes, central heating pipes and cables under boilers. Surely these should have all been neatly boxed in? Regrettably, unless clearly specified by the client, these are items commonly charged as 'extras'. It's amazing how expensive a bit of 2 by 1 timber covered with plywood can suddenly be.

Photo: Wooden Hill

Photo: EGLO

Quotes from specialist package-deal loft conversion firms often assume that clients want to do their own decorating, along with any tiling to bathrooms. This arrangement may not suit everyone, in which case the contractor will normally put you in touch with a local decorator so that a price can be negotiated independently for the work.

People easily forget what a skilled job good decoration really is, because anyone can buy a can of emulsion and start slapping paint on a wall. Achieving good results requires not just skill but also a lot of hard graft. The old cliché is still very true – decoration can only be as good as the preparation. Which means plenty of laborious rubbing down, followed by filling and then rubbing down again before going anywhere near a can of paint.

Bad paintwork will manifest itself in the form of runs, bubbles, streaks and gaps. There'll be rough lumpy surfaces and trapped dust. Poor varnishing will appear patchy and after the first few months may start to blister and peel off. Good decoration, on the other hand, can hide a multitude of sins, although obviously there are limits. Because this is the final finished surface that the client sees, decorators are sometimes unjustly put in the frame for everybody else's rubbish work.

The decorating trade is usually carried out on a labour only basis. Decorators normally supply their own brushes, filler and sandpaper etc, but the paint will be supplied by the main contractor, or by the client if the trades are being employed directly.

Preparation

New timber surfaces should be rubbed down to a smooth finish before the first coat, using medium to fine paper of about 120 grade, and then rubbed down again between coats. After initial sanding there may be small indentations, such as from nail heads, which need to be filled. It's a bit of a DIY myth that paint alone can fill holes; you really need to apply a suitable filler. For surfaces to be varnished, a wood filler should be used which matches the colour of the wood as closely as possible. There may be larger gaps where skirting and architraves meet slightly

uneven wall surfaces, which can be filled using flexible filler or decorators' caulking from a sealant gun.

Painting softwood

Time was when all the visually important internal joinery – the doors, skirting, architraves etc – was universally finished in good old gloss white. Today, preserving the natural beauty of the wood using a stain, wax or varnish finish is a popular alternative. A matt white or soft sheen cream finish can also add an element of charm to the interior design. Where bare timber is to be painted (as opposed to stained or varnished) it will typically require one or two coats of primer, after any knots have been treated. It should then be undercoated before the final coat of gloss, silk or matt paint is applied.

Knotting solution is used on resinous areas of bare wood, to prevent resin leaking and discolouring the subsequent layers of paint. Aggressive resins can force the paint surface to separate entirely from the timber. Knotting solution takes approximately three hours to dry. Alternatively, a 'self-knotting' primer can often be used.

Wood primer is a thin paint that soaks into the grain, making new timber less absorbant. This seals the surface to prevent further coats of paint soaking in. If you skip this and apply an undercoat or topcoat directly to bare wood the moisture is sucked out of it too quickly and the paint dries on the surface but is poorly bonded, and may quickly peel.

Painting new softwood
- Rub down with glasspaper to get a smooth finish over the entire surface.
- Apply knotting solution to any knots.
- Apply a coat of wood primer or universal primer.
- Fill any voids with a suitable filler and smooth using glasspaper.
- Brush off all dust.
- Touch up any exposed knots.
- Apply undercoat.
- Apply at least one topcoat.

Varnish and wood stain

Instead of conventional gloss paint you may prefer a transparent varnish, or a stain or waxed finish that enhances the timber rather than hiding it. But this means any faults and blemishes in the joinery will stand out, so extra careful preparation is needed.

Varnish is popular for joinery and especially for timber floors as it protects the wood and highlights the natural beauty of the grain. It's often applied before the walls are decorated, since careless emulsioning could leave visible marks showing through on the finished product. Varnish combines polyurethane with wood stain, so that the stain effectively sits on the surface of the timber rather than being absorbed into it. If you want to modify the colour of the joinery to blend in with other woods, coloured varnishes can be used, for example giving softwood the appearance of oak.

Preparation is similar to that for painting, but the sanding process needs to be more thorough, finishing off with a fine grade of paper. Note that sanding across the grain can leave scratches that may later become exaggerated. Varnish is applied in layers of two to four thin coats. To achieve a

durable finish, the bare wood should first be sealed with a thinned coat of varnish diluted with about ten per cent solvent to key into the timber. Allow to dry and apply a further two coats of undiluted varnish. Remember that each coat applied will darken the wood, so once the desired shade has been achieved, subsequent coats of clear varnish can be applied. It's important to apply an even film to avoid patchy colours and brush marks, and not to double-coat the varnish (or wood stain) where it overlaps.

Wood stains are easy to use and resistant to fading. They consist of dyes that are spirit or water based. The technique for applying wood stain is different from painting since the dye is much more fluid than paint and will dry very quickly into the wood. It can be applied quickly and evenly using a clean rag or brush after the surfaces have first been sanded. Note that water-based dyes can cause the grain of the wood to temporarily swell when applied, so the wood should not be sanded directly afterwards.

Paint safety

Gloss paints and spirit stains contain chemical cocktails known as VOCs (volatile organic compounds). From a

health risk point of view, as well as an ecological perspective, it's better to specify low VOC paints, or water-based gloss paint. Water-based acrylics are more user-friendly and make washing out your brushes dead easy. Despite some trade prejudice against them, they perform as well as oil-based paints, but won't give a highly shiny gloss finish (but silk or matt is often preferred anyway).

When the job's done, flammable or polluting materials such as white spirit and paint should not be chucked away down drains – Local Councils should provide special waste disposal facilities.

Emulsioning

Skimmed plasterboard surfaces can normally be decorated within a couple of days of being plastered, once fully dry. It's important not to slap paint onto a freshly plastered surface, otherwise it will shrink, crack and peel. For the first coat on new plaster, non-vinyl water-based paint should be used rather than vinyl emulsion.

Colour therapy

It's well established that the colours around us can affect our moods. So interior designers don't just pick a colour they like as much as one that will set the atmosphere for the room. So with your bank balance by

now on life-support, creating a soothing, otherworldly ambience with subtle pastel-colours, might just help regain some sanity. True, estate agents routinely advise playing safe and sticking to neutral colours, and property developers rarely venture beyond the safer shades of magnolia, but hey, this is *your* home, so why not try something more original? A little colour therapy could be just what the doctor ordered after months of coping with builders on site.

Ceramic tiling

Wall and floor tiles come in a bewildering variety of shapes, sizes, colours, textures and patterns, yet nothing seems to date quicker than last year's tile styles. Indeed, you can

often guess the age of a house fairly accurately from its wall tiles alone. But don't let that put you off. Wall tiling should be well within most DIYers' capabilities. Fortunately you'll be off to a flying start working with smooth new wall surfaces rather then having to stick reluctant tiles to uneven prehistoric plasterwork on old bowed walls.

Wall tiling is normally carried out after the plasterwork is fully dried out. It typically takes a tiler about an hour to fix a square metre of tiles plus another ten minutes to grout them. The use of the correct tile spacers is important to help even out any inconsistencies in tile shapes. Tiles should be set out starting from a line drawn centrally down the room. If timber panelled surfaces or boxed-in pipes are to be tiled, they're best made from water-resistant plywood.

Although floor tiling is fairly rare in attic rooms, ceramic, quarry or stone tiles can be laid on timber floating floors as long as the surface is as rigid as possible. There may be some initial movement due to shrinkage, so it's important to use the correct flexible adhesive. If you're installing electric underfloor heating, the mats can be laid within the adhesive.

External finishing

It's important to make sure that all the outdoor finishing work can be done whilst the scaffolding is still in place. Of course, you may have selected UPVC dormer windows, fascias and cladding, with a view to a maintenance-free future. However, in most conversions there'll be at least some external timbers that require decoration, or perhaps some rendered wall surfaces in need

of finishing. Clearly, working on such tasks at high level is always going to be considerably easier from scaffolding than when balancing on ladders.

External timbers

The traditional way of finishing external timbers is with oil-based gloss paint, applied in three coats – primer, undercoat and gloss. Today, however, new timber windows and doors should arrive on site ready-primed with a honey-coloured

stain basecoat, just awaiting their finish coats of stain or paint. If you want a painted finish it can save time and money to specify joinery ready-primed with paint, rather than the standard stain basecoat. However, any bare planed timberwork, such as at roof level (where it will be most exposed to the weather) won't have been ready-primed and will need the full treatment – which means knotting and priming, or a stain basecoat.

Primer should be carefully brushed into all the corners and joints, working along the grain. Once dry, it can be rubbed down, and then the undercoat applied. This in turn is allowed to dry and is then sanded down. Finally the surface coats of gloss paint are applied. The key to cutting decorating costs is reducing the number of coats needed to get a good quality finish, such as by using 'one coat' paints that let you dispense with the undercoat.

The main alternative to paint is wood stain. Varnish is not widely used externally as it can be prone to flaking or blistering. Stains are dearer to buy than paint, but quicker to apply, and modern stains should let you dispense with the traditional third coat. Because stain soaks into the timber it's far less prone to peeling than paint or varnish.

The thicker stains are classed as 'medium build' and have a light, treacly consistency. The thinner 'low-build' variety is used on sawn timber, which can guzzle a surprising amount of the stuff. Traditionally stains have been spirit based, but like paint they're now available as water-based acrylics and normally contain a fungicide to inhibit mould growth.

So far so good. The only snag with having immaculate, gleaming new paintwork tastefully adorning your freshly constructed dormers is that it might make the old house look a teeny bit shabby in comparison. Nowhere is this more obvious than at eaves level, where somehow the flaking paintwork wasn't so obvious before. This is why many loft converters decide to grasp the nettle and give the old timbers a good rub down and a lick of paint whilst the scaffolding (and decorators) are at hand. But apart from the well-known risks of working at height, there are other potential dangers lurking here. Using a flame gun or hot-air burner on old paintwork can release particles of poisonous lead from old lead paint, which was widely used up until the 1960s. Worse, it's not unknown for a momentary lapse of concentration to cause tinder-dry eaves and rafter feet to become engulfed in flame.

Tidying up

Now that the building works are largely complete, it's tidy-up time. You may notice a marked lack of enthusiasm amongst site personnel by this stage. But a good contractor will see the job through to the bitter end, which not only means tidying up and removing rubbish and scaffolding, but also cleaning all the dust and debris both indoors and out, and generally leaving the house clean and the new loft ready for occupation.

Any splashes of paint or plaster over indoor joinery and fittings must be cleaned off and sticky labels removed from new glazing. Lastly, that industrial-sized Dyson must be put through its paces. Then, with hands all a-tremble, the protective covers can finally be whisked away, including those to smoke alarms and lights.

Completion

The job is not officially done until you've notified Building Control and the final inspection has been carried out to their satisfaction. You'll then need to formally request that a completion certificate is issued. The completion inspection should always be carried out before the contract with the builders has terminated and they've vanished off-site. Failing this, any remedial work required will be your responsibility to complete.

Unless already inspected at a previous stage, the Building Control Officer may want to check that any new plumbing is connected up and works satisfactorily, and

Photo: EGLO

will most definitely want to be assured that the protected fire escape route is fully in accordance with the approved drawings. But what Building Control consider complete, and what you regard as complete, can be two very different things. For example, they won't be terribly interested in all the cosmetic stuff, like whether the decorations have been done neatly or the skirting boards are secure. Remember, the Building Regulations are only the minimum standard acceptable for health and safety purposes. They aren't a guarantee that the builders have finished everything they were supposed to have done. That's where snagging comes in. Which is pretty much down to you.

Snagging

The objective of the snagging inspection is to draw up a list of all remaining defects. These are normally very minor things, like paint blemishes, sticking doors and windows, loose joinery, missing mastic to joints, messy tile grouting and wonky wall sockets – in fact, anything that doesn't look too clever. It's always best to go round the building unaccompanied as you write out your list, so that you can really concentrate and methodically inspect each component of the building work. Surveyors have a trained eye and are the best people to do this job, but if none are available ask a friend or colleague to take an independent look, in addition to making your own inspection. You'll then need to provide the contractor with a copy of your list, and together take a long hard walk around the building to agree all the points. Later, all the snagging items that have been satisfactorily completed can be checked off the list.

Practical completion and final payments

You may recall that useful 'builder-motivating device'

Cartoon: ODPM licence C2007000130

known as a retention. If you don't, the builders will certainly remember if any money was retained by their client. But now's the day of reckoning. It's at this stage – known as 'Practical Completion' – that, in accordance with the contract, you may be required to release half of the retained moneys. This payment can now be made together with the builder's final payment.

If you have an architect or surveyor who's been monitoring the job, they may be willing to issue and sign the certificate of practical completion once you're happy the snagging has been substantially completed. This will formally trigger the release of funds. However, the final totting up process can be quite complex, since any extras or changes instructed will need to be taken into account. It's not unusual for there to be small differences of opinion, often due to fading memories, so some degree of compromise may be needed on both sides. After all, everyone now wants to get on with their lives rather than bickering over the last 99p.

There may then follow a period known as the 'defects liability period', normally three or six months depending on what was written in the contract. It's during this period that any latent defects that appear – typically things such as minor shrinkage cracks to plasterwork and small leaks –

should be made good, with the help of a final snagging list. The architect or surveyor can ultimately issue and sign the appropriate certificate triggering the release of the remaining retention money due to the contractor.

Insurance

Just to put a dampener on things, if your house suddenly burned down right now your insurance company could conceivably wriggle out of paying the full amount. Why? Because you've just massively boosted the value of your home and your house insurance hasn't been increased to reflect it. Calculating the rebuild insurance cost shouldn't be too hard, since it would normally equate more or less to the total amount you've paid for the build (unless, of course, you got an amazing bargain from the builders). Simply tot up all those cheques that you've been handing over to the contractors these last few weeks and then add the retention and VAT. Oh, and those nice people at the Council may have already clocked your increased property value and are right now busy upping your Council tax band.

Topping out ceremony

You don't need a Haynes manual to help celebrate, but you do deserve warm congratulations for seeing the job through. There's no such thing as a stress-free building project. There will always be challenging moments and potential for disputes. So if you've survived the job reasonably unscathed – well done! Hopefully all the expense, hassle, dust, dirt and noise will have been worth it. Not just in terms of added property value and improved lifestyle but also in terms of experience gained and one or two new friends made.

Photo: Velux

Photo: South London Lofts

Photo: Wooden Hill

GLOSSARY

Alternative escape routes Twin escape routes sufficiently separated by fire-resisting construction, or by direction or space, to ensure that should one be affected by fire, the other is still available for safe escape.

Alternating tread A special paddle shaped tread with the wide portion alternating from one side of the stair to the other. Designed to save space. Used in both straight flights and spiral stairs.

Angle fillet A small strip of timber typically placed under the felt covering of a flat roof where it is folded up an adjoining wall, to reduce the sharpness of the bend, reducing the risk of splitting.

Approved documents A series of technical documents issued by the Government explaining the practical details of The Building Regulations and suggesting how they should be interpreted.

Architrave A plain or moulded decorative strip, normally of timber, fixed around a door or window opening, to hide joints.

Attic The room or space below the rafters in a roof and above the ceiling.

Attic truss See 'RIR' truss.

Background ventilation Permanent ventilation consisting of airbricks, grilles and 'hit' & miss' ventilators, required in all habitable rooms under the Building Regulations.

Baluster One of several vertical 'spindles' used to infill a balustrade, *eg* to stairs.

Balustrade A protective barrier on a staircase formed by a series of balusters capped by a handrail. The height of balustrades and spacing of balusters are given in Approved Document K.

Bargeboards Decorative boards placed along the verges of a roof, usually at gable ends, usually of timber or UPVC, a.k.a. 'vergeboard'.

Base plate In a timber stud wall, this is the length of horizontal timber that forms the base of the studwork wall, usually to a floor, a.k.a. 'soleplate'.

Batten A small strip of sawn timber fixed across the rafters on a roof to provide support for tiles or slates.

Binders Thin strips of timber nailed across the tops of ceiling rafters in lofts to strengthen the structure.

Birdsmouth joint A 'V' shaped cut to the inner face of rafters near their feet, so they can connect to the timber wall plate.

Blockwork Wall construction formed in concrete blocks, normally finished externally with render, tile or timber cladding.

Boarded roof A roof structure in which the rafters are covered externally with timber cladding (boarding) before the roofing felt and tile/slate battens are fixed. See 'sarking boards'.

Bottom rail In a timber stud wall, the bottom strip of horizontal timber that forms the base of the studwork wall, a.k.a. 'base plate', 'soleplate', 'floor plate' or 'sill plate'.

Box frame A simple square frame made from four members (usually timber) joined together, such as around a loft access hatch or a roof window.

Breather membrane A sheet of material that repels water penetrating the face of the outer cladding (*eg* tiles) but is permeable to water vapour escaping from inside the structure. It is defined as a material with a vapour resistance between 0.1 and 2.0 MNs/g, although the norm is for breather membranes to have a maximum vapour resistance of 0.6 MNs/g.

BTU British Thermal Units. The output of radiators and boilers is measured in BTUs.

Butterfly roof Common on Georgian and early Victorian town houses these are 'M' shaped roofs comprising 2 lean-to roofs, one either side, with a valley in between. Normally hidden from view from street level by a parapet front wall.

Cat slide Steep subsidiary roof that sweeps down from the ridge (or close to it) nearly to the ground, often covering a single storey extension. Can sometimes apply to steep mono-pitched dormer roofs.

Centres The distance between joists, or between rafters, measured from the centre of one to the centre of the next one.

Cheeks The side walls of a dormer window.

Cold bridging A cold bridge is formed when there is a poor thermal insulation between the exterior and interior faces of a wall. It allows a path through which heat is lost with potential for condensation to form on the inner side of a wall.

Collar A horizontal timber member that joins and restrains opposing roof slopes, tying them together.

Condensation Water droplets deposited from warm, moist air when it comes into contact with any cold surface.

Counter battens Sawn timber strips fixed down the outer face of the rafters over a boarded or felted roof – *ie* in the opposite direction to the main battens from which the tiles or slates are fixed. This allows improved natural ventilation. May also be provided to tiled dormer cheeks.

Creasing tiles Courses of projecting tiles laid under a line of bricks, commonly found towards the top of parapet walls to deflect rainwater .

Cripple studs Short vertical load-bearing timber studs, typically found either side of a window opening to provide a bearing for a lintel.

Cut roof Traditional roof structure made from individually cut timber rafters and purlins.

Dead load The total load of a building comprising the weight of all the elements of construction including the walls, partitions, floors, beams, roofs, finishes and services.

Dormer A window structure projecting out of a roof slope in order to admit light and provide ventilation to a room, and/or to provide additional headroom to a loft conversion.

Drips Expansion joints in the form of steps in leadwork to flat roofs, where lead is lapped over a step in the flat roof structure (substrate).

Durgo valve An air admittance valve to secondary internal soil stack.

Dwangs Another word for noggins (or noggings), traditional cuts of wood fixed between joists to improve rigidity.

Eaves The lowest part of a roof around its periphery, which projects beyond the face of the wall below.

Egress window Another name for 'escape window' .

Escape route Any route forming part of the 'means of escape' from fire, leading from any point in a building to the final exit.

Eyebrow window A traditional dormer roof window with a gently curved roof, found in some thatched roofs but can also be formed in plain tiles.

Extract ventilation A means of mechanical extraction of stale air such as from a bathroom, cloakroom or kitchen.

Fascia Horizontal timber boards that run along the eaves at the base of roof slopes. They normally cover the ends of the rafters and have gutters fixed to them.

Felting Sheets of traditional roofing felt soaked in bitumen and laid over the rafters to line the roof before the tile/slate battens are fixed. Widely installed in roofs from 1950s to 1990s, but now superseded by breather membrane roofing underlay.

FD Fire Door - as in 'FD 30' for a door providing minimum 30 minutes fire resistance – see 'fire-check' door.

Final exit The termination of any escape route from a building giving access to a safe passageway, street or open space and sited so that persons are not in any danger from fire or smoke. Normally refers to a main entrance door such as the front door.

Firecheck door A door designed to withstand the passage of fire for a given period of time (*eg.* an FD20 door will resist fire for 20 minutes).

Firrings Pieces of tapered timber fixed to the top of joists to adjust their slope, such as to flat roofs. Can also be used under decking to give a drainage fall or to make a sloping surface level.

Fish plate Steel plates used to join two lengths of timber or steel end to end. The plates (one on each side) overlap both pieces and are secured using bolts through.

Flange A flat plate at the end of a beam or pipe through which a bolted joint can be made, so 2 lengths can be joined together.

Flashings A thin strip usually of lead used to cover joints to roofs and chimneys to prevent leakage.

Flight The series of consecutive treads and risers which make up a stair.

Flitch beam/flitch plate A timber beam which has been strengthened by the insertion of a metal plate sandwiched between the strips of timber.

Floor plate See 'sole plate'.

Framing anchors Metal fixings used to join timber studs together.

Gable The triangular upper part of a wall under the verges at the edge of a pitched roof ('gable end wall').

Gablet A 'baby gable' or small gable, sometimes found above a hipped roof slope.

Gallery An internal balcony (or projecting landing) running along an inside wall, found in some period houses, churches, barns etc. Also means a long, narrow room, such as within a loft space.

Going A stair tread minus its small projecting front 'nosing' – equivalent to the horizontal distance between the risers of two consecutive stair treads.

GRP Glassfibre Reinforced Plastic. A modern sheet material used as a cheaper substitute for lead, such as when lining valleys etc.

Habitable room A room used, or with the potential to be used, for dwelling purposes, including kitchens, but not bathrooms, conservatories or utility rooms.

Half-dormer A traditional roof window built up from a main wall.

Half-hip A traditional barn-style roof treatment in which a side gable wall is only partially built up, finishing instead with a small hipped roof at the top.

Hanger A vertical component found in some traditional timber roof structures, commonly hanging from the ridge down to the ceiling joists.

Head of water The vertical distance between the water in a storage tank or cistern (*eg* in a loft) and the fitting or appliance it feeds, such as a shower or bath. The greater the height of the tank above the fitting, the better the 'head' of water pressure for it to operate correctly.

Head beam or head The top member of a stud partition or of the frame/lining around a door or window.

Header plate A header beam.

Header The end of a brick, visible in solid walls when laid crossways, as opposed to its side, the 'stretcher'.

Header tank A small open-topped cistern (tank) containing water with which to top up a central heating system.

Headroom The clear height in a room or doorway to allow a person to stand without bending.

Hip A hip is the external junction where two roof slopes meet. A hipped roof has a roof slope instead of a gable wall, hence its distinctive pyramid shape.

Hit & miss ventilator A special ventilator grille built into an external wall to provide background ventilation and which can be opened and closed (see rapid ventilation).

'I' beam A structural beam of steel or timber with a central spine and top and bottom flanges in the shape of a letter 'I'.

Imposed load The load produced by the intended occupancy or use, including the weight of all movable partitions, furniture, persons, distributed, concentrated, impact and snow loads, but excluding wind loads.

Jack rafters On a hipped roof, these are the short rafters cut to fit the angle of the hip structure, spanning from the wall-plate to a hip. Also used to describe rafters that span from a valley up to a ridge.

Jambs The vertical side members of window frames or door frames/linings .

Joist A structural member of timber or steel, usually to a floor or ceiling, that spans between supports and is designed to carry loads. See also RSJ.

Joist hanger A metal bracket designed to support the ends of timber joists where they cannot be built into the supporting wall or other structural element.

Knee wall An alternative name for a 'purlin wall' built of timber studwork between the loft floor and the rafters at purlin level, roughly knee high. Usually load-bearing, these timber framework structures look similar to a ladder on its side, forming the eaves cupboards. .

Ladder wall As per 'knee wall'.

Laminated timber beam A timber beam made up of relatively thin strips of wood, glued together.

Landing A level platform at the top of a flight of stairs or at a change of direction in a stair.

Lath & plaster The traditional method (now obsolete) of covering walls and ceilings, in use until the 1930s when it started to be replaced by plasterboard sheeting.

Layer boards Another name for timber valley boards that form the base to a roof valley .

Light tube A tube, normally made of metal, through which daylight from the roof surface is channelled down to a room or landing below.

Lintel A timber, steel or concrete structural member used to span an opening and support the load above, such as over a window or door.

Live load See imposed load.

Loadbearing Any structural part of a building designed to carry imposed loads, *eg* a brick wall or a steel or timber post.

Loft The space in a roof below the rafters and above the ceiling, commonly used for storage.

Mansard A roof constructed so each slope has two different pitches – a shallow or flat upper part and a very steep lower part - so as to provide a top floor of useable space within a roof structure.

MoE 'Means of Escape'. Often refers to 'escape windows' which comply with minimum dimensions set out in the Building Regulations.

Newel post A post supporting the strings and banisters of a staircase, normally at the top and bottom of a flight of stairs.

Noggins, Also known as 'noggings' or 'nogs', these are short timber battens fitted between a pair of joists or timber studs to add strength.

Nosing The projecting front edge of a stair tread, often rounded.

OSB Oriented strand board. A multi-layered board manufactured from strands of wood or fine timber waste mixed together with a binder. The strands are aligned and parallel to the board length or width.

Packing Any material used to fill a gap between two adjacent surfaces.

Padstone A hard stone or very strong piece of masonry, such as an engineering brick or a dense concrete block, laid under the end of a beam or steel joist to help distribute the load.

PAR timber PAR (planed all round) timber has been machined on all four faces to precise dimensions. For example 50mm x 100mm sawn timber will reduce to 45mm x 95mm (approx) after machining.

Parapet Low wall along the edge of a roof or balcony.

Party wall The wall that separates adjoining semi-detached or terraced houses. Part walls are built on the boundary between two properties, although shared by both, and subject to legislation in The Party Wall Act and Building Regulations.

PFC beam Parallel Flange Channel – a steel beam designed to extend telescopically .

Pitch The angle or slope of a roof, technically the ratio of span to height, expressed in degrees (eg a 30° pitch.).

Plasterboard A sheet material used for ceilings and stud walls consisting of compressed gypsum plaster between two sheets of tough building paper.

Plate A horizontal beam that provides structural support, eg a timber wall plate that supports rafters and floor joists.

Protected escape route A route protected by fire-resistant material that can be used in the event of fire to provide escape to a place of safety.

Protected stairway A stair that discharges to a final exit and place of safety, and is adequately enclosed by fire-resisting construction.

PSV 'Passive stack ventilation' is a system of ventilation that uses ducts from the ceilings of rooms to terminals in the roof and operates by a combination of the natural movement of warm air, and the effect of wind over the external surface of the roof (see also Approved Document F).

Purlin The large horizontal timber or steel beams that provide support to the rafters of a roof slope.

Purlin wall A wall normally of timber studwork constructed to support roof purlins, built up from the loft floor (normally supported on a beam) to the rafters at purlin level. Usually load-bearing and often about knee high. See 'ladder wall' and 'knee wall'.

Rafters The main sloping roof timbers which form the roof structure of a building, to which the tiles or slates, battens and felt are fixed. Typically sized about 4 x 2in.

Rails The top and bottom horizontal members of a door or window. These combine with the two vertical members known as 'stiles' .

Rapid ventilation A permanent method of ventilation, such as a window, that provides a natural flow of air (see Approved Document F).

Restrictive covenants Legal conditions sometimes written into the deeds of a property by the original developer at the time of construction to prevent future residents carrying out inappropriate activities, or building extensions, making alterations etc.

Ridge The apex of a pitched roof where the two slopes meet. The ridge is commonly formed by a timber ridge board to which the tops of the rafters are joined, which is then clad on top with curved or angled 'ridge tiles'.

Ridge board or plate The horizontal strip of timber which spans the length of the roof at its apex supporting the ends of the rafters.

Rise The vertical distance between two consecutive treads in a stair (see 'going' and Approved Document K).

Riser The vertical portion of a step between the stair treads above and below.

Rising butt hinge A special type of hinge which operates as a very simple self-closing mechanism when a door is open.

Rising main The pipe supplying mains water through a house, usually terminating in the loft at a cold water storage tank.

RIR ('room-in-roof') truss A modern variant of the manufactured trussed rafter, but with the central area clear of any webbing or obstructions. These 'attic truss' roof structures provide the skeleton of a loft room ready for easy conversion to accommodation (subject to planning and access etc). .

Rolls In leadwork to flat roofs, rolls are a type of expansion joint. A wood roll is formed by dressing the edges of adjoining sheets over a wooden 'broom handle' core whereas a hollow roll has an empty core.

Roof dome A clear plastic dome for flat roofs, normally made from polycarbonate.

Rooflight A window, or similar element, that allows daylight through a roof, such as a roof window fitted flush to a roof slope. Traditionally non-opening, serving the purpose of attracting light into a building, but often now used interchangeably with the words 'roofwindow' or skylight'. Can also refer to a variety of glazed lights, such as lantern lights, domes, or glazed barrel vaults.

Roof truss A traditional roof structure comprising a framed assembly of structural members consisting of ceiling joists, rafters, struts and ties.

Roof window An opening skylight window fitted into the roof slope and parallel with it. See also 'rooflight' and 'skylight' .

RSJ Rolled Steel Joist. Very strong, long manufactured beams used to provide structural support to walls, roofs or floors, capable of spanning wide openings.

Sarking felt A sheet of bituminous felt traditionally laid over the rafters to provide a weatherproof barrier under the battens and tiles/slates. Provides a secondary defence against rain, but was not widely fitted until the 1950s.

Sarking boards A layer of timber cladding traditionally laid to the outer face of the rafters under the battens and tiles/slates in better quality properties.

Sawn timber Timber in its rough state prior to being machined. Sawn sizes are nominal, whereas machined sizes are actual and referred to as PAR.

Secret gutter A hidden gutter typically formed at the edge of a dormer cheek, party wall or a valley and concealed by tiles. Individual strips of lead or GRP are fixed underneath the tiles and turned up at the sides.

Sill or cill The lower horizontal member at the bottom of a door or window frame. Externally it should throw water clear of the wall below. Inside the house it refers to a 'shelf' at the bottom of a window .

Sill plate See 'sole plate.

Skew nailing A method of nailing timbers at an angle when constructing stud partitions.

Skirting A narrow moulded or plain strip of timber fixed around the base of walls internally to protect the wall finish from being kicked or damaged, and to conceal gaps. In a kitchen or bathroom skirtings may sometimes be of tiles.

Skylight A general term for a window inserted in a roof slope, flat roof or ceiling, that admits daylight to the room below. Can be fixed or opening. See 'roof window', and 'rooflight'.

Slate A fine-grained rock capable of being easily split into very thin layers and used for roofing and flooring tiles.

Snagging The process of making good outstanding minor works, such as loose fittings, paint marks, shrinkage cracks etc, carried out towards the end of a project.

Soakers Small strips of metal sheet (usually lead) inserted under overlapping courses of plain tiles or slates to provide a waterproof joint at the junction of a roof with a wall, chimney or certain roof windows. Sometimes also overlaid with flashings.

Soffit The underside of an overhanging part of a building. An 'external ceiling' found at the eaves (between the fascia board and the external wall) or to balconies.

Soleplate In a timber stud wall, the bottom strip of horizontal timber that forms the base of the studwork wall, a.k.a. 'base plate', 'bottom rail', 'floor plate' or 'sill plate'.

Spine wall The main internal load-bearing wall commonly found in pre-1970s properties, especially older houses with traditional roof structure. Usually the wall that divides the front and rear reception rooms and the main bedrooms taking loadings from roofs, floor and ceiling joists.

Stanchion A vertical supporting beam usually made from steel.

Stretcher The side of a brick, visible in walls when laid lengthways.

Soil pipe/Soil vent stack A vertical pipe designed to carry away effluent from bathrooms, cloakrooms, kitchens and 'soil' waste from WC's over one or more floors of a building, terminating above the eaves level of the roof. Provides ventilation to the foul water drainage system into which it discharges. Typically of plastic or cast iron. See 'SVP'.

SVP Soil and vent pipe. See 'soil pipe'.

Span The clear distance between two supports or bearings measured along the length of a structural member such as a floor joist.

Spiral stairs A circular staircase with tapered treads assembled around a central column. Also referred to as a helical stair.

String The two main structural side members of a staircase into which the treads and risers are fixed.

Strut An upright or angled structural member, normally of timber, typically used to prop up and support roof purlins etc and resist compression stresses.

Stud A vertical timber used in the construction of stud partitions.

Stud partition A series of vertical studs and horizontal noggins nailed together to form a framed partition covered with plasterboard on both sides.

Suspended ceiling A lightweight, non-structural ceiling framework clad with plasterboard and insulated, constructed independently below an existing ceiling. The sound and fire resistance to a room will be improved at the expense of loss of height in the room.

Tanalised timber Timbers used in construction, typically for floor joists, which have had tanalith-oxide preservative driven into their cellular structure under pressure.

Tapered treads Triangular shaped stair treads that are wider at their outer edge. Used in spiral stairs and as winders where stairs turn a corner without a flat landing.

TDA truss A bolted timber roof truss structure used in some roofs built between the late 1940s and 1960s. Designed by the Timber Development Association, forerunner of TRADA (Timber Research And Development Association).

Tie A structural member designed to resist tension stresses and used in roof trusses.

Tiles Very popular and durable weatherproof roof coverings, traditionally made from burnt clay, or since the 1930s from concrete. Tiles are laid with their projecting nibs on the inner face hooked over battens of the roof.

Top head On a typical dormer window structure, the vertical front studs support a horizontal timber beam known as the 'header', also referred to as the 'head beam', 'window header', 'top head' or 'head plate'.

Tread In a staircase, the treads are the horizontal parts of each step that you tread on.

Trimmer A small piece of structural timber joist run at right angles across the cut ends of floor joists or rafters to form an opening, such as for stairs, chimney breast or a roof window.

Trussed rafters A modern method of roof construction (post c.1965) using pre-fabricated triangular frames incorporating 'W' shaped webbing timbers fixed together with metal nail plates. The manufactured frames are placed at regular intervals (normally 600mm) along the supporting walls of the building.

U-value A measure of the rate of heat loss of a building component. The U-value is calculated by taking the reciprocal of all the combined thermal resistances of the materials in the element, including air spaces and fixings. It is a measure of the rate at which heat passes through one metre^2 of any material, when the air temperature on either side differs by one degree. The value is expressed in Watts per square metre/temperature difference in degrees Kelvin. ($U = W/m^2 /K$). See Approved Document L.

Universal beam (UB) A steel beam similar to an RSJ but with flat top and bottom flanges.

Universal column (UC) A steel beam similar to an RSJ but square in section.

Upstand A vertical element that laps up a wall, such as where the felt covering to a flat roof is dressed up an adjoining wall by at least 150mm and fixed into a mortar joint.

Valley The external junction between the two inner slopes of a pitched roof which form the valley gutter.

Valley gutter Gutter at the external junction of two roof slopes – at the bottom of a 'V'.

Vapour Control Layer A material that substantially reduces the water vapour transfer through a building element into which it is incorporated *ie* polythene sheet materials or foil backed plasterboard. Vapour control layers are sometimes required on the warm side of the insulation, to reduce the possible risk of interstitial condensation forming within the building's structure.

Verge The edge of a roof, especially over a gable.

Wall plate A timber beam placed along the top of main structural walls. It is a load-bearing timber member onto which the ceiling joists and rafter feet are fixed.

Welt In leadwork, welts are a type of 'folded' expansion joint. They are formed by turning up the edge of one sheet of lead (the undercloak) by approx 25mm (1in), and then turning up the edge of the adjoining lead sheet (the overcloak) by 50mm (2in). The overcloak is then folded over the undercloak and pressed flat.

Winder A tapered triangular stair tread which allows a change of direction in a stair and used where space is restricted.

Window header In the construction of large dormers, a horizontal timber beam runs along the top of the studwork front wall. Referred to also as 'head beam', 'top head' or 'head plate'.

INDEX

Author	Ian Alistair Rock MRICS
Technical Editor	Basil Parylo MBEng
Photography	Basil Parylo, Dave Davies, Helen @ The Rooflight Company, Peter Morgan @ Kingspan Insulation, and the Author
Project Manager	Louise McIntyre
Copy Editor	Ian Heath
Page Build	James Robertson

INFORMATION SOURCES

Fire Safety and Loft Conversions — Leeds City Council
Loft Conversions — J Coutts — Blackwell
LABC Building Control Guidance — LABC
Home Extension Manual — Ian Rock — Haynes
Loft Conversions — Laurie Williamson — Crowood
Roof Construction and Loft Conversion — C.N. Mindham — Blackwell
The Housebuilder's Bible — Mark Brinkley — Ovolo
www.aboveitall.co.uk